How Good Teachers Thrive

How Good Teachers Thrive

Flourishing Long Term in a Noble Profession

Ken Badley

BLOOMSBURY ACADEMIC
NEW YORK • LONDON • OXFORD • NEW DELHI • SYDNEY

BLOOMSBURY ACADEMIC

Bloomsbury Publishing Inc, 1359 Broadway, New York, NY 10018, USA
Bloomsbury Publishing Plc, 50 Bedford Square, London, WC1B 3DP, UK
Bloomsbury Publishing Ireland, 29 Earlsfort Terrace, Dublin 2, D02 AY28, Ireland

BLOOMSBURY, BLOOMSBURY ACADEMIC and the Diana logo are trademarks of
Bloomsbury Publishing Plc

First published in the United States of America 2026

Copyright © Bloomsbury Publishing Inc, 2026

Cover images: © istock/Yurii Karvatskyi, © istock/FORGEM

All rights reserved. No part of this publication may be: i) reproduced or transmitted in any form, electronic or mechanical, including photocopying, recording or by means of any information storage or retrieval system without prior permission in writing from the publishers; or ii) used or reproduced in any way for the training, development or operation of artificial intelligence (AI) technologies, including generative AI technologies. The rights holders expressly reserve this publication from the text and data mining exception as per Article 4(3) of the Digital Single Market Directive (EU) 2019/790.

Bloomsbury Publishing Inc does not have any control over, or responsibility for, any third-party websites referred to or in this book. All internet addresses given in this book were correct at the time of going to press. The author and publisher regret any inconvenience caused if addresses have changed or sites have ceased to exist, but can accept no responsibility for any such changes.

A catalog record for this book is available from the Library of Congress

ISBN: HB: 9781475874716
PBK: 9781475874723
ePDF: 9788765160954
eBook: 9781475874730

Typeset by Deanta Global Publishing Services, Chennai, India
Printed and bound in the United States of America

For product safety related questions contact productsafety@bloomsbury.com.

To find out more about our authors and books visit www.bloomsbury.com
and sign up for our newsletters.

*To the Bachelor of Education graduates from
Mount Royal University in Calgary.*

Contents

Introduction 1

1 Snapshots of Teaching 7

2 The Language of Teaching: Vocation, Calling, Work, Career, Job, Profession 17

3 Teachers' Day-to-Day Work: A Model 29

4 Teaching: Intense and Complex with Mixed Rewards 39

5 Teachers' Worldviews, Teachers' Identities 47

6 Classroom Ideals and a Philosophy of Education 59

7 Metaphors for Flourishing 71

8 Flourishing in the Induction Years 83

9 The Middle Years 95

10 Voices from the Classroom 107

11 The Summit Push 127

12 Six Kinds of People One Meets on the Road 139

13 Supporters 153

14 Dispositions That Foster Flourishing 167

15 Staying Focused on the Journey 183

16 Nurturing the Teacher's Core 191

Bibliography 205
Index 214
About the Author 218

Introduction

This book represents a dance between two purposes. I want to present the kind of grand vision of teaching that will grip my readers and deepen their desire and their capacity to flourish until the day they retire. A book that presents a grand vision is likely not a how-to book or anything that might get shelved with self-help. And that's the kicker. Flourishing long-term—thriving in this profession—does entail having a grand vision. But it requires more than that. Grand visions are realized only when people take the right steps, follow life-giving routines, work with the right mindset, find allies, and know what to do in a wide variety of situations. In educational work, grand visions are realized in the daily nitty-gritty of curriculum, instruction, assessment, classroom climate, record-keeping, and other administrative details.

We should all celebrate that thousands of teachers have gotten these details right and have flourished until the day they retired. May we all keep learning from those thousands of teachers. If, in these pages, I can bring some of what they have learned to you, the book will be a success. A teacher colleague recently said to me that most teachers would like an educational revolution along with smaller classes. I agreed. But to her first point and to my point in this book, short of a revolution in education, what can teachers do, what must teachers do? Even without an educational revolution, teachers can take the necessary steps to flourish until the day of their retirement tea.

Two Alberta teachers inspired me and might inspire you. To protect their privacy, I will omit their names here, and to help you, my readers, not feel like I'm repeating myself too much, I will not mention them again. But their stories are the kind of soil from which this book has grown. May these stories trigger your own memories of outstanding teachers who have inspired you.

The first story comes from a remote school situated on a remote religious colony in northern Alberta. For several years, I served the Alberta Minister of Education on a committee that helped select the twenty teachers who would receive an outstanding teacher award each year. My committee colleagues and I would sift through several hundred nomination packages until we had agreed on the twenty whom the Minister would recognize that school year. I experienced great joy serving on this committee because I was able to read letters about great teachers written by their students, parents, colleagues, principals, and superintendents. One piece of background information will help you understand the significance of this story. Members of this religious sect ordinarily pull their children from school as soon as the Alberta Education Act permits them to do so (sixteenth birthday or completion of ninth grade). As was the case in most such colonies of members of this sect, the village school ran only to ninth grade. The core event in this story surprised my colleagues and me when we read the letters that came in support of this teacher's nomination: the elders in this community had requested that the school board add grade ten to the school on their colony so that this teacher could continue to teach their children. The question for teachers who want to thrive and flourish is this: How did she run that one-room school so that the village elders were led to ask the school district to add grade ten? What was her classroom program like? Worded most simply, what did she do?

Through the same teaching excellence program, I met another teacher who, at the time of being honored as an outstanding teacher, worked hundreds of miles north of Edmonton and, in the year of her nomination, had only a few more weeks to teach before she would retire from teaching. For years, she had used her spring breaks to travel to Edmonton for university courses or other forms of professional development. When I read her nomination package, I knew immediately that I wanted to ask her why she had come to Edmonton to take a course in the final term of her career. The Excellence in Teaching awards banquet gave me my opportunity to ask her that question. Without a gram of irony, she answered that she still had several weeks to go before the end of the school year and she wanted to learn how to teach better. I tried not to set my face to stunned, but I could not help but wonder what kind of teacher—what kind of person—gives up her spring break in her final year of work and drives several hundred miles to participate in professional development? This woman had flourished; she was still thriving in the last weeks of her teaching career.

All teachers need inspiration, perhaps not that they will be asked by village elders to add grade ten to the school or that they will be registering to take more professional development three months before they retire. But all teachers need inspiration so they can avoid the cynicism and weariness that some experience toward the end of their careers and so they can thrive and flourish through to the day of their retirement. My goal in this book is to bring my readers some of that kind of inspiration, along with suggestions about the strategies and routines that give that inspiration legs to run on.

Throughout this book, I will use the tone I would use if a few of us were sitting in a coffee shop or pub on a Friday afternoon after a week of teaching. We might be expressing gratitude that we finished another week of this amazing and complex work we've been given to do. And we might be a little bit awestruck that mere humans like ourselves were able to do it. We might complain in passing about the antics or answers of some of our students, or the decisions of our administrators or board. We might simply be wondering if we're downright bonkers for continuing to go back to work day after day and year after year when our work is so difficult. In this book, I write the way I talk in conversations like these, where we simply gather as teacher colleagues and friends. Thus, my tone is on the informal side. But I do not want my conversational tone and these personal pronouns to diminish the importance of what I write in these pages.

What Follows in This Book

If you glance at the Table of Contents, you will see that the book begins with four chapters related to various images of teaching, what you might call the exterior landscape of teaching. How do teachers frame their work in light of how both non-teachers and they themselves view teaching? The book begins by exploring these images because they are an important part of the context of teaching work.

Chapter 1 of that section deals with some of the ways filmmakers portray teachers—what some call *reel teachers*—and also examines how journalists and bloggers write about education and teachers. In other words, what is teaching in the popular imagination?

Chapter 2 examines teaching in relation to six key words people use with reference to all forms of work: *profession, vocation, calling, work, career,* and *job*. I argue there that flourishing long-term in the teaching profession requires viewing teaching as a vocation or calling, not only as work or as a career.

Chapter 3 deals at some length with a graphic model of the core cycle of educational work: curriculum, instruction, and assessment. After arguing that those core teaching activities take place in a classroom ethos or climate that teachers must build, I situate the core cycle and classroom ethos in the context of three wider questions: How do we teach who we are? How do we teach who they—our students—are? How do we teach where we are (i.e., the social and political contexts of educational work)?

In Chapter 4, I argue that teaching work is complex, intense, and sometimes frustrating. Connected to the periodic frustrations, teaching also has mixed rewards. Be assured that Chapter 4 is the only chapter in the book that focuses on the difficult and even negative aspects of teaching. After all, this is meant to be a book on thriving and flourishing, not on why teachers burn out and leave the profession. You are welcome to skip Chapter 4 if you sense that you already know what you need to know about the challenges of teaching.

The second section of the book treats what one might call the interior landscape of teaching, starting with Chapter 5's treatment of teachers' worldviews. Why worldviews? Because teachers' worldviews heavily influence how they view and carry out their classroom work. That chapter ends with the claim that teachers can frame their work in ways that foster long-term professional flourishing.

Chapter 6 treats teachers' philosophies of education, connecting those philosophies to their worldviews as well as to their classroom ideals. It builds on both Chapter 5 and on decades of classroom conversations and workshops where pre-service and in-service teachers have identified the classroom ideals that led them into teaching and that help them get up each morning and go to work. With the goal of long-term flourishing, the chapter invites readers to identify ways to realize their ideals in the core cycle of curriculum, instruction, and assessment.

Our metaphors for schools, students, curriculum, instruction, assessment, and other aspects of our educational work also work powerfully to shape how we carry out that work. Chapter 7 focuses on how educational metaphors influence cognition, and it includes brief explorations of several metaphors and what new perspectives they might offer classroom teachers. The second section of the book closes with this examination of educational metaphors.

The third section includes four chapters that focus on different stages of the teaching career. Chapter 8 focuses on the induction years, identifying factors typically associated with novice teachers who stay in teaching for at least five years, which is the standard period used by researchers studying teacher attrition among novice teachers.

Chapter 9 frames the experiences of the mid-career within the literature on middle age. Some psychologists refer to *the middle passage* as a specific task that middle-aged people must accomplish, a task related to the self and to identity. Teachers who continue to thrive in mid-career typically have navigated the middle passage and have developed a number of life-giving dispositions and practices that foster flourishing.

Chapter 10, "Voices from the Classroom," addresses questions raised for both novice and mid-career teachers. It focuses on the structures, routines, and habits of a number of mid-career teachers who responded to an invitation to answer these two questions: What do you do to keep your brain alive? What do you do to keep your ideals alive?

Chapter 11, the final chapter in the third section, goes by the title "The Summit Push" because of the many similarities between the final years of the teaching career and the final push for the summit of big mountains.

The fourth section, "Companions for the Journey," consists of two chapters meant to confirm the view that almost all teachers already hold: they need support. In Chapter 12, "Six Kinds of People One Meets on the Road," I make comparisons between teachers and six kinds of people one actually meets on the road—tourists, travelers, adventurers, pilgrims, refugees, and guides. I argue in that decidedly metaphorical chapter that the same postures and dispositions that enrich travel and make it more fulfilling also lead to long-term flourishing in teaching. The chapter concludes by recommending that teachers spend their time with colleagues who will inspire them rather than drag them down.

Chapter 13 begins with a nod to the volume of research on how both administrators and teaching colleagues can support the work of teachers and can function as valuable resources for educators who flourish on the journey. But most of the chapter focuses on two possibilities one hears less often. First, students can also become their teachers' allies. Granting that school teachers must respect the professional boundaries that separate them from students, I describe in this chapter those characteristic attitudes and postures toward students typically taken by flourishing teachers and how those teachers gain students as supporters. The chapter ends with the second somewhat unusual possibility: that readers pull together a team, a small group of colleagues, family members, and friends who will agree to support their work and help them stay accountable.

The last section of the book focuses on some of the resources flourishing teachers typically bring to their vocation. It begins with a chapter on the dispositions most likely to contribute to long-term flourishing. Chapter 14 begins with reference to Michelle Hughes' 2024 volume on teachers' dispositions and the importance of framing teaching work in life-giving ways.[1] The chapter includes brief treatments of several dispositions and extended treatments of gratitude and remembering rightly. That section asks readers to list times and events during which they felt the call to teach most deeply and to list some of their great moments in teaching.

Chapter 15 continues in the spirit of Chapter 14. It uses the geological concept of *the angle of repose* to address the question of flourishing while teaching in less-than-ideal school cultures. A plain English definition of the geological concept might be that *things are as they are*. Chapter 15 encourages teachers to let their school be what it will be—at least to some degree—and to focus their energy on their own instructional program in their own classroom.

Chapter 16, "Nurturing the Teacher's Core," returns to some of the questions raised early in the book, as well as to some of the ideas offered by the teachers who contributed to Chapter 10. It argues that teachers who would thrive and flourish to the end of their careers must attend to both the details of their classroom program and their own interior being. Chapter 16 concludes the book with an extended "you've got this." The phrase has become a cliché in our time, but I want to assure my readers that they can thrive and flourish long term in this challenging profession.

Note

[1] Michelle C. Hughes, *Dispositions Are a Teacher's Greatest Strength: Mindful Pedagogical Practices to Develop Self-Awareness to Flourish in the Classroom* (New York: Routledge, 2024).

1 Snapshots of Teaching

Several questions drive this chapter about images of teaching and teachers. What pictures of teaching and teachers do teachers and non-teachers hold, and what is the mix of positive and negative depictions? Who and what are the primary sources and shapers of contemporary portrayals of teachers and teaching? What are some of the effects of those images on the public at large and on teachers themselves?

After examining some possible answers to those three questions, the chapter concludes by returning to the theme of the book: how do good teachers thrive and flourish through to the end of their teaching career?

Images of Teaching and Teachers

What do non-educators—ordinary people—think about teachers and the work teachers do? And how do teachers view themselves and their work? Consider these two opposite views, roughly representing the extremes of a whole range of views. At one extreme are the familiar and pernicious claims that "anyone can teach" and "those who can, do, and those who can't, teach."[1] After all, teaching cannot be that much more complicated than babysitting, especially considering that governments and school boards provide the curriculum and that students are almost always required by law to attend school until a specified age or until they complete a certain grade. And the holidays teachers get!

At the other end of the scale is a view held by many teachers and those who know them best, that teachers are underpaid, and that teaching is so complex, intense, and often frustrating that, given its mixed rewards, it's a surprise anyone goes into teaching these days.[2]

To help explain the first view (without defending it), consider the fact that nearly all critics of schools and teaching have attended schools. Decades ago, in his book, *Schoolteacher: A Sociological Study*,[3] author Dan Lortie identified what he called the *apprenticeship of observation*. Lortie meant by this phrase that all who have attended school have seen teachers work and therefore have, in some sense, apprenticed—or at least they think they have apprenticed—as teachers and therefore think they know how to teach. Lortie's particular focus in that volume was on teacher education and the difficulties of helping new pre-service teachers accept the fact that they might not already know everything they might need to know to succeed as classroom teachers. But, for our purposes, his conclusion also applies to those not aiming to become teachers. If everyone has already apprenticed as teachers then, arguably, everyone is already knowledgeable about the ways teachers should do their work.

The claim that anyone could teach may be more widespread in our own era than at any previous time. In 2017, author Tom Nichols identified the growing public sense that experts of all kinds do not deserve the public's trust. In his book, *The Death of Expertise*,[4] Nichols described the growing suspicion that not only climate scientists and medical researchers, but even electricians and plumbers are not as good at their jobs as they want everyone to think. "They" are beholden to some shady group or other who operate in secret or they pretend their work is complicated when in fact it is simple. Nichols reports seeing a noticeable rise in this suspicion of claims to expertise over the last few decades. That the negative tropes about teachers have persisted for decades indicates that the death of expertise regarding educators has persisted for many years before Nichols published his book. After all, as Lortie pointed out, everyone has been to school and watched teachers do their work; thus, in the public imagination, or at least for a proportion of the public, teachers' work cannot be that difficult.

The opposite view of teaching—that it's so challenging it's a surprise anyone goes into it—becomes easier to understand with each passing year. Increased regulation discourages teachers. For example, Florida's Stop WOKE Act ("Wrongs to Our Kids and Employees") requires that teachers keep no books on their classroom shelves not vetted by persons approved by school boards.[5] The sheer workload teachers carry leads many teachers to question their choice of professions.[6] As my readers know, compared to many other professionals who work similar hours, teachers receive relatively modest salaries. Because some schools have insufficient funds to supply teachers with the classroom resources they need, some teachers purchase classroom resources out of those modest salaries. Related to the death of expertise, criticism of teachers has increased and respect for the teaching profession has declined in recent decades. My readers already know enough of this bad news.

Somewhere between those views—but closer to the view that teachers are underpaid for doing demanding work—is another view of teachers as hard-working, caring experts who go beyond what anyone could expect in their efforts to help give children and adolescents the resources they need to become good citizens and to function successfully in the world of work. We regularly hear stories of how someone's life was turned around because a teacher cared about them. Teachers—likely along with almost all members of the public—take for granted the truth of the bumper sticker that reads, "if you can read this, thank a teacher." But how do critics of teachers and teaching reconcile that bumper sticker with the negative images so many hold?

Obviously, more images of teachers than these are available. But consider the two extreme views with the teacher-as-hero image one is more likely to see in a feature film. The gaps between these three images raise important questions about teachers and their vocation. Obviously, the gaps raise questions for the public. But focusing on how teachers can flourish long term in their vocation implies that, here at least, the questions the gaps raise for teachers are of greater importance. In the remainder of this chapter and in Chapter 2, we will continue to examine how we view, think about, and talk about teachers and teaching.

Shaping the Image of Teachers

Consider for a moment some of the best-known teacher films. For example, think of *To Sir with Love* (1967), *Mr. Holland's Opus* (1989), *Dead Poet's Society* (1989), *Freedom Writers* (2007), and *Abbott Elementary* (2021 to the present).[7] Spanning six decades, these films and television series all portray the teacher as some combination of hero and martyr. All of them show people who care about students and who go out of their way to help students succeed. While feature films, documentaries, and television series about teachers and classrooms may have less influence on the view of teachers than they once had, their influence remains significant. In fact, a subfield of educational research has produced a significant body of commentary on teachers in film, or what some call *reel teachers*.[8]

The films listed all portray teachers who brought some combination of charisma, dedication, mystery, creativity, and courage to class (as well as other virtues). Other films offer negative portrayals of teachers, ranging from incompetent, addicted, or lazy to disorganized. Many of these films, such as the movie *Bad Teacher* and the series *Bad Education* (2012–24),[9] are presented as comedies, presumably leaving it up to viewers to infer that such films are not meant as critiques of teachers in general.

For both good and ill, and although its importance is declining, the traditional press also shapes the public's image of teachers and teaching, and people can still hear news about amazing teachers who do amazing things in classrooms. The press also reports those teachers who have been released from their duties for this or that reason. Because negative news travels fast and therefore tends to dominate traditional news outlets, one may have to dig hard to find good news about education, but the news is there for those who persist.[10] For example, at the time of writing, UNESCO has just awarded Panama, Ghana, Austria, Egypt, Nigeria, and Indonesia awards for their outstanding initiatives in literacy.[11] The word *teachers* might not appear in the headlines of news about increased literacy rates, but one does not have to be a genius to make the connection.

Members of the traditional press do not always go easy on teachers, an impression borne out by Australian researcher, Nicole Mockler's analysis of printed reporting on teachers and education in twelve major Australian newspapers from 1996 to 2022.[12] She concluded that reporting tended to focus on teaching quality to the relative exclusion of reporting on other social and systemic factors that affect educational outcomes. Related to that statistical conclusion, she suggested that such a focus makes it easier for educational policymakers and politicians to ignore those wider factors. Another of Mockler's conclusions bears on the question of how people's views of teachers and teaching are shaped. She concluded that the media play an important role in establishing a link between teaching quality and educational accountability.

Kathryn Shine analyzed educational coverage in three major Australian newspapers and drew conclusions similar to those of Mockler. In the newspaper coverage she analyzed, Shine found a picture of teachers as resistant to testing, teaching to tests and, in some cases, even cheating. Furthermore, she found the overall presentation of teachers to be that they were simply inadequate for the task; they were to blame for any shortcomings in Australian education.[13]

Arguably, online influencers have become an influential alternative to the traditional press. These self-appointed experts—and, often, non-experts—gather a following and shape public opinion. Especially among young people, a platform such as TikTok has a significant influence on public opinion about many topics, including education. For good or ill, materials created by means of artificial intelligence will also function as shapers of people's views of education and teaching.

Another obvious source of influence is people's personal experience. Some people have good experiences with school and teachers, and therefore have memories of their own; others do not. More typically, parents and former students have a mix of experiences, some with good teachers and some not so good. Many teachers first considered teaching because they had a good teacher themselves, perhaps as early as primary school.

To conclude this section, note the range of sources of people's opinions about teachers. And note the range of views, from decidedly negative to the teacher as a hero.

Effects of the Images

Positive and negative images of teachers and teaching have quite predictable effects. One undeniably positive effect of teaching immediately comes to mind. Teachers have taught billions of children to read, write, and count. And teachers have taught most of these children how to think, an important skill in a time when thinking seems to be less important than it once was. Such positive information about teachers and the image of teachers it helps produce—along with positive personal experience—draw younger people into the teaching profession. The 2021 *Global Report on the Status of Teachers* reports that 29.9 percent of participants in one study thought the teaching profession was attractive to young people.[14]

Among a portion of the non-teaching population, positive images of, experiences with, and news about teachers also create a generalized feeling of warmth toward teachers and schools. Teaching has historically been considered a noble and important profession and remains so in several nations.[15] In fact, Aristotle believed that those who teach children should receive more honor than those who produce them because teachers teach children how to live well (with Aristotle, we know that parents do that too).[16]

Negative images also do their work. Contra Aristotle, and millennia before teachers got caught in the culture wars, St. James warned that not many should become teachers because they would face a stiffer judgment (Jas 3:1). His warning has come true with a vengeance as changes in the cultural and political atmosphere have eroded the morale of teachers and led many teachers to wonder if they should leave the profession.

Consider for a moment the famous "anyone, anyone?" scene in the 1986 film, *Ferris Bueller's Day Off*.[17] By giving us such a negative instantiation of the instruction-as-transmission metaphor, the screenwriters and actor Ben Stein gave viewers a powerful counter-example of good instruction. I do not offer *Bueller* as an argument against direct instruction. But it serves as an example of a negative image of teaching that, in this case, has become a meme in the culture.[18]

One challenge facing teachers is that while teaching is complex work,[19] the best teachers make it appear deceptively simple, an observation made by many researchers and one that accords with the claim Lortie made decades ago about the apprenticeship of observation.[20] In *The Tact of Teaching: The Meaning of Pedagogical Thoughtfulness*, Max van Manen identifies *teacher tact* as that ability possessed by the best teachers to know intuitively what is happening in their classrooms at all times and what move to make next.[21] In essence, the high-tact teachers Van Manen describes are the ones who make teaching look easy.

Consider this parallel from the world of sports. Hockey great Wayne Gretzky used to claim that the good hockey player always knew where the puck was and the great player knew where it was going. If the parallel to his words applies to teaching then one is led to wonder why those who saw Gretzky play watched in awe, coveted his skill, and knew they could never match his level of play, but those who see similarly great teachers conclude that teaching must be easy. The irony that many critics of teaching apparently miss is that making teaching look simple is actually a sign of great expertise.

Conclusion

Views of teachers and teaching range from extraordinary real teachers such as Erin Gruwell, whose work is celebrated in the feature film *Freedom Writers*,[22] to the common untruths that "anyone can teach," "those who can, do, and those who can't, teach," and "if you're teaching, this must be plan B then, right?"

How can teachers flourish regardless of what opinions members of the public hold about them, about schools, and about what people typically call the education system? How can teachers continue to thrive when some influencers, some filmmakers, and some in the traditional press shape opinion as powerfully—and often as negatively—as they do? These are ongoing challenges for teachers, and they are the challenge this book addresses.

Most teachers have days when they sense deeply that teaching is their vocation. On those days, they might say to themselves, "I could do this for free." While I believe most teachers should be paid much more than they now earn, my wish for my readers is that this book will help them enjoy more days when they think they could work for free.

Notes

1. At the time of writing, Google returned 723,000 hits for a search of the phrase "anyone can teach." The nasty extension of the second familiar phrase is ". . . and those who can't teach, teach phys ed." See Bryan McCullick, Don Belcher, Brent Hardin, and Marie Hardin, "Butches, Bullies and Buffoons: Images of Physical Education Teachers in the Movies," *Sport, Education and Society* 8, no. 1 (2003): 3–17.
2. The intensity, complexity, frustrations, and mixed rewards of teaching are the subject of Chapter 4 in this volume. Here I deliberately echo the language in the title of Nicole Mockler's article, "No Wonder No One Wants to Be a Teacher: World-first Study Looks at 65,000 News Articles about Australian Teachers," *The Conversation*, July 10, 2022, https://theconversation.com/no-wonder-no-one-wants-to-be-a-teacher-world-first-study-looks-at-65-000-news-articles-about-australian-teachers-186210.
3. Lortie, Dan. *Schoolteacher: A Sociological Study* (Chicago: The University of Chicago Press, 1975).

4 *The Death of Expertise: The Campaign against Established Knowledge and Why It Matters* (Old Saybrook, CT: Tantor, 2017).

5 For example, see Tesfaye Negussie and Rahma Ahmed's article, "Florida Schools Directed to Cover or Remove Classroom Books that are Not Vetted," https://abcnews.go.com/Politics/florida-schools-directed-cover-remove-classroom-books-vetted/story?id=96323.

6 Type "research teacher work week" into your browser to get a sense of the number of studies showing that many teachers work fifty or more hours per week.

7 *To Sir with Love*, directed by James Clavell (Los Angeles: Columbia Pictures, 1967); *Mr. Holland's Opus*, directed by Stephen Herek (Los Angeles: Hollywood Pictures, Buena Vista Pictures, 1995); *Dead Poet's Society*, directed by Peter Weir (Los Angeles: Touchstone Pictures, Buena Vista Pictures, 1989); *Freedom Writers*, directed by Richard LaGravenese (Los Angeles: Paramount Pictures, Double Feature Films, MTV Films, Jersey Films, Kernos Film, 2007); *Abbott Elementary*, directed by Randall Einhorn, Jennifer Celotta, Jaime Eliezer, et al. (Los Angeles: Warner Brothers, 2021–2024).

8 For examples, see William Ayers, "A Teacher Ain't Nothin' but a Hero: Teachers and Teaching in Film," in *Images of Schoolteachers in America*, ed. Pamela Bolton Joseph and Gail E. Burnaford (Mahwah, NJ: Lawrence Erlbaum, 2001), 201–9; Robert C. Bulman, *Hollywood Goes to High School: Cinema, Schools, and American Culture* (New York: Worth, 2005); Adam Farhi, "Hollywood Goes to School: Recognizing the Superteacher Myth in Films," *The Clearing House* 72, no. 3 (1999): 157–9; R. Lowe, "Teachers as Saviors, Teachers Who Care," in *Images of Schoolteachers in America*, ed. Pamela Bolton Joseph and Gail E. Burnaford (Mahwah, NJ: Lawrence Erlbaum, 2001), 211–25; and W. Reed Scull and Gary Peltier, "Star Power and the Schools: Studying Popular Films' Portrayal of Educators," *Clearing House* 8, no. 1 (2007): 13–17.

9 *Bad Teacher*, directed by Jake Kasdan (Los Angeles, CA: Sony/Columbia Pictures, 2011); *Bad Education* (series), directed by Freddy Syborn, Elliot Hegarty, Ben Gosling-Fuller, and Al Campbell (Endemol: Tiger Aspect Productions, 2012–2024).

10 Several good news sites attempt to present a different picture from the bad news one typically finds online. See these, for example: https://fixthenews.com/ and https://www.goodnewsnetwork.org/.

11 Award recipients named in October, 2024. See https://www.unesco.org/en/articles/2024-unesco-international-literacy-prizes-reward-six-groundbreaking-initiatives?ref=fixthenews.com.

12   Nicole Mockler, *Constructing Teacher Identities: How the Print Media Define and Represent Teachers and Their Work* (London: Bloomsbury, 2022). An earlier project of Mockler's also connects to the question of how the press shapes the popular imagination regarding teachers. In her earlier volume, see Nicole Mockler and Susan Groundwater-Smith, *Questioning the Language of Improvement and Reform in Education* (New York: Routledge, 2020). They compare how the language of teacher quality is used differently in K-12 education compared to how it is used in higher education. They conclude that the Australian conversation about teaching quality has become politicized, a state of affairs characteristic of many nations at this time.

13   Kathryn Shine, "Are Australian Teachers Making the Grade? A Study of News Coverage of Naplan Testing," *Media International Australia* 154, no. 1 (2015): 25–33, https://doi.org/10.1177/1329878X1515400105.

14   Greg Thompson, https://www.ei-ie.org/en/item/25403:the-global-report-on-the-status-of-teachers-2021.

15   It is not by coincidence that the word *noble* appears in the title of this book. See comparative international data on the status of the teaching profession. Tim Walker, "Where Do Teachers Get the Most Respect?," *NEA Today*, April 1, 2018, https://www.nea.org/nea-today/all-news-articles/where-do-teachers-get-most-respect.

16   Aristotle, *The Nicomachean Ethics*, ed. Robert C. Bartlett and Susan D. Collins (Chicago, IL: The University of Chicago Press, 2011).

17   *Ferris Bueller's Day Off*, directed by John Hughes (Los Angeles, CA: Paramount Pictures, 1986). Several clips from the film are available on YouTube. Type "boring economics teacher anyone?"

18   Having used that clip quite regularly in teacher education courses, I find that the question "anyone?" has the power to cause a whole class of pre-service teachers to break out in laughter.

19   In Chapter 4, I deal at greater length with the complexity of teaching.

20   See, for example, Pam Grossman, Karen Hammerness, and Morva McDonald, "Redefining Teaching, Re-Imagining Teacher Education," *Teachers and Teaching: Theory and Practice* 15, no. 2 (2009): 273–89.

21   Van Manen, Max. *The Tact of Teaching: The Meaning of Pedagogical Thoughtfulness* (Albany, NY: SUNY Press, 1991).

22   *Freedom Writers*, directed by Richard LaGravenese (Los Angeles, CA: MTV Films, Jersey Films, 2S Films, Paramount Pictures, 2007).

2 The Language of Teaching
Vocation, Calling, Work, Career, Job, Profession

How do we talk about teaching? Identifying the right language for what teachers do shouldn't be that difficult. After all, we get up in the morning and go to work in classrooms. If we left some other profession to become a teacher, we might say that we switched professions or changed careers and no one would misunderstand what we meant. Many teachers say they teach because it is a calling or it is their vocation; teaching is the reason they are on this earth. And without doubt, teaching is a profession; one usually has to train to become certified as a teacher, and most teachers join a professional teachers' organization. Fresh graduates of education programs looking for a teaching position commonly use the language of *finding a job*. In light of the clear meanings these ordinary words carry, why give a chapter over to discussing them?

How do people ordinarily use the six words listed in the first paragraph, and how do those words affect how teachers frame their work? To the point of thriving as teachers—of long-term flourishing—what language should teachers use? And how should teachers use that language to nourish their own sense that they indeed are professionals and thereby give themselves more joy and satisfaction in the work they do day to day and year to year? Teachers are more likely to flourish long-term if they can get the words *profession*, *vocation*, and *calling* so centrally fixed in their language and thinking that they never think of teaching simply as a job or as work, even though, as Chapter 4 makes clear, it is complex, intense, and challenging work.

Job

This small word is capable of accomplishing big things, both positive and negative. On the positive end of the continuum, I noted that fresh graduates of education programs looking for a teaching position commonly use the language of finding a job, and they get excited when they find one. A more neutral sense of the term might be in teachers' planning of their work weeks; they know they cannot usually take off and go to the beach on a Wednesday or do a grocery run at 11:00 a.m. The word *job* in that sentence is not necessarily negative; it is simply the reason that one cannot do something else because one is otherwise occupied, a reality experienced by all kinds of people every day, all over the world. We also use the word in a neutral sense when we talk about job descriptions, sometimes saying aloud or under our breath that some particular task is "not in my job description," perhaps even using that intentionally shocked look in case our conversation partner is not clear about our meaning.

The word *job* also has the potential to connote judgment and negativity, notably when it appears in such phrases as *dead-end job* or *stuck in this job*. Teachers should take joy that most people consider teaching to be noble work and so few people consider a teaching position to be a dead-end job (although "teaching must have been Plan B" persists in the language). Perhaps the whole ranking system by which some jobs enjoy greater prestige than others actually is a disservice to a culture. After all, everyone needs the food picked by low-prestige workers. Everyone enjoys the hotel rooms typically cleaned by immigrants. This book is not the right venue to argue that all work should be considered noble if it contributes to the common good. Still, teachers can perhaps take heart that in a culture with a ranking system firmly in place, teaching is considered good work.

What else does this word mean in relation to teaching? What are its connotations? With reference to teaching, it most typically carries neutral or positive connotations. In common usage, claiming that one has a teaching job does not diminish the unspoken fact that teachers are professionals or that most teachers feel that by teaching they are fulfilling their vocations.

Work

Teaching is work. And teachers know that. Those in many other professions work as hard as teachers. Real estate agents, for example, meet clients when their clients need them, often in the evening. Construction workers do physically demanding tasks. Forestry workers have accident and fatality rates that make teaching look easy. Teachers do not envy people working graveyard shifts. These comparisons notwithstanding, teaching is hard work. As I noted in the introduction to the book and in the introduction to this chapter, I deal at length in Chapter 4 with the complexity and the intensity of teachers' work. That chapter also treats some of the frustrations inherent in teaching and the reality that teaching pays mixed rewards. Anticipating the conclusions of Chapter 4 here, anyone who has taught and still claims that teaching is not hard work must have missed not only the memo but several crucial aspects of teaching itself.

In ordinary usage, the word *work* has a range of connotations from negative, through neutral, to positive. Starting with the negative connotations, think about these two sentences: "Work sucks!" and "I have to go to work" (usually accompanied by a slight drop of the head and a frown). The word also has neutral connotations where it refers to an activity one does at one's job or in one's profession. Think of this reply to a query about meeting for coffee: "Sure, how about tomorrow after work?" And it can have positive connotations. Think about the new graduate of an education program. Or think about the person who has landed a job after a period of unemployment and reports to family members along these lines, "I found work so we're going to be okay."

How should we characterize our work as teachers? And how well does the word suit teaching work? Chapter 3 presents a model of teaching that places a teacher's tasks related to curriculum, instruction, and assessment at the center, as what I call the core cycle of teaching. Teachers carry out these tasks in a classroom environment or climate that they have built, to some degree, with their students. Building that environment is also work. From almost any perspective then, referring to teaching as work seems appropriate. Teaching work is more than simply dealing with instruction. Teachers need to complete their grading in a timely manner. They attend meetings, and they call parents and guardians. They attend to professional reading. They respond to curriculum revisions, and they develop new instructional strategies. While none of these activities is as physically demanding as construction or felling trees, anyone who thinks that teaching is easy ought to try it for a day or two ... or maybe for a year.

Career

The word *career* has contrasting connotations from both the words we briefly examined above. First, it connotes longevity. People with a career or in a career have been and likely plan to be in the same profession or the same kind of work for some time. The person who claims to be starting a career or starting out in a career has similar plans. Unlike the connotations of the phrase *it's just a job*, the word *career* connotes direction; few people stay in a career by accident. Some may start into a new type of work by some unforeseen circumstance, but to claim that such work has become a career clearly implies a degree of intentionality. If someone left another profession to become a teacher, they might say they had switched professions or changed careers and no one would misunderstand what they meant. So far, the connotations of this word seem to range from descriptive and neutral to positive.

But the word sometimes carries a more ambitious or even aggressive semantic load. For example, *career path* might strike some as an indicator of overweening ambition. New teachers in their mid-twenties who say they plan to be school principals by age thirty-two or education professors by age forty may reveal this kind of ambition. Similarly, "I need an MEd degree to become a principal" may sound overly instrumental or slightly calculating to some ears. In such a frame, teaching positions and even relationships may become simply stepping stones on a career path. But there is another way to hear such statements. If it is ambition that gets teachers out of bed and back to work each morning, then perhaps setting vocational goals and taking the necessary steps to accomplish those goals should not be viewed negatively. Even for those teachers who have set themselves on a clear career path, one hopes that they get out of bed in the morning because they want to support students and be part of a learning community.

Profession and Professional

Teachers wonder periodically if, as teachers, they are actually entitled to consider themselves professionals. Do teachers rank with such easily recognizable professionals as doctors, lawyers, engineers, and dentists? What criteria should one use to answer that question? Salary? Supervision and oversight of the profession? Required education and training to enter the profession? Autonomy in the execution of responsibilities? Complexity of the work? These five questions represent objective criteria. Public opinion bears on teachers' views of their own work as well, and although it is more subjective, it is as measurable as any of the five more objective criteria. Including public opinion places the issue of perspective squarely in view. Many teachers see themselves as specially trained professionals, and the public may give lip service to that view, but teachers' salaries and the commonplace criticism that teachers have summers off indicate that another view is actually at work in many societies.

Beginning with salary, teachers fall below the other four professions listed. For many, that criterion eclipses all other means of judging whether teachers are professionals. This fact points to the double meaning that the word *profession* actually carries. First, it denotes the work one does to earn a living. Think, for example, of an application form that requires someone to identify their profession. Answers could range from chambermaid to university president. Its second meaning is connotative and bears centrally on the question of whether teachers qualify as professionals. If teachers are professionals, then their salaries typically rank at or near the bottom compared to other professionals.[1]

Among the many findings of a 2018 study of 35,000 adults in 35 countries conducted by the Varkey Foundation,[2] in only seven countries (Italy, Finland, Portugal, Singapore, Spain, Germany, and Switzerland) were teachers being paid more than what study participants thought they should be paid. The study also found a correlation between teacher salaries and student achievement (and status, which we will come to shortly). Not to be overly unkind, but perhaps those in the press or in government who berate teachers for students' performance ought to connect some of the dots the Varkey research has made plain for all who would read their research.

Most professionals are members of a society that oversees the profession. Thus, we have medical associations, law societies, engineering societies, and so on. One Canadian province, Ontario, allows teachers to govern their own profession. Nine provinces do not; the Department of Education in those provinces governs teachers' certification and work. Evaluated this way, one is likely to conclude that Ontario treats its teachers more as professionals than do the other nine provinces. How important is this criterion? Engineers, doctors, and lawyers who oversee their own professions consider it very important; they do not want to be beholden to civil servants who they would claim do not understand their work. I am not suggesting here that teachers ought to be up in arms. But I am suggesting that when jurisdictions withhold this aspect of professional supervision from teachers, they send a message to both teachers and the wider public. In most jurisdictions, nurses and social workers also do not govern their own professions, implying that governments view them in about the same way that they view teachers.

Considering the level of education required to enter the profession reveals some interesting differences between teaching and the paradigm examples of recognized professions. Teaching licensure programs in many countries typically follow two paths. Many teachers finish a four-year undergraduate degree that leads to licensure. Some complete a three- or four-year undergraduate degree in another field and then study for two more years in a licensure program that leads to a Bachelor of Education (BEd, After-Degree) or a Master of Arts in Teaching. So far, the Master of Education degree has remained the advanced or second degree one might take in education and is not required to secure a position. How does this level of education compare to what is required in other professions? Engineers typically study for four years but have as many as three full-time placements in engineering firms between their academic years. Lawyers typically do their law degree after a Bachelor's degree. Stopping to compare momentarily, we see that engineers have roughly the same amount of education as teachers who are licensed after a first degree. And lawyers spend about the same number of years in training—five or six—as do teachers who complete an after-degree licensure program. Medical doctors typically study for about six years but work under supervision beyond their studies for many more hours than teachers, lawyers, or engineers.

On the face of it, the education and training of teachers should qualify them to consider themselves professionals. And most teachers do view themselves that way. But because of the dangerous idea that anyone can teach, requirements are sometimes lowered or shelved altogether during teacher shortages. One story related to these lowered requirements perhaps bears witness to the complexity of teaching work. Florida, facing a teacher shortage, declared that military veterans could be fast-tracked into teaching. That this move attracted only three candidates in a state with a population of over 26,000,000 might warm qualified teachers' hearts. With a handful of exceptions, people who presumably were prepared to be shot at in their previous work did not find teaching enticing.[3]

Nevertheless, no jurisdiction facing a shortage of engineers or doctors would ever decide that, really, anyone can design a bridge or diagnose a tumor. That governments facing teacher shortages are willing to compromise on the education and training of teachers reveals something important and sobering about the view in some quarters of teachers' status as professionals.

To the fourth criterion listed above, teachers do have a high degree of autonomy regarding how they carry out their day-to-day responsibilities. As my readers know quite well, the curriculum is largely in place, implying that teachers' autonomy about what to teach is restricted; the Department of Education or a local educational authority has specified what students are supposed to learn. And the school that a teacher works in reports to a school board. Thus, the curriculum has a quasi-legal status. But how teachers help their students learn the curriculum materials and achieve the specified outcomes remains largely within teachers' own hands. Were teachers' status as professionals to be judged on this criterion alone, there would be no doubt; teachers are professionals.

The last criterion relates to the complexity of teaching work.[4] Knowing nothing about dentistry, law, medicine, engineering, nursing, or social work, I will make no comparisons. But I need not bother even trying because teachers know how complex their work is. Those who have done other kinds of professional work are entitled to make such comparisons.

Using only five criteria—salary, oversight of the profession, required education and training, autonomy, and complexity—teachers qualify as professionals. Claiming that casts a particular light on the sixth criterion, public opinion and the status of the teaching profession. Respect for teachers varies dramatically within and between countries. The 2018 Varkey Foundation study mentioned above with reference to salaries showed that people in China, Malaysia, Taiwan, Russia, and Indonesia have the greatest respect for teachers.[5] In China, in fact, teachers enjoy the same prestige as doctors. That study showed Canada, the United States, and the United Kingdom ranking eleventh, thirteenth, and sixteenth, respectively. Of the thirty-five countries studied, Israel and Brazil ranked lowest in public regard for the teaching profession. That study's participants typically ranked the status of teaching in the middle among the fourteen professions listed.

The Varkey study contains some nuanced findings about respect for teachers, and those are worth reporting here. Besides the differences between countries, the study found that older people have more respect for teachers than younger people. Respect for teachers is higher among those who have finished school, and men respect teachers more than women do. Those with children tend to respect teachers more than those without. Ethnic minorities tend to show less respect for teachers, while followers of the Islamic faith tend to respect teachers more. These sub-trends indicate the naivety of generalized statements such as, "No one respects teachers anymore." Clearly, respect for those in the teaching profession varies along a large number of lines.

As I did with the discussion of teachers' salaries, I note that the 2018 Varkey study revealed that teacher status, as measured by positive regard for teachers among members of the public, also correlates with student achievement.

Vocation and Calling

The word *vocation* comes from the Latin word for *voice*. While contemporary language users are not bound by etymology, the origins of words still inform usage and, in this case, help clarify that having or following a vocation implies that one has heard a voice or a call. Some teachers joke that they received a literal call—on a telephone—from a principal or from the Human Resources Department of a school district and therefore became teachers. This language of vocation and call actually has religious origins. Someone would follow a religious vocation in response to some kind of divine call or urging. Today, in non-religious settings, people might speak of "having a strong sense in their heart" that they should become teachers, or of "simply knowing they were on this earth to teach." They might say that "teaching fits me" or that "teaching seems to come up from the deepest parts of my being."

Parker Palmer explores this sense of vocation in *The Courage to Teach*. He writes that for the teacher who has a call to teach, "every major thread of one's life experience is honored, creating a weave of such coherence and strength that it can hold students and subject as well as self."[6] When he uses the language of "every major thread," Palmer does not mean that one gets married to one's job. But he does mean that those teachers who are clearly called can take all of themselves to work. That is, they can teach who they are, an idea I treat in greater depth in the next chapter.

Given the substantial overlaps in the meanings of those two terms, let us explore further the question of teaching as a vocation and a calling. Because the two terms, although they are not synonymous, are used interchangeably, I will treat them together here. We start with this assumption: anyone who understands the character of teaching work will know that it cannot be simply work or a job; there are easier ways to earn the same salary. If it cannot be simply work or a job, can it be a profession? Specifically, can one flourish in the teaching profession if one does not sense that teaching is one's vocation or calling? My thesis is simple: teachers who do not sense that teaching is their vocation will likely not flourish long-term in the teaching profession. On its face, this thesis has a sobering implication, one with two aspects. First, teachers must teach only if teaching is their vocation or they will likely be unhappy teaching. Second, they likely should teach if it is their vocation or they will be unhappy doing whatever it is they do other than teaching.

Beginning with the first aspect, someone who knows they are called to teach will be more capable of accepting the work of teaching and its mixed rewards. They will find a measure of contentment in teaching. They can engage in the artistry of curriculum and instructional design. They can take joy in their teaching and can give the gifts of learning to the next generation of children and young people. They can participate in and know they are participating in building a better world.

Someone who has never sensed that they are responding to some kind of inner voice or calling will more likely get fed up quickly and leave the profession early. They will not find contentment. If they stay in teaching, they will probably make themselves unhappy and bring little life to their students. In the words of one teacher colleague, teaching for the money, for the adrenaline rush, or to gain affirmation is a recipe for pain.

How can someone know that they are called to teach? One measure relates to the rewards: if the rewards of teaching are inherent in the activities of teaching, one is likely responding to a vocation. Teachers who enjoy trying new instructional strategies and who attend to their own professional development are likely fulfilling their teaching vocation. Teachers who feel like they have found their place in teaching are likely responding to a calling. Still, teachers who become somewhat uncertain after experiencing disappointments in their first years may still be responding to a calling.

One question that readers should consider only as a thought experiment is this: "Would you teach for free?" Almost all teachers would answer that they cannot teach for free because they need their salary to live on. But as a thought experiment, the question can still help teachers think about the concept of vocation. Of course, most people would teach a younger sibling to drive or teach a parent or grandparent how to post a picture online without charging. But aside from the need for a salary or the obvious cases where one helps a loved one learn how to do a task, asking about teaching for free can help teachers reflect on the joy they derive from teaching. Those who take real joy from teaching are probably called to teach. The teaching-for-free question may seem fairer if we specify some conditions. What about on a service trip to support teacher colleagues in another country? What about helping immigrants learn a new language through a program at the public library? What about in a club or voluntary organization? Teachers who would never dream of teaching for free five days a week in a school might answer yes to some of the scenarios I suggested. Such teachers are likely called to teach.

Confirmation of the call to teach can come from external sources as well. Student reviews and evaluations of supervisors tell teachers something about the quality of their work. Family members and trusted friends who listen to teachers talking about their work can reflect on the tone of such conversations and the persistent themes that emerge.

The second aspect of the calling to teach is not teaching if one is called. Presuming the readers of this volume are teachers, I will not treat this aspect of calling at length. At its simplest, someone who is called to teach should teach; they will not be content with life unless they do.

Conclusion

My goal in this chapter was to frame teaching in a way that lifts it well above the status of jobs and work. People use words other than those I have examined here when they talk about their work. At minimum, those who have a strong desire (in the non–Lady Macbeth sense) to enjoy a teaching career and those who view themselves as professionals are more likely to flourish as teachers. Beyond those two categories, thriving in the teaching profession almost always requires that one senses it is one's calling or vocation to teach. Expressed hyperbolically, one should be able periodically to say these words: "All the DNA that ever existed existed so I could be doing this work with these students today." In its more subdued form, the sentiment might run like this: "I simply cannot believe they are paying me to do this work!" Teachers who flourish long-term experience those moments, not every day but often enough to continue responding to their calling to teach.

Notes

1. See Taylor Mali's comedy routine, "What Do Teachers Make?," https://www.youtube.com/watch?v=RxsOVK4syxU Type in "clean version" in YouTube for a rendition with less colorful language than the one listed here.
2. Varkey Foundation, *Global Teacher Status Index, 2018*, https://www.varkeyfoundation.org/global-teacher-status.
3. Scott Maxwell, "Florida Teacher Shortage: Veterans Take a Pass on Filling the Gap," *Orlando Sentinel*, May 3, 2024, https://www.orlandosentinel.com/2024/05/02/teacher-shortage-veterans-say-no-maxwell/.
4. I deal with the complexity of teaching work at length in Chapter 4.
5. The Varkey report is summarized by Tim Walker, "Where Do Teachers Get the Most Respect?," *NEA Today*, April 2019. Also see Education International's, *Global Report on the Status of Teachers*, 2021, https://www.ei-ie.org/en/item/25403:the-global-report-on-the-status-of-teachers-2021.
6. Parker Palmer, *The Courage to Teach: Exploring the Inner Landscape of a Teacher's Life* (San Francisco, CA: Jossey-Bass, 1998), 15.

3 Teachers' Day-to-Day Work
A Model

An online image search of *models of teaching* or *curriculum models* will yield hundreds of images, most of them produced by education professors and meant to illustrate how the component parts of teaching should work together. This chapter focuses on a model that presents the central aspects of teaching in a simplified way (Figure 3.1). This graphic representation provides a framework for discussion of the details of teaching at various points in the chapters that follow and thereby contributes to the overall purpose of this book, which is to encourage teachers to keep on teaching, to enjoy teaching, and to flourish professionally.

Why does a search of curriculum models or models of teaching return as many records and images as it does? In short, models are the mental constructs by which teachers think about how the component parts of teaching fit together. Educators may not recognize that they work day after day within and out of a model of teaching, but they do. That is, teaching models are necessary and not just nice.[1] Despite being essential parts of teachers' thinking and daily work, models of teaching often receive little attention once they have been dealt with in educational foundations courses at the university.

A model of teaching can begin in several places. It could begin with the prevalent views of education in a given era in educational history. It could begin with the mandates of a state, province, or school jurisdiction. This model begins with the three central parts or aspects of teachers' work: curriculum, instruction, and assessment. These core aspects of teaching take place in a classroom ethos or climate that teachers must build, and which, in turn, is situated in the context of three wider questions: How do teachers teach who they are? How do teachers teach who their students are? How do teachers teach where they are? That is, how do they suit their classroom programs to the social and political contexts in which they work?

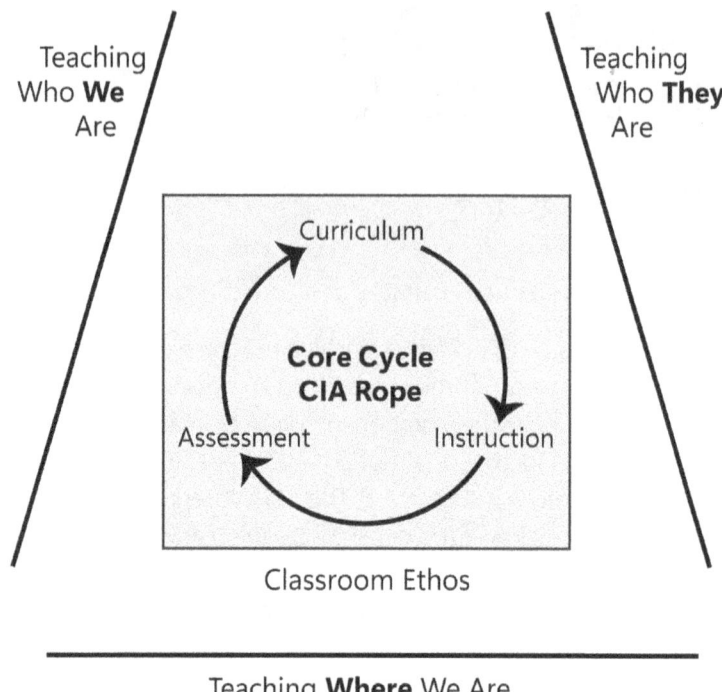

Figure 3.1 A model of the teacher's work. Model by author: Kristen Badley.

All teachers would benefit from taking time to articulate their own model because working consciously within and out of a model can nourish their understanding of and vision for their day-to-day work. That is, having a simple, visual understanding of one's work helps one get up in the morning and go back to work. Obviously, a visual model is not all a teacher needs, but it helps.

The key elements of teaching work are curriculum, instruction, and assessment. Teachers give most of their teaching day to these three elements. In this model, these three elements appear in the immediate context of teaching work: the classroom ethos, culture, or climate, three terms I use interchangeably throughout this book. On the outer sides of Figure 3.1 are three important matters that necessarily shape how teachers view the central elements in the graphic: teachers need to teach who they are, out of their own being. They need to teach who their students are, recognizing both individual differences and cohort characteristics. And they need to teach where they are, taking seriously their social and political context.

Chapter 4 treats the complexity of teaching work in more depth, but Figure 3.1 makes clear some of that complexity, inasmuch as the central aspects of teaching function as a part of a cycle, connecting to each other in a classroom environment. The environment itself is framed within at least three larger questions. The center of the graphic represents the main features of a teacher's work. A jurisdiction or school board prescribes a curriculum. For a couple of obvious examples, teachers are mandated to teach certain content such as a unit on the water cycle in year seven science, or the French Revolution in grade eleven Social Studies. With the prescribed content, outcomes, or standards in view, teachers prepare for and carry out several days or weeks of appropriate instruction. And they assess how well their students have learned the prescribed contents.

The three-stand rope in a sheath (Figure 3.2) serves as a simple symbol for the core cycle of teaching activities. The three elements in the core cycle function like such a rope. The rope is stronger with all three strands than it would be if any one of the strands were missing. The strands are woven together and no strand functions independently of the other two. The name *CIA rope* is memorable because it sounds like a spy agency.

In a physical rope, the sheath protects the inner strands of the rope from wear and tear, abrasions, and decay due to weather. It is not too much of a stretch to argue that teachers who succeed in building a positive and inviting classroom climate protect and facilitate the central tasks they need to do each teaching day. In a positive classroom ethos, most students willingly join their teacher in the core activities of curriculum, instruction, and even assessment.

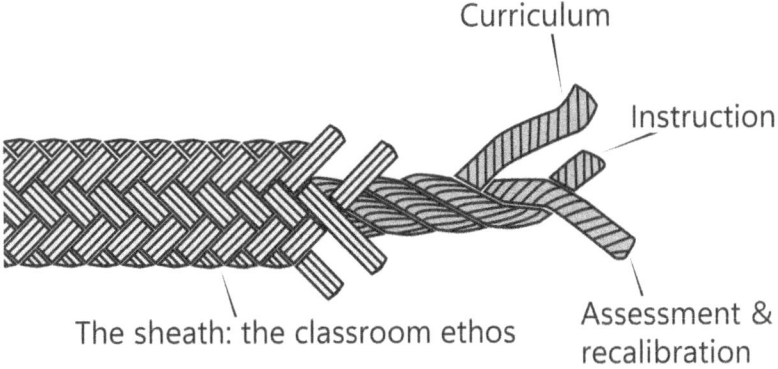

Figure 3.2 The CIA rope consisting of three strands: curriculum, instruction, and assessment. The strands are wrapped in a sheath, the classroom ethos. Kristen Badley.

The Core Cycle: Curriculum, Instruction, and Assessment

Readers of this volume do not need the core cycle of curriculum, instruction, and assessment explained to them; that is the work they do every teaching day. Nevertheless, in its treatment of the complexity and intensity of teaching, Chapter 4 does deal with the trio of curriculum, instruction, and assessment. Before moving to the outer parts of Figure 3.1 however, one note is in order. If one additional aspect of teachers' work were to be added to this model, it would appear between assessment and curriculum, in the upper left part of the core cycle. That addition would be *revision* or *recalibration*. That is, teachers critically evaluate their students' success in meeting the learning outcomes of a given portion of the curriculum, and they make adjustments to their teaching materials and strategies before teaching those materials again. They recalibrate and revise. Having noted that possible revision, we move the conversation about this model to the classroom ethos and the three questions lying outside the core cycle.

The Classroom Ethos

In-service teachers have all worked at building a positive classroom ethos or shaping a classroom culture, and they know already the challenges of doing so. During their in-school placements, pre-service teachers may already have had a taste of this challenging construction task; they will certainly have observed their cooperating teacher attending to the crucial matter of classroom climate. It is not necessary here to catalog the challenges teachers encounter as they try to construct and protect a space where they and their students will want to work, teach, and learn (challenges which are catalogued in Chapter 4).

On the other hand, readers can recall the moments when their students were fully engaged with their learning tasks. In 2020, my colleague Susanna Steeg Thornhill and I published *Generating Tact and Flow for Effective Teaching and Learning*.[2] In this book, we presented dozens of teachers' accounts of classes in which their students got into what Mihaly Csikszentmihalyi calls a *flow state*.³ That is, these students were totally focused, they were unaware of the passage of time, and they were enjoying the inherent rewards of learning. A thread runs through most of the narratives our teacher colleagues provided us for that book: students found the classroom climate safe and invitational. Almost all teachers have experienced such moments.

With another colleague, Margaretta Patrick, I published *The Complexities of Authority in the Classroom: Fostering Democracy for Student Learning*.⁴ In this volume, we and our contributors specifically address the question of classroom climate, focusing our attention on the character of teacher-student relationships and how we as teachers exercise our authority in ways that create trust and increase students' desire to learn. I will not repeat here what my colleagues and I presented in the two volumes I have mentioned. But in just six words, I will summarize one conclusion of those two books: a positive classroom climate is essential.

Teaching Who We Are

Our work with the three elements of the core cycle needs to arise out of who we are as teachers. I return to this idea repeatedly in this book and will treat it only briefly here, starting with a negative example. I recently insulated part of my basement with pink fiberglass insulation. As it happens, I am not allergic to fiberglass insulation, and so I suffered no ill effects from installing the batts between the studs in the utility room wall. In fact, when I was a university student, I insulated seventy-two houses for a summer job; I knew I could manage one small room. To the point of this book, though, and to the questions about teaching as a vocation or calling, installing pink fiberglass insulation in my utility room walls was simply something I needed to do so I could install the wallboard. It was just a job that needed doing; it did not arise out of the deepest parts of my being. Insulating is not who I am. Insulating is not my vocation, a fact I knew with certainty when I insulated those seventy-two houses.

So, what is the opposite of insulating for a teacher? For you? What does it mean to teach who we are? I cannot add much to what Parker Palmer wrote decades ago in *The Courage to Teach: Exploring the Inner Landscape of a Teacher's Life*.⁵ The second part of Palmer's title is perfect inasmuch as he examines in detail teachers' interior processes—both mental and emotional—and how those processes connect to the joys and sorrows of our daily work.

Why claim that an essential part of a model of teaching must be to teach who we are? The answer is simple: for our own mental health. If I am forced to become someone other than who I am, if I am required to become inauthentic to keep my position then I ultimately will end up unhappy. When my colleague Gordon T. Smith and I interviewed nineteen educators in their final decade of work, we concluded, among other things, that if one truly does not fit where one is employed then one needs to seek employment elsewhere.[6] Fit, fitting . . . that is why teaching who we are figures so prominently in my model.

Teaching Who They Are

What does it mean to claim that teachers need to teach who our students are? First, and obviously, we need to be aware of individual differences. My readers have attended enough professional sessions on differentiation that they already know they should respond appropriately to the wide range of skills that any given group of students brings to class on any given day. The phrases *differentiated instruction* and *trauma-informed practice* have become as naturally at home in the educational lexicon as the words *desk* and *text*. So, yes, to teach who they are implies that we need to recognize our students' individual differences and the contexts from which they come. Such language reminds us that our job is not simply to focus on getting through to some kind of generic student with the curriculum contents we have planned for the teaching day or the week.

Rather, we must attend to the individual characteristics of our learners. This student comes to class with this particular learning difficulty. That student carries to class the burden of a family issue, the details of which we may or may not know. And that student has difficulty focusing today because of an upcoming play, concert, game, or even a major assessment in another class. That other student has difficulty understanding oral instructions or, for that matter, listening to an explanation of anything for more than ten minutes. Some other students come with extraordinary learning strengths. In short, good teachers attend to the individuals in their classrooms.

Teachers also need to attend to cohort and generational characteristics. As I write this (in 2024), climate change, wars, and politics have led many adolescents to adopt a more pessimistic view of the world's prospects than the view held by the generation that preceded them. Today's students have a keener sense of irony than previous generations of students. For them, technology is ubiquitous. Most of them have reduced financial expectations than did their parents. Factors such as these characterize whole cohorts of students.

To refer to popular culture for a moment, at the time of my writing this paragraph Taylor Swift is perhaps the pre-eminent popular singer in the world. If I had written this Chapter 10 years earlier I might have named Miley Cyrus or Beyoncé instead of Taylor Swift. But now, in 2024, she has captured the hearts of millions of fans and given them a way to identify themselves with something both larger than themselves and more positive than the apparent state of the world. These claims may not be true at the time you read this, but my point is that they are true in 2024 and that most teachers and students during this academic year know who she is and most students would love somehow to get tickets to a Taylor Swift concert. To my point, given this cohort's interest in her, can teachers find ways to incorporate her fame, her lyrics, her economic impact, and other aspects of her rise into their instruction and thereby teach who their students are? Incorporating her in such ways would be one way to teach who our students are.

Regarding a cohort of students younger than those who adore Taylor Swift, some teachers may be finding ways to incorporate Minecraft into their instruction. In this context, the word *incorporate* definitely does not mean giving over instructional time to playing Minecraft. But at this moment in the history of online entertainment some teachers will be making connections between Minecraft and curriculum and thereby getting some of their students' attention. To recall John Dewey's instructions from more than a century ago, educators should start with their students' interests.[7] The year two or three curriculum should not be all Minecraft all the time,[8] but making some connections to this popular game (popular in 2024 at least) might be an effective way to teach who students are.

The previous section ended with the question why it was essential for teachers to teach who they themselves are. This section ends with a similar question: why is essential to teach who our students are? Among the several available answers, the best one seems to lie along the lines of this: if teachers focus only on the curriculum contents and forget who those contents are for, then they will bore their students and ultimately themselves. Teaching who our students are is a necessary pre-condition for student engagement. And student engagement is most typically a pre-condition for teacher flourishing.

Teaching Where We Are

By *teaching where we are* I mean two things. First, teachers teach in an educational jurisdiction. That could be as wide as a national education system, a state or provincial system, a school board with a dozen or several hundred schools, or a single, independent school. Long-term flourishing as teachers implies coming to terms with the legal setting in which they teach and the expectations of those to whom they report.

This first sense of *teaching where we are* is easier to understand with a Venn diagram. In the first circle are the teacher's own vision of life, educational philosophy, and pedagogical ideals. The other circle represents the vision of education, pedagogical ideals, and (let's be honest) the rules and regulations of the setting in which that teacher works. To what degree do these circles overlap? Teachers who see that the two circles barely overlap should—for their own mental health and long-term flourishing—likely seek other employment opportunities. The sobering corollary to that conclusion is that if the two circles overlap completely then, while that teacher may be very happy at work—he or she may find little challenge at work and may not have much life outside of work.

Second, teaching where we are implies that teachers recognize their location in a cultural history and in both the nation and local setting in which they teach. In my own case, I have taught in two American states and four Canadian provinces. I have also worked with teacher colleagues in Kenya and the Philippines. I have taught secondary students, as well as university students from undergraduate to doctoral. In every case, whether paid or as a volunteer, I have had to recognize—and even perhaps honor—the settings in which I was working. That implied, for example, not cracking classroom jokes about the national president in either Kenya or the Philippines. It implied not criticizing my host country's passion about sports when I taught in the United States. It implied doing my best to learn about the history, traditions, and social mores of all the places I taught, even the regional differences between provinces in my native Canada.

Teaching where we are implies respecting local traditions and local interests. And, in turn, that kind of respect may imply learning things one did not know before and showing interest in sports or local celebrities about which one did not previously care. If I may be allowed one tautology, teaching where we are implies being where we are.

To conclude, teachers' contracts and the teaching standards documents of the jurisdictions in which they work almost certainly state that they must carry out specified responsibilities in specified ways. That is, they are legally bound in some sense to teach where they are. Second, teachers who want to flourish long term in the profession need to be able to focus on student success and not be distracted by their discomfort with their school's ethos or their disagreement with a school jurisdiction's published goals. And, as I argued in Chapter 2 regarding teachers' finding their vocation, if they find themselves unable to teach where they are because they simply do not fit there then—for their own flourishing—they need to find positions where they do fit.

Notes

1 To gloss an old phrase often applied to a related essential to thought: metaphors. Search "metaphors necessary nice" online and notice the agreement on their importance.
2 Susanna Thornhill Steeg and Ken Badley, *Generating Tact and Flow for Effective Teaching and Learning* (New York: Routledge, 2020).
3 Mihalyi Csikszentmihalyi, *Flow: The Psychology of Optimal Experience* (New York: Harper and Row, 1990).
4 (New York: Routledge, 2022).
5 (San Francisco, CA: Jossey-Bass, 1998).
6 "Called to Teach," *Teaching Theology and Religion* 1, no. 3 (October 1998): 171–6.

7 John Dewey, *The Child and the Curriculum* (Chicago, IL: The University of Chicago Press, 1902).

8 My eight-year-old grandson says it would be good if school were all Minecraft all the time. On this point he disagrees with almost every teacher in the world. When pressed, he admitted that at the end of the school year he would not know very much.

4 Teaching
Intense and Complex with Mixed Rewards

Teaching is intense work, and it is complex. It can be deeply frustrating and, as all teachers know, it comes with mixed rewards. In the introduction to this volume, I promised to include only one chapter focused on the challenges and sorrows of teaching. I repeat what I noted there: that readers are welcome to skip this chapter if they wish, especially given that much of the chapter could have been written by almost anyone who has worked in a classroom for at least a year.

The title of this chapter arises out of the description the Director of Child Protection for one Canadian province gave of her work, that it was complex and intense. Legally, she was ultimately responsible for the welfare of thousands of children who, for a variety of reasons, ended up in the care of the government. By poaching her use of the words *intense* and *complex* I do not mean to diminish the scale or seriousness of her responsibilities. After all, she had a budget in the hundreds of millions of dollars and oversaw the welfare of these thousands of children and youth. But those two words struck me as applicable to the work of teachers.

Both teachers and non-teachers sometimes describe teaching work as hard, demanding, or wearying. While not suggesting the removal of those words from our lexicon, to my ears, the trio of intense, complex, and mixed rewards offers more specific insight into the character of teachers' work. The three main sections of this chapter explore some of the ways that these three descriptors suit the work of teachers.

Complexity

Interlocking jigsaw puzzles provide a helpful image to represent the complexity of teaching. Imagine a 500-piece or 1000-piece puzzle called curriculum. The teacher's daily task is to put all the puzzle pieces in place. Like other puzzles, the curriculum puzzle has a picture on the box showing what the final product should look like.

Unlike puzzlers who relax with a puzzle for an evening, teachers need to work on the curriculum puzzle at the same time that they are working on several other puzzles. Thus, to complete the curriculum puzzle, for example, they must be multitaskers. In the previous chapter, Figure 3.1 offered a model of teaching meant to represent both the core cycle of activities that teachers engage in every day and the context in which they carry out the activities of the core cycle. As a reminder, the three components of the core cycle were curriculum, instruction, and assessment. Figure 3.1 situated that core cycle in the immediate context of a classroom culture and then situated all those components within three larger and very important questions. And therein lies the challenge of the curriculum puzzle.

At the same time that teachers are attending to the elements of the core cycle, they are doing so in a classroom climate that they construct day by day with their students. And all that work is done in light of three large questions: How do teachers teach who they are, authentically and from the deep parts of themselves? How do they teach who their students are, attending to individual differences as well as cohort characteristics? And how do they teach where they are, recognizing that they work in a social and political context that assumes or specifies in writing a whole set of expectations.

Each of these elements is a puzzle in itself. Many teachers claim that they did not really figure out how all the pieces of the instruction puzzle—preparation, instruction itself, record-keeping, administration, and the like—until their second decade of teaching. Some say it took longer than that. Assembling the pieces of the assessment puzzle can take just as long. The classroom climate puzzle—constructing a space in which both teacher and students want to work—can take a lifetime. In effect then, teachers are not like puzzlers who can clear the dining room table after dinner and relax for the evening. Rather, all the puzzle pieces from seven or eight puzzles are spilled into a single pile on the table. And the teacher's job is to construct each puzzle. Even with a photo on every box, the challenge would feel overwhelming to an actual puzzler. And it does for many teachers.

While this metaphor has some weaknesses, on the whole, it helps make the case that teaching is complex. The fact that so many teachers not only survive for decades but actually thrive while doing such complex work speaks to both their commitment and their resilience.

Intensity

The metaphor of interlocking jigsaw puzzles could also be used to argue that teaching is intense. After all, teaching involves simultaneously navigating all the components of teaching shown in Figure 3.1 and likely listed in most teachers' job descriptions.

Several specific aspects of teaching illustrate intensity. For example, confrontations with students—and sometimes their parents and guardians—add to the intensity of teaching. Teachers must deescalate when a student seeks a confrontation or behaves in a way that may endanger other students. Thus, teachers do not assemble the puzzle of instruction in a vacuum. Rather, they assemble that puzzle in a room with children or young people, some of whom are dealing on any given day with any number of unhappy personal or family issues. An outburst adds to the intensity. The teacher wants to lower the temperature and return the class to instruction. The student acting out wants any number of other results, none of which perhaps overlap with the teacher's goal of carrying on with instruction. One might even argue that students are puzzles themselves. Readers could add dozens of other reasons that instruction can add to the intensity of teaching.

Ordinary, completely non-confrontational interactions with students also add to the intensity of teaching. Think for example of the student who asks, "Do you have the assignment that I missed last Thursday?" That student, who asks such a question without ill intention, has no idea of the complexity and the volume of distinct details that teachers carry through a typical teaching day in their heads. Doubtless, some teachers can instantly report to a student the status of the assignment from last Thursday because they have exceptional memories. But for some teachers, such a question may add to a sense that they are overwhelmed, not only because they don't know the answer to that particular question but because they may hear the question as evidence that students have no awareness of the true scope of their teacher's job.

What some call *initiative fatigue* adds to the intensity of teachers' work.[1] Most teachers recognize that as cultures and societies change, school curricula need to be updated. Curriculum change implies more work for teachers because they must develop new materials and adapt their instructional strategies to suit the new curriculum. Likewise, teachers need to give time to understanding how new reporting requirements and new software work. School jurisdictions make decisions about new emphases that need to be integrated into or layered onto existing curriculum, again requiring work from classroom teachers.

Many secondary teachers have as few as four minutes between classes. Elementary teachers are typically required to change subjects on the fly, presumably invisibly and seamlessly, without even a moment to breathe between one subject and the next. Toss just one or two off-the-wall student questions into this hurried mix, and you have some key moments of frustration for many teachers who were focused on getting the next part of the day started and instead are dealing with questions residual from the last period. Students often ask those questions only because they did not understand something and haven't detected that the teacher is moving along. Without assigning blame for the lack of understanding, the effect of the question is still to reduce substantially the smoothness of the transition (and the teacher's breathing time).

Assessment also contributes to the overall intensity of teaching, with the sheer volume of grading students' work perhaps being the main aspect of assessment that makes teaching intense. Many teachers do not typically complete their grading by the time they leave their school building after their teaching day. Along with their preparation for teaching, their grading may take several hours at home on many weeknights of the school term.[2] The intrusion of artificial intelligence into student work adds to the intensity of teaching as well (and possibly to the matter of teaching's rewards). Teachers have always had to deal with plagiarism but now have the added challenge of working with students who have relied more than they should on AI to produce their work. Teachers who believe that completing assignments is a source of learning—and that is almost all teachers—will experience disappointment when students submit plagiarized and AI-generated assignments.

Some teachers experience a persistent sense that they could and should be doing more. Again, they entered the teaching profession with humanistic motives; they wanted to make the world a better place. As is the case with social workers and members of several other professions, by definition they could do more. And, as happens to people working in those other professions, could turns into should, and some teachers feel like they have never done enough.

Mixed Rewards

Teaching pays mixed rewards. Students and family members will thank teachers for their amazing classes. These teachers will receive greeting cards, coffee cards, kind emails, and home-baked treats. On the other hand, some people will post comments expressing surprise that teachers are bright enough to tie their shoes. These critics will express their certainty that people who do such easy work for so few days a year should not get anywhere near that much pay. Such is the range of rewards for the complex and intense work of teaching.[3]

Teachers' periodic frustrations with teaching perhaps lie right in the gap between the things they feel like they would do for free and the things they feel they should be paid $320,000 per year to put up with (a non-arbitrary amount I will come back to shortly). Teachers know that both feelings come with the teaching territory; they're both part of the job. But most teachers love their job and don't want to shove it.[4] If they had wanted to make money, they would have gone into orthodontics or commercial real estate. They have humanistic motivations and they teach because they want to leave the world a better place than they found it. On the other hand, no one thinks of grading assignments when asked for a paradigm example of a good time. But, as it turns out, changing the world through teaching is not only more complex and intense than most teachers knew when they started, but there are real frustrations; the rewards for teaching are mixed. Teachers know about the mixed rewards and frustrations inherent in the work they do.

Most teachers have days when they succeed in their craft and can take joy in the sense that they are fulfilling their vocation. They enjoy the creativity and innovation they can bring to their planning and instruction. They enjoy the buzz of teaching well. And they often can take deep satisfaction with the outcomes of their work as they see students make leaps in their learning. Elementary teachers know they cannot put a price on the light in children's eyes when they make a reading breakthrough. And secondary teachers love to share the mirth of a whole class rapping a mnemonic for the quadratic equation. They recognize that they are privileged to be able to influence and shape cohorts and even generations of students. And of course, teachers can recall moments when individual students made progress because of their teacher's efforts or when a student shouted a greeting to them on the street or inside a shopping mall.

Another of the mixed rewards relates to the reality that teachers' students—their clients if you will—keep leaving regardless of how well those teachers do their job. There are obvious exceptions; teachers in one-room schools may see their students year after year, and teachers in small schools and subject-area specialists may teach some students for several years in a row. But most grade-level teachers will say goodbye to their students at the end of the academic year and quite possibly not teach them again, a reality quite different from that of people in many other professions. Plumbers, lawyers, real estate agents, and landscapers who do a good job usually retain their clients. Year after year, they are rewarded by their clients' loyalty and return business. Many teachers must satisfy themselves only with the fact that they did a good job, perhaps being reminded of that good job when a former student greets them in the school hallway or somewhere off the school property.

Elsewhere in this book, I treat the rather widespread assumption that anyone can teach, an idea that leads some teachers to laugh and demoralizes others. At the time of writing, teachers are caught in the crossfire of the culture wars; their autonomy as professionals is being reduced as they hear demands from across the political spectrum that they teach this but not that or that but not this. And no one enjoys being bullied or threatened by students, parents, administrators, or governments. Criticisms of entire education systems and individual teachers wear teachers down and lead some to consider leaving the profession. Increasingly, teachers face public criticism and backlashes on social media and websites (such as ratemyteachers.com), which can be troubling and isolating, leading to deep vocational questions.

The pandemic led a number of teachers to take early retirement, partly out of concern for their own health, given their possible exposure to the virus in their school buildings. Their early retirements led some other veteran teachers to wonder if they too should leave the profession. Also as a result of the pandemic, the available pool of retired teachers who previously acted as substitute teachers shrank, meaning that administrators and classroom teachers now had to cover classes for which no substitute teacher could be found.

Conclusion

This book arises out of the obvious need for teachers to find more ways to support themselves and for people outside school buildings to support teachers. This chapter arises out of the need to make clear that such support needs to extend far beyond giving teachers yet another World's Best Teacher coffee mug at the end of the school year. Teaching work is complex and intense. And the rewards are mixed.

Most people admit that teachers do noble work and that society could not make any progress without them. Most teachers actually want to do this work; it is why they show up at school every day. For most teachers, teaching is a vocation. In some sense, teachers do their work in response to a voice, and they know this is what they need to do.

Teaching is intense, consuming work and teachers need deep reasons to keep doing it. One analysis of effective teachers caught educators' attention in 2010 when economists suggested that kindergarten teachers should perhaps earn US$320,000 per year.[5] Based on a study of 12,000 students who had reached the age of 30 by the time of the study, Raj Chetty and some colleagues at Harvard University calculated that amount as the difference in lifetime income a whole class of kindergarten pupils would likely earn as a result of having had a great kindergarten teacher. Chetty and his colleagues did not address the economic dimension of other social goods such as improved health and decreased crime, so one may consider $320,000 a conservative estimate. Teachers would gladly accept such a salary but, amazingly, they continue to return to their school buildings day after day and do the intense work of teaching for so much less than that.

Notes

1 Regarding initiative fatigue, see the work of Doug Reeves, for example, https://www.creativeleadership.net/resources-content/overcoming-initiative-fatigue-focusing-time-energy-and-resources-for-student-results.

2 Researchers have studied teachers' work weeks for decades. For an early example, see John D. McAulay, "A Teacher's Week," *Peabody Journal of Education* 33, no. 5 (1956): 308–10. More recent studies include this one: Greg Thompson, Sue Creagh, Meghan Stacey, Anne Hogan, and Nicole Mockler, "Researching Teachers'

Time Use: Complexity, Challenges, and a Possible Way Forward," *The Australian Educational Researcher* 51 (2024): 1647–70.

3   Privacy considerations prevent my posting a screenshot of a Facebook page that listed the names of an entire elementary school staff and their actual salaries. This table of information that should never have been made public was titled "Are They Worth It?" The member of that school staff who showed me that page said these words as she showed it to me: "This is what we put up with!" As a result of that interaction, I began a book project called *Pissed With Teaching*... which turned out to be too discouraging to write.

4   Here, I obviously borrow language from the title of the 1981 movie, *Take This Job and Shove It*, directed by Gus Tomkins (Los Angeles, CA: Metro-Goldwyn-Mayer, Embassy Pictures). The film was named after a 1977 country and western song with the same name, written by David Allan Coe and sung by Johnny Paycheck (Los Angeles, CA: Columbia Recording Studios).

5   David Leonhardt, "The Case for $320,000 Kindergarten Teachers," *New York Times*, July 27, 2010, https://www.nytimes.com/2010/07/28/business/economy/28leonhardt.html.

5 Teachers' Worldviews, Teachers' Identities

Viewers of the opening credits of Tom Tykwer's breathtakingly fast film, *Run Lola Run*,[1] hear a narrator ask several questions. He precedes his first question by observing that the human is the most mysterious species on the planet . . . because we love to ask questions. He then asks the film's viewers, "Who are we?" "Where do we come from?" and "Where are we going?" The inquiries end with the epistemological question, "How do we know what we think we know?" The narrator ends by suggesting that all our human questions come down to one question. *Run Lola Run* refuses to tell us what that question is—at least directly—but the camera zooms in on a policeman holding a soccer ball. He looks straight into the camera and makes three short statements: "The ball is round. The game lasts 90 minutes. That's a fact." With his three assertions, the credits end and the film begins.

Two and a half decades after that film's release, Murray Sinclair, a career judge in Canada and co-chair of Canada's Truth and Reconciliation Commission, frames his 2024 book *Who We Are: Four Questions for A Life and A Nation*[2] by asking very similar questions: Where do I come from? Where am I going? Why am I here? Who am I? That he starts a book dealing with the challenges facing a nation needing to reckon with its own treatment of its Indigenous peoples with these worldview questions ought to tell us something about the importance of the ways we answer these questions and the importance of the ways our views of the world shape our day-to-day lives.

Everyone has pondered similar questions at some point in their life. Anyone who has suffered loss, felt heartbreak, sensed the presence of the numinous amidst the stars or the birth of a newborn, or enrolled in Philosophy 101 will have begun to ask such questions. People do want to know where they fit. People do want to find out what life means. People do need ways to see the world that are true to the character of that world. Throughout what historians refer to as the modern period (beginning in the early 1600s), many have argued that empirical answers were the only acceptable answers to such questions.[3] Yet, most people suspect the existence of, and spend considerable energy seeking something with more heft than simple empirical claims. Modernity also produced a less communitarian and more individualistic understanding of the person or the self, leading to a shift by which the question "Why are we here?" has often become "Why am I here?"

Everyone, including teachers, lives within and lives out of a worldview. Teachers' worldviews include their answers and approaches to questions central to the work of teaching. What are students like? What motivates them? And what are schools for? As they are presently organized, do schools serve society's most pressing educational needs? What should the prescribed curriculum include, and what can be omitted? Teachers who want to live well in the world and flourish in their professions ask such questions as these. They also look for life-giving ways to understand their own work as educators and to reflect on their own sense of vocation, especially at those times when they experience weariness or frustration and wonder if they have chosen the right profession. How can teachers learn to live well in the world in which they find themselves?

For teachers to respond intentionally and thoughtfully to the questions of worldview, they need at least two things. First, they need to be able to identify and articulate their own worldview. This will require understanding what forces have shaped and shape that worldview, what forms it takes, and how it expresses itself in the world in which they find themselves.

Second, they need to understand how their worldviews resemble and differ from the worldviews of other people they meet in their individual contexts and in society as a whole. As people understand the worldviews of others better, they typically understand better what forces and motivations are at work in themselves and why they themselves respond in the ways they do to life's events and to world affairs. Understanding our own worldviews and the worldviews of others makes it more possible to live in and respond to our circumstances intentionally, consistently, and with some joyful calm.

What Is a Worldview?

At its simplest, a worldview is a person's or society's way of seeing the world. A worldview provides a total, comprehensive way of looking at everything—knowledge, ethics, humanity, meaning, and even the divine. In the early twentieth century, anthropologists and sociologists brought the German word *Weltanschauung*, which simply means *worldview* or *viewing the world*, into English. They found it useful to identify that every society has its own way of seeing and living in the world. For over a century now, scholars in diverse academic disciplines have utilized the concept for their own purposes, and some have explored it in depth.[4] For our purposes as educators, I will first introduce the concept, follow that introduction by exploring briefly the forces and influences that shape worldviews, and then note how and why people maintain and change their worldviews.

As do all people, teachers live life with all its day-to-day parts, big and small, within a mental framework or worldview. A worldview includes uncounted assumptions, convictions, ideas, prejudices, old sayings and proverbs, tendencies and habits of mind, the sources or sometimes even the existence of which people might live unaware. Although some teachers may not often reflect explicitly on their worldview, how they view the world nevertheless shapes how they respond to that world outside and inside their classrooms.

The popularity of the concept of worldview derives in part because it reminds us that everyone operates out of some vision of the good life and views the world in one way or another. An atheist goes through the day without seeing the hand of any god at work, while a religious believer perhaps sees a divine hand at work in the presence of natural beauty or in the kindness of a friend. Canadians tend to hold an image of themselves as a polite people. Japanese people tend to believe that Japanese cars are as good as or better than German cars. These examples illustrate that worldviews have to do not only with people's answers to the big questions but also with their everyday lives. In the most general terms, a worldview guides people's thoughts and actions from day to day. It guides and gives meaning to their actions. And it helps people perceive, filter, and classify the world they live in.

Similarly, teachers' worldviews affect how they view their world, both inside and outside schools. Teachers' worldviews influence their views of the nature and purposes of curriculum, the best ways to carry out classroom instruction, and the most effective ways of assessing student learning. For members of the wider public, teachers' views on these matters obviously do not rank in importance with the big questions of, for example, the meaning of life. However, for teachers wanting to succeed and thrive professionally, the answers to these questions matter a great deal every teaching day. One's worldview and one's identity are clearly intertwined, implying that teachers should reflect on their worldviews and on the connections between their worldviews and their day-to-day practices as educators.

Characteristics of Worldviews

Worldviews characteristically range from the simple to the complex. The moral claim that one should pay it forward[5] represents what seems to be a simple idea but one that some people adopt as a philosophy of life. Arguably, bumper stickers making such claims as "Whoever gets the most toys wins" and "A bad day skiing is better than a good day at work" may also qualify as philosophies of life even though they do not address all the bigger worldview questions. On the other hand, a bumper sticker reading "Co-Exist" clearly addresses one of the big questions, not unlike students enrolled in a 400-level senior seminar course in the humanities or social sciences who may be dealing with the deepest worldview questions week to week in their classes.

People hold their worldviews somewhere on a continuum that runs from consciously held to subconsciously held. Children who by age four think that *Damn Liberals* is the actual name of a political party have been conditioned by the natural language of their home; they have grown up in a linguistic environment that reflects and perpetuates a specific worldview. Such children illustrate the unconscious end of the continuum. Young adults who reject one political affiliation for another typically have identified the worldview they grew up in and are making a conscious decision to reject that worldview or at least part of it. Those same adults may also come to view stuffed toys as dust collectors instead of as the cherished friends they once were.

People also typically hold some parts of their worldview firmly and other parts more tentatively. Some characteristics or convictions that people think deeply reflect who they are may turn out to be more negotiable than we imagined. For example, the person convinced that interracial marriage is simply wrong may fall in love with someone from another race.

Some parts of people's worldviews clearly rest on evidence and personal experience; other parts rest on assumptions or on the word of others. These two continua—conscious-to-unconscious and firm-to-tentative—are helpful in defining and redefining what professional flourishing looks like at different stages of one's teaching career. Teachers require new ways of framing their work at different points in their careers. From time to time, they need to realign their classroom practices as their worldviews and core beliefs undergo change.

Where does one have to stand to judge a worldview? Almost all—do we dare hope all?—science teachers believe the earth to be round, not flat. From the perspective of those who believe the earth to be flat, such science teachers are simply wrong. That is, everyone is located somewhere intellectually, politically, and socially, and those locations shape how people view the views held by others, often making dialogue impossible. Many readers' first encounter with Shirley Jackson's short story, "The Lottery," leaves them in shock at what they consider the patently stupid practice of regularly killing someone to get good crops.[6] For many of Jackson's readers, more shocking than the practice itself is the story's characters' almost nonchalant approach to the killing. Jackson presents the killing as if it were just another day in the town square. Such shock may help us understand the power of worldviews and the difficulties that those who hold their worldviews deeply encounter when they try to engage in dialogue with others who, bluntly, consider them wrong. Language like "It was like talking to a brick wall" expresses some of these difficulties.[7]

Listen and read carefully and you will notice dozens of different adjectives preceding the word worldview. A few obvious examples include urban worldview, primitive worldview, ecological worldview, capitalist worldview, feminist worldview, technological worldview, Chinese worldview, Hindu worldview, children's worldviews, and, for our purposes, teachers' worldviews. Taking note of these many adjectives reveals something important: we might not notice that the many singular nouns seem appropriate when in fact they are anything but. There are many worldviews held by urban people, by feminists, by Chinese people, by Hindus, and by teachers. We make a big mistake if we let our worldview language lead us into thinking that worldviews are singular. The worldviews of city dwellers may share some themes or common threads, but there is no singular urban worldview. And there is no singular teacher worldview. Most teachers agree on many things, but a careful look will reveal substantial differences as well. The agreements and the differences both contribute to the richness of educational culture, and sometimes to the liveliness of staff-room conversation. And those agreements and the differences also have the potential to help teachers frame their own work in ways that foster long-term professional flourishing.

People's worldviews change over time, sometimes because they undergo what some call a *worldview crisis*.[8] In such a crisis, individuals or whole societies confront undeniable evidence that their view up to that point has been wrong. It turns out that the earth is round. It turns out that all rappers do not have tattoos. It turns out—contrary to popular images—that some teachers are hardcore rock climbers, stock car drivers, or opera singers. In popular speech, we say that people can write or rewrite their own story. That is, they have the capacity to change their worldviews. That capacity leads to the next two sections of the chapter.

Forming, Maintaining, and Changing Worldviews

The feature film *The Truman Show*[9] tells the story of someone raised from birth as the main character in a television series about his life. For the creators and viewers of the television series (not the movie with the same name), part of the conceit is Truman's unawareness that he literally lives his whole life in and on a massive television stage, that those he considers his friends and even his wife are in on the plot, and that everything around him is, in effect, artificial. At one point in the movie (not the television series), one of the television show's staff asks why Truman (played by Jim Carrey) never questioned the nature of his world before age thirty. Christoff, the show's director (played by Ed Harris), offers this sobering answer: "we accept the reality of the world with which we are presented." Notice this paramount characteristic of a worldview: we accept the view of the world that we do because that is the view that our world first presented to us.

Societies enshrine their values and ways of life in a million structures, seen and unseen. They reproduce themselves. Individuals follow the group in which they find themselves. And if the society or group believes the world to be structured in a certain way, the individual is likely to believe that the world is structured in that way.

Many forces combine to produce our worldviews. First and obviously, one's family (or the absence of family) powerfully shapes how one views the world.

Several other factors, such as birth order, work to shape who we become. Clearly, no one grows up only in a family, and some do not grow up in families. We also grow up in a neighborhood, among friends. We grow up in a culture, speaking one or more languages. Our native language introduces us to the world with a pre-made set of organizing categories whose terms and prejudices we adopt before we are even old enough to question whether the world might be otherwise. We grow up identified by gender, by race, by ethnicity, by religion, by nationality, and by social class. We cannot avoid these influences as we grow into and develop our ways of seeing the world.

We should not ignore a second group of shaping influences. Most people (including all who read this sentence) have their worldviews shaped by media,[10] and many have their views shaped by such practices as journaling, meditation, prayer, and reading. Societies establish formal school systems to socialize and to shape the worldviews of children. Although school costs keep education out of reach for an alarming number of the world's children, in those places where education is available to all, older adolescents and young adults are able to choose the point at which they will take or not take further formal education. In so choosing, they exercise a measure of control over the extent to which their worldview will be shaped by that set of structures for the reproduction of society's norms and values. Some point to positive or negative watershed personal experiences and personal crises as important turning points in the development of their worldviews. In short, many influences shape worldviews, some of which are increasingly within people's control as they age.

How do individuals and whole societies maintain their worldviews? Anthropologists and sociologists have cataloged how groups develop, enforce, and perpetuate structures to keep their members in line and to make their norms acceptable to the next generation. As part of that research, linguists have described how the language we are born into—appropriately called our mother tongue—contains within it a whole cognitive structure or worldview that is inherently self-affirming. George Orwell illustrates such enforcement and perpetuation in his dystopian novel, *1984*.[11] In the society he portrays, Newspeak controls what can and cannot be thought. Despite the many instruments of control being firmly in place, Orwell's protagonist Winston deviates from the societal norms, risking corporal punishment by doing so. Orwell's Winston and *The Truman Show*'s Truman illustrate that even though societies and groups put structures in place to bolster their legitimacy in their members' eyes and perpetuate their own existence, some people still deviate. They reject the established worldview and social norms of their society or group.

Why and how do people change worldviews? According to social scientists and historians, worldviews change for several reasons. An individual falls in love with someone who thinks differently from themselves. Initially, they may tell themselves they are simply going along with the other person's views in the interest of continuing the relationship. Over time, they may start to think that their loved one's views on fashion, politics, sports, religion, or car brands make sense. In other words, they convert. Social scientists sometimes adopt the views and social patterns of the population whose lives they are researching. The worldviews of the society they are studying—that group's explanations of everyday life—come to sound increasingly plausible. The individual researcher may decide that, in fact, the patterns and explanations of the studied group make more sense than the patterns and explanations of the group from which he or she came.

Some people change their worldviews because of travel, study, or reflection.[12] Rationalists would take comfort if this were always the case, but people's ability to resist worldview change in the face of overwhelming evidence that contradicts their views indicates that, in fact, rationality may not be the strongest suit of the human species. Still, one regularly hears of people who changed their politics because of one event, changed car loyalties because of one television program on car safety, or adopted different religious views as a result of a romantic involvement. Unlike the fictional characters Winston and Truman, some people's changes in worldview do not lead them to liberation from a society's strictures. Rather, they abandon a relatively freeing worldview for one that places restrictions on them. In short, people change not only for many reasons but also in many directions.

Finally, and obviously, people and societies change their worldviews because they end up in a worldview crisis. Personal bankruptcy or divorce can induce a worldview crisis for an individual. An accident or the unexpected onset of serious disease can induce a worldview crisis in oneself or those nearby. The death of a loved one often causes a worldview crisis. And such crises sometimes lead to dramatic changes in people's worldviews, which one sociologist has called *alteration* or *rewriting* one's biography.[13]

Whole cultures or societies sometimes undergo a worldview shift, for example, from a heliocentric to a geocentric worldview at the time of Galileo. And such shifts happen when two civilizations clash, as occurred in pre- and post-Spanish Mexico.

Teachers' Worldviews

Like everyone else, teachers have worldviews. But on the practical economic question of the importance of earning as much money as one can, teachers obviously share more in common with social workers than they do with investment bankers or stock market traders. That is, typically one of their fundamental commitments is to make a better world, what we usually call a humanistic or a moral commitment.[14] Because of these commitments, teachers forgo the salary they might earn because of their stronger desire for the moral rewards of humanistic work. To play with two English phrases, teachers are usually more interested in doing good than in doing well, although most teachers think that doing well by doing good would be an appropriate reward.

To some degree, teachers—nearly alone among all professionals—have a public mandate to pass along a society's worldview. At points, their own worldview will vary from that of the larger society, leading to tensions for both teachers and those issuing the mandate. For example, teachers have been fired for using books alleged to be based on critical race theory (CRT). That is, what they understand to be their mandate as teachers is not what their state government or local school board considers appropriate. Such firings bring into focus the irony that some who call for teachers to be armed with guns do not grant teachers the same level of trust regarding books.[15]

Teachers' worldviews embed and express themselves in the metaphors within which they understand and think about such important parts and aspects of their educational work as children, themselves (teachers), schools and schooling, teaching and learning, assessment, and curriculum. These metaphors warrant our careful examination, and I will consider them further in Chapter 7.

Conclusion

A basic question to ask about a teacher's worldview is whether or not he or she likes to be with students. Is a student's question at the teacher's desk an interruption of the teacher's work, or is it part of the teacher's work? A teacher's unspoken and spoken responses to such a question will reveal some parts of that teacher's worldview. For example, what subterranean currents regarding gender, skills, disabilities, and race affect a teacher's response to a particular student? Reflecting on worldviews in general and on one's own worldview—with all its classroom-related particulars—can help teachers understand better why they do some of the things they do and why they resist some of the things they resist.

Reflection on worldviews will never cure all the ills that any group of teachers might list on a given Friday afternoon in a coffee shop or bar. But worldviews shape our philosophies of education and our educational ideals, ultimately driving our day-to-day classroom practices. To follow up on this chapter, in Chapter 6 we turn to questions of teachers' philosophies of education and their educational ideals.

Notes

1. Tom Tykwer, director, *Run, Lola Run* (X-Filme Creative Pool; WDR, Arte, 1998).
2. Murray Sinclair and Mazina Giizhik, *Who We Are: Four Questions for a Life and a Nation* (Toronto: McLelland and Stewart, 2024).
3. I recommend here Sam Keen, *Apology for Wonder* (New York: Harper and Row, 1969); Anthony Giddens, *The Consequences of Modernity* (San Francisco, CA: Stanford University Press, 1969); Albert Borgmann, *Crossing the Postmodern Divide* (Chicago, IL: The University of Chicago Press, 1990); and Charles Taylor, *The Malaise of Modernity* (Toronto: Anansi, 1991).
4. German philosopher Wilhelm Dilthey (1833–1911) noted that many people do not give much attention to questions of worldview. He suggested that some people use a *Weltbild*, a rather simple world-picture. See *Wilhelm Dilthey: Selected Works, Volume VI, Ethical and World-view Philosophy*, ed. Rudolf A. Makkreel and Frithjof Rodi (Princeton, NJ: Princeton University Press, 2019).
5. A phrase made more famous by an eponymous feature film, *Pay It Forward*, directed by Mimi Leder (Bel-Air Entertainment, Tapestry, Warner Brothers, 2000).

6 The non-fictional Aztecs used live sacrifices to appease their gods, although they usually killed captives from other tribes.

7 When I last saw the flat-earther whom I know personally, I literally did not know where to start, so I didn't. For the simple reason that he is committed to this view, a person we normally call a true believer, I knew there would be no purpose. I even refrained from asking why, if the world was flat, there was no glass skywalk at the edge, with T-shirts for sale and expensive snacks.

8 In his book *Between Man and Man* (New York: Macmillan, 1965), Martin Buber notes the tendency for societies to ask worldview questions only when they experience loneliness and uncertainty. As long as their present worldview passably answers life's questions, people tend to take that worldview for granted.

9 Directed by Andrew Niccol (Los Angeles, CA: Scott Rudin Productions, Paramount Pictures, 2000).

10 For many people, constant exposure to only a single type of media source leads them to develop a largely false picture of the world. For example, many believe to this day that the Sandy Hook school shooting did not happen. See Chris McGreal, "It Got Vile very Quickly': How Alex Jones Turned a Tragedy into a Battleground," *The Guardian*, March 26, 2024, https://www.theguardian.com/tv-and-radio/2024/mar/26/alex-jones-sandy-hook-shooting-documentary.

11 George Orwell, *1984* (London: Secker & Warburg, 1949).

12 Hongyu Wang explores how travel or study abroad transforms one's worldview. See *The Call from the Stranger on a Journey Home: Curriculum in a Third Space* (Lausanne: Peter Lang, 2004). The *third space* in the title refers to the new place created in the cross-cultural encounter as both parties experience transformation.

13 Peter Berger, *Invitation to Sociology* (New York: Doubleday, 1967).

14 Amitai Etzioni, *A Comparative Analysis of Complex Organizations: On Power, Involvement, and Their Correlates* (New York: Free Press, 1975).

15 See, for example, Hannah Natanson and Moriah Balingit's article, "Caught in the Culture Wars, Teachers are Being Forced from Their Jobs," *Washington Post*, June 22, 2022, https://www.washingtonpost.com/education/2022/06/16/teacher-resignations-firings-culture-wars/.

6 Classroom Ideals and a Philosophy of Education

This chapter builds on the discussion of worldviews in Chapter 5 and on hundreds of pre-service and in-service teachers' answers to my question about what led them into teaching and what ideals help them get up every morning and go to work. Noting my overall goal of seeing teachers flourish long-term, I begin by encouraging you, my reader, to think about your own ideals and the ways you approach your work in the core cycle of curriculum, instruction, and assessment in ways that will help you realize those ideals in your own educational practice. In the second part of the chapter, I introduce the idea of a personal philosophy of education and ask readers to identify ways we can work to align our philosophies of education with our classroom program and practices.

Teachers' Classroom Ideals

Everyone has ideals, a vision of what they would like to do or be. Some young adults use the phrase *30 by 30* to express their travel goal of traveling to thirty countries by age thirty. Some people work toward their *ticket* in a trade such as electrical, carpentry, or plumbing. Some high school students identify a life goal or ideal in the grade twelve yearbook. In ordinary speech, our sentences sometimes begin with the word *ideally*, followed by our naming or describing a state of affairs we wish were true. Put simply, ideals are a normal part of our thinking. Many teachers identified a vocational goal or ideal while still young. They knew at an early age that they wanted to become teachers, perhaps because of a relative who worked in education or a particularly inspiring elementary or secondary teacher; a significant proportion of those who knew early on that they wanted to teach also envisioned the kind of classroom they wanted to have. That is, they had already thought about their ideals.

In very general terms, many teachers express their purpose for entering the teaching profession in language such as *making the world a better place* or *helping children find their way*. In fact, teachers often describe their profession as noble because of such ideals, in contrast, say, to someone who aims to become a billionaire by age forty. In general, like social workers and nurses, teachers choose the vocation they do for what we generally consider humanistic ideals or goals, as opposed to financial goals. And on the days when students really get it—when their eyes shine—teachers take satisfaction in their work even though they know it will not lead to their owning a show garage full of Lamborghinis. From this point forward in the chapter, I will work with the assumption that my readers find themselves somewhere in the general comments I have just made about teachers and the typical ideal of making the world a better place. Yet, my main interest in our teaching ideals is more specific.

Teachers hold specific ideals regarding the ways they want their classrooms to work and how they want their students to carry out their tasks. The obvious corollary of teachers holding those ideals is that they usually work day to day in ways meant to realize those ideals. Those ideals drive and shape teachers' day-to-day work. And what are those ideals? Table 6.1 contains a selection from a much longer list assembled from in-service teachers in workshops and pre-service teachers who completed a course assignment related to the classroom they envisioned once they began teaching. Several features of this composite list deserve our attention. First, some of the words and phrases, for example *self-regulation* and *minds-on*, have appeared in the educational lexicon relatively recently compared, for example, to the ideal of building *character*. In addition, notice that different educators use different words for similar ideals. *Curiosity* and *wonder* both appear; these are related concepts that carry somewhat different meanings. The presence of both *playful* and *serious assignments* on this list also confirms what most teachers already know about schools: that all teachers do not envision the ideal classroom in the same way.

My own list of classroom ideals changes slightly from time to time but I find that I keep returning to the same central themes and ideas. My ideals relate to a rather stable vision of the kind of classroom in which I want to teach and in which I want my students to do the great work of learning. Like most teachers, I have more than twelve ideals, but prioritizing a list of twelve helps me stay focused from week to week and from year to year. Shortly, I will invite you, my reader, to take time to produce your own annotated list of ideals. Here is my own list of ideals that illustrates how naming and describing one's

Table 6.1 A List of Pre-Service and In-Services Teachers' Classroom Ideals

A Composite List of Classroom Ideals			
accepting	excitement	literacy strategies	relevant to life
accountability	experiential	loving	resilience respect
achievements	learning	make choices	responsibility reverence
adventurous	expert researchers	maturity	for ideas
aesthetic/artistic	faith	meaningful work	rewards
appreciative	flexible	metacognition	risks
ask why	flow (zone)	minds-on	routines
assess for learning	focused	movement	safe
attentive	forgiving	multiple	secure
authenticity	formative	intelligences	see
awareness	assessment	music	self-aware
beauty	free to disagree	natural intelligence	self-control
calm	friendly	no excuses	self-critical
care	generosity	on task	self-direction
celebrate	give reasons	open to surprise	self-discovery
centered	goal-oriented	optimism	self-efficacy
challenge	grace	organized	self-evaluation
character	gratitude	our own referees	self-motivation
choice	grounded	pacing in learning	self-regulation
clean	hands-on	panache	sensitive
clear expectations	hard work	passing on heritage	serious assignments
collaboration	hear complaints	patience	service
comfortable	helpful	peaceful	shared authority
committed	honesty	peer coaching	smell
community	hope	perceptive	speak directly
compassion	hospitality	perseverance	start new things
confidence	human flourishing	persistence	stimulating
connection	humility	personal growth	student ownership
cooperation	humor	playful	supportive
courage	imagination	polite	teacher is learning
creation-care	inclusive	pondering	team-work
creativity	innovative	positive attitudes	thankfulness
critical thinking	inquisitive	practical	thoughtful
curiosity	insightful	preparation	touch
dedication	intentional	present	transformation
dignity of all persons	integrity	pride	transparency
disciplined	intellectual depth	professionalism	trust
discretion	interdisciplinary	purposeful	truth
discursive	interiority	questions	try again
empathetic	internal controls	rapt up (flow, zone)	unwrapping gifts
empowering	internal motivation	reading	verve
encouragement	intuitive	ready when bell	volunteerism
engaged	invitational	rings	welcoming
enquiry learning	joy	realistic expectations	win-win
environmental care	justice	recognize limitations	wonder, wondering
equality	kindness	recognize people	working atmosphere
ethical	leadership	reflection	writing
listen	learning styles	relational	

own ideals can help fill out a picture of a teacher's desired classroom space and, one hopes, help shape one's classroom practice.

First, I want to see myself and my students work as partners in the tasks of learning and teaching, building what Parker Palmer calls a community of trust.[1] To continue with his language, I want to approach *the big subject* together with my students so they do not always have to go through me to get to the curriculum and so they get a sense that they share responsibility for the course with me; the course will be our course, not mine. I want to become a *co-learner* with my students and work alongside them, as Carl Rogers puts it in *Freedom to Learn*[2] and as my colleague Margie Patrick and I developed it at length in an edited book on classroom climate.[3]

I want my students to be struck with wonder because of the curriculum materials we use in class and the ways we approach those materials. The instructional strategies I use ought to invite students into the curriculum in ways that engage, intrigue, and excite them. For example, knowing the composition of ordinary salt ought to induce wonder. After all, sodium and chloride are both toxic if ingested. But humans need the combination to live.

As individuals and as a class, can we produce excellence in our work; can we produce better work than we even imagined we could? This kind of excellence is unavoidably tied to my creating the kind of space where critical thinking and creative thinking flourish (the next ideal below).

Together, can we think critically and creatively within flexible structures? Much of my thinking about thinking critically and creatively has been shaped by my study of the Skunk Works, a not-so-secret research division called the Advanced Development Program at Lockheed Aerospace in Burbank, California.[4] Kelly Johnson, the founding director of the Skunk Works, created reporting structures so that those who worked there could unleash their creativity and think of that which had never been thought of before in aerospace.[5] Most of this creativity was directed toward making better weapons of war. I want to unleash my students' creativity so they can help build a better world. With my colleague Amy Dee, I have written about this in detail elsewhere.[6]

I want my students to adopt an attitude of stewardship toward the earth's condition and its finite resources. Although they sometimes tease me in a friendly way about it, I invite my students to submit their work on recycled (good one side) paper. This invitation might result in one tree being saved in my lifetime, but it serves as an inviting way to place an important question in front of my students.

I want my students to embrace humble service as a mode of living among our neighbors, both here and abroad. This implies that the teacher is also the servant of the students. Perhaps counterintuitively, I have discovered—for example, by periodically picking up trash in my classrooms—that humble service to one's students actually increases one's authority.

I want to authorize my students so that they generate much of the learning power in the classroom. That implies that I share with my students some of the authority and responsibility for learning, for classroom ethos, and for classroom procedures.[7] Obviously, as the teacher, I have a measure of authority in a classroom, but I do not take that authority for granted. I want to exercise my classroom authority in such a way that my students give me their consent, that they authorize me to teach. In my view, the corollary of their giving me their consent is that I will authorize them, that they will become authors and experts.

I want my students to find joy in learning, in part because the work we do together is relevant to them and engages their interest. Joy is connected to satisfaction; I want them to take satisfaction in what they accomplish. As I note in Chapter 14, joy in the classroom contributes both to students' learning and to teachers' flourishing.

I want my classroom to be a place where people can laugh. Structured correctly, a fun classroom can be a classroom with increased engagement and deeper learning. All teachers can recall a time when a whole class burst out laughing and the energy that laughter brought to the room for some minutes afterward. I give a couple more paragraphs to this in Chapter 14 and I make reference to a doctoral dissertation on the connections between laughter and student achievement.

I want my students to know that our classroom is a safe place for all who enter it, and that all have the right to just and fair treatment, especially regarding assessment. Safety entails more than physical safety; it implies emotional safety, which in schools often expresses itself in a class's agreement that mistakes are a way to learn, not an occasion for ridicule.

I want my students to learn to show respect for others, ourselves, ideas, and property. This four-clause list came from a colleague with whom I worked on one of my trips to work with teachers in Kenya, and I hung a poster with those words on my classroom wall from that year forward.

I want to create a classroom where we celebrate the varieties of gifts and strengths reflected in individual differences in capacity, in thinking and learning styles, in backgrounds, in interests, and in schedules. Classroom community is built and learning is enhanced when teachers and students celebrate the varieties of interests, strengths, and gifts students bring.

Do I always reach the twelve ideals I've listed above? Of course not. An additional ideal that I have never achieved, likely because it is impossible, is that "I want to reach 100% of my students." I've discussed this ideal with many educators and received mixed responses. Some say I should let it go. Others say, with poet Robert Browning, that one's reach should exceed one's grasp. I stick with Browning, although I also commit to sleeping at night without feeling like a failure. Recognizably, this ideal is lofty, but it has the power to motivate one to return to work each day and to give one's best.

Aligning Our Practices

In Chapter 4, where I discussed the complexity and intensity of teaching, I noted some of the difficulties of achieving our classroom ideals. In some aspects of our classroom program, we will achieve high alignment with our ideals. In other aspects, we will see areas where we need to make adjustments. In fact, veteran teachers know that we always need to make adjustments. In the opening paragraph of the introduction to this book, I noted the tension between the grand vision educators might have for their work and the daily tasks and routines through which they try to realize those grand visions. Identifying our ideals relates most closely to those grand visions that we need year to year if we are to fulfill the educational vocations in which we have found ourselves. The daily tasks we engage in and the routines we establish and follow are the ways we realize those grand visions. These ideals and visions can sustain teachers in a complex and complicated profession!

As one might expect, when asked to list their ideals, teachers often list such words as joy, curiosity, creativity, music, movement, and reading. Most teachers get up in the morning because they want to realize those ideals;

we wouldn't have gone into teaching without them. Recall from the model presented in Chapter 3 that teachers need to work where we are. Working where we are implies that we may work with colleagues and administrators who aim at ideals different from our own. We may work in a jurisdiction with whose educational ideals we have major difficulties. And we certainly work within finite budgets and with students who come to class with a range of abilities and varying levels of energy for their learning tasks.

Also recall from Chapter 3 that the core cycle of curriculum, instruction, and assessment implies the presence of a fourth element. Assessment of students' work actually shows teachers what adjustments they need to make before they teach that particular material again. Teachers readjust. Teachers realign. We do so because we are teachers.

In this discussion of classroom ideals, I have tried to be clear that even when we don't reach our ideals, we keep aiming at them. We keep going back to work day after day because we want to accomplish these ideals. I doubt that you, having chosen to read this book, are a lazy teacher who does not care if you ever succeed in your classroom. So, while I am not a priest, I do want to tell you to go, to carry on teaching, and not to carry a burden of guilt because you regularly do not achieve all you set out to achieve. Keep teaching, please. Your students need you to show up.

The Philosophy of Education Statement

For many students in teacher-education programs, the phrase *philosophy of education* induces an eye-roll. Under their breath, some students say things along the lines of "Here we go, Greece, Rome, Rousseau, Montessori, Dewey, Maslow, Bloom, Skinner . . . blah, blah, blah." I lament that some philosophy of education courses earn a bad reputation, in part because all teachers have a philosophy of education, whether they have articulated it or not. Having had the delightful task of teaching foundations of education courses for many years and leading professional workshops for in-service teachers, I have enjoyed hearing teachers at all stages of their careers describe their philosophies of education with reference to the reasons they keep getting up and going to work in the morning. Most of them can recite a list of the big names in educational history, but they don't end their comments with "blah, blah, blah."

That is, implicitly or explicitly, teachers have answered the big questions of philosophy of education. What did they think were the purposes of education and schools? What did they want to accomplish in their own classrooms, and how did they frame their teaching work? Why did they become teachers? What difference did they think their work would make in the world if they taught this way rather than that way? What are students like? What should we teach students? And what classroom characteristics would induce students to want to be at school rather than somewhere else? The important connections between teachers' philosophies of education and their classroom ideals become obvious when we start to answer some of these questions.

Some schools require that their teachers post on their classroom wall a philosophy of education statement. For nine years I taught in such a school, and for the last six of those years, I posted only nine words. Because my original statement had been so long that I didn't even want to read it, I eventually lifted the nine words verbatim from Gordon Matties, a friend and colleague from Winnipeg, Manitoba. Those nine words were *Nurturing the mind, Minding the heart, Mending the world.*

Students would sometimes ask me why my statement was so short compared to my previous statement or those posted on the walls in other classrooms. My answer was always that I wanted my students to read my statement all the way through rather than stopping because the lunch break had ended before they finished. But I had a non-comic answer as well: I knew that the students coming into my room day after day were not robots; they were people with hearts as well as minds, and they wanted the world still to be there when their grandchildren came of school age. In my view, Gordon Matties had captured in those words the essence of what I wanted to do in my classroom. For the record, no students ever asked me what that philosophy of education statement meant; it was clear. Whether alone or with colleagues, in the years since I posted that statement, I have continued to work out what those nine words mean for classrooms, teachers, students, and myself.[8]

Having invited you to list your classroom ideals, I now invite you to take a few minutes and try to get your philosophy of education encapsulated in as few words as possible. I suggest using paper because it facilitates a messier process and, for many of us, forces a slower and more reflective process.[9] However, if you find editing to be easier on the keyboard, then please work on a keyboard. My interest here is that you allow yourself the freedom to get into what Csikszentmihalyi[10] calls *flow* and athletes call *the zone* while carrying out this exercise. I promise not to change the rest of the book while you step away for a few minutes.

Landing on the Ground

Ultimately, we need to realize and bring our classroom ideals and our philosophies of education to fruition in the day-to-day life of our classrooms. We certainly need to do this for our students. We want them to want to come to our classroom. We want them to want to engage with the curriculum and with our instructional plans. We want them to succeed. This chapter appears in a book about thriving in a noble profession; we also need to realize our ideals and our philosophy of education in our classrooms because doing so will help us flourish long-term as teachers. We become more satisfied educators when we can see day by day that our instructional plans are working and that our students are making progress. Seeing our classroom take the shape we want it to take brings us rewards (for sure), but it also confirms that we have followed our vocation and that we are doing what we are on this planet to do.

Having invited you to list some of your classroom ideals and to produce at least a rough draft of a working philosophy of education, I now want to ask you to engage in one more activity. Select one unit from one of your current courses or classes and spend a few minutes addressing the following question: What small changes could I make in this unit to align it more closely with one or more of my ideals or with my philosophy of education statement? You do not need to look for an educational revolution here, only for an adjustment that would bring your classroom program one notch closer to your grand vision. Much later in the book (in Chapter 13), I recommend that you build a team who will support you in your work and hold you accountable. I recommend that if you do identify a point in a unit where you will attempt to achieve greater alignment, you share with some members of your team what you hope to do, and then tell them how it went.

Conclusion

In this chapter, I argue that we need educational ideals or classroom ideals to help us get up in the morning and go back to school. I have also argued that whether we think about it very often or not, we all conduct our educational work based on a philosophy of education. My hope is that you have experienced this chapter not as "Greece, Rome, Rousseau, Montessori, Dewey, Maslow, Bloom, and Skinner . . . here we go again," but as a contribution to and source of motivation for your flourishing as a teacher.

In the next chapter, I will turn to educational metaphors, another aspect of teachers' philosophies of education. We express our philosophies of education in our classroom ideals and in the ways we execute our classroom programs. And we also express them in the metaphors we choose as we connect the strands of the CIA rope—curriculum, instruction, and assessment—and as we answer such questions as who or what students are, what are schools, and who we are as teachers.

Notes

1. Parker Palmer, *To Know as We Are Known* (New York: Harper, 1983).
2. Carl Rogers, *Freedom To Learn: A View of What Education Might Become* (Indianapolis, IN: Merrill, 1969).
3. Margie Patrick and Ken Badley, *The Complexities of Authority in the Classroom: Fostering Democracy for Student Learning* (New York: Routledge, 2022).
4. The Skunk Works website is at https://www.lockheedmartin.com/en-us/who-we-are/business-areas/aeronautics/skunkworks.html.
5. Kelly Johnson, *Kelly: More than My Share of It All* (Washington, DC: Smithsonian, 1985).
6. Amy Dee and Ken Badley, "Creating an Educational Ethos Where Innovation and Accountability Flourish: A New Model for Transparency in Educational Organizations," *The International Journal of Educational Leadership Preparation* 5, no. 4 (October–December 2010), https://digitalcommons.georgefox.edu/soe_faculty/52/.
7. I argue this view at length in the edited book I mentioned in footnote 3 in this chapter: *The Complexities of Authority in the Classroom: Fostering Democracy for Student Learning.*

8 In a series of books, typically written or edited with colleagues, I have worked out in great detail the nine-word philosophy of education statement I had posted on my secondary classroom wall. I will not repeat here what appears in those volumes. *Engaging College and University Students: Effective Instructional Strategies* (New York: Routledge, 2022); *Joyful Resilience as Educational Practice: Transforming Teaching Challenges into Opportunities,* edited with Michelle C. Hughes (New York: Routledge, 2021); *Generating Tact and Flow for Effective Teaching and Learning,* with Susanna Steeg Thornhill (New York: Routledge, 2020); and *Curriculum Planning with Design Language: Building Elegant Courses and Units* (New York: Routledge, 2018).

9 Juhani Pallasma, *The Thinking Hand: Existential and Embodied Wisdom in Architecture* (Chichester: Wiley, 2009).

10 Mihalyi Csikszentmihalyi, *Flow: The Psychology of Optimal Experience* (New York: Harper and Row, 1990).

7 Metaphors for Flourishing

Like all specialized fields, education has its own specialized language. For example, a list of common education-related phrases at the time of writing includes *trauma-informed practice*, *assessment for learning*, *growth mindset*, *backward design*, and *fail forward*. Not one of these phrases was in the educational lexicon four decades ago. Also like the language of other specialized fields, educational language contains a number of metaphors. In fact, it is packed with metaphors.

Examples abound. The curriculum is like a map, or curriculum is like a guidebook. Assessment is measurement. Teaching is like babysitting. Teaching is socializing. Schools are like factories. Schools are like gardens, and students are like plants (thus the word *kindergarten*). Students are blank slates.[1] Instruction can be a dance. Education is for equipping students. In catalyst metaphors, teachers are like burglars; they break into students' heads and mess things up. Teachers are bridge builders; they connect students and curriculum. Readers may like or dislike any of these metaphors, but at some point in educational history, and perhaps even to this day, these metaphors and comparisons have been part of the language of education.

Because the driving question of this book is how good teachers can thrive, the metaphors teachers use warrant examination, in part because the metaphors we use as educators can, in a sense, use us. To name a very simple example, if teachers view students as tender little plants to be protected and nourished, they will treat—teach—them differently from how they will treat and teach them if they think students are little animals who need to be controlled. The first metaphor has the power to confuse teachers who don't understand why some students do nasty things to each other. The second metaphor has the power to blind educators to some of the wonderful people who come to their classrooms day after day.

Obviously, educators need to think about schools, classrooms, students, curriculum, instruction, assessment, and record-keeping (among other things). Educational language is rich in images for all these aspects of educational work, implying that my thesis here is relatively straightforward: some metaphors have the potential to lead to flourishing, and others have the potential to lead to cynicism. Teachers wanting to flourish long term in their profession need to find and use the right metaphors, the ones that lead to flourishing.

Views of Metaphor

In the traditional view of metaphor, metaphors are helpful devices for explaining complex processes by comparing those processes to simpler processes. For example, as a secondary student, I was told that electricity flows through a wire the way water flows through a pipe. As I learned much later, that simple comparison is wrong. Nevertheless, it illustrates how metaphors function; in this case, they function to mislead. Incidentally, the fact that I still can't get that image out of my head also illustrates the power of metaphors.

That bad metaphor for electricity leads to two observations about metaphors. First, metaphors highlight certain aspects of the thing compared, and they place other aspects in the background. Second, metaphors all land on a scale with accuracy at one end and misleading at the other.

Some use the word *nice* to refer to the traditional understanding of metaphor.[2] That is, some salient point of comparison between two objects or ideas allows us to understand the more complex one better because we already understand the simpler one and can recognize the parallels between the two. Something is missing from or misleading about this understanding of metaphors: that they help us think more clearly, but they do not determine our cognition.

This view that metaphors are helpful or *nice* has faced a serious challenge over the last half-century, with many people claiming that metaphors do much more than usually meets the eye. Paul Ricoeur, for example, argued this stronger view in *The Rule of Metaphor: Multidisciplinary Studies in the Creation of Meaning in Language*.[3] Two years after Ricoeur's book appeared, George Lakoff and Mark Johnson released *Metaphors We Live By*, which remains one of the most influential presentations of the strong view of metaphor.[4] Their argument is simple: metaphor is ubiquitous in our thoughts and metaphors shape cognition.

Simply put, human cognition—how we conceptualize our world—is metaphorical. I will not repeat here what my readers can read firsthand in

Lakoff and Johnson's book, but one of their examples clearly pertains to the work of educators. Without making specific reference to schools and students, they discuss how the words *top* and *bottom*, and *up* and *down* function in our language. To bring their discussion to educational work, think about how many times teachers say something along the lines of, "She is one of the top students in my class." As educators, we use this language without even recognizing it as metaphorical, confirming Lakoff and Johnson's thesis that metaphors are deeply at work in our thinking, but for the most part, we do not even recognize them.

On *the nice* account, we will understand such aspects of teaching as curriculum and instruction better if we can find helpful metaphors to give us new insights. On the strong account, the metaphors we use do not simply help us understand such aspects of education; they actually shape our thinking and practice, and we can't think without them. Semanticists refer to metaphors as *dead metaphors* once they have become so deeply embedded in language that people treat them as natural language. For example, a table leg no longer strikes any language user as metaphorical. To use a second metaphor, that metaphor has found a natural home in our language. Such is the power of metaphors; they shape our thinking without our even noticing.

Throughout this volume, I repeatedly suggest that teachers who want to flourish should try this idea, read such-and-such author, or develop systems to get this or that aspect of their classroom program humming more smoothly than it perhaps already is. Here I will explore and recommend five metaphors, all of which do not typically appear in the educational conversation. In each case, I want to explore where these metaphors might lead and ask how they might change our thinking and, as a result, our classroom practices. How might these metaphors lead teachers to think differently about some aspect of teaching? What new insights might these metaphors give us into instruction, curriculum, assessment, classroom climate, or students? How might these metaphors enhance our work? Ultimately, how might these metaphors sustain us as teachers and help us flourish?

Curriculum Planning as Design

We begin with the image of curriculum and class planning as a design task. In the years since Jay McTighe and Grant Wiggins introduced the phrase *backwards by design*,⁵ many teachers in both K-12 education and higher education have given less attention simply to getting through their material or their plans and more attention to what they expect students to know by the end of a course, unit, or lesson. This shift in attention was needed, especially in higher education where some educators tend to focus on their content without giving sufficient attention to students' learning.

In the years since this language became popular and partly because of the popularity of backwards by design, educational uses of the word *design* itself have narrowed so that other senses of the word have been pushed into the background, even out of sight. Thus, while McTigue and Wiggins' contribution was and still is needed, it has had at least one negative effect. How often do educators view course or curriculum design as a design task requiring attention to aesthetic and design principles in the way they would view planning and designing a building, a kitchen, a garden, or a city-center plaza? Almost never. And the failure to think about course design in those ways points both to the power of language and to the possibilities that might open up for educators willing to consider this metaphor.

For example, the work of a famous American architect and philosopher of design, Christopher Alexander, could inform curriculum and course design with a series of design concepts, possibly aiding educators at all levels with their planning and, ultimately, in their flourishing.⁶ Alexander offers what he calls a *pattern language* by which he means a comprehensive and connected set of rules which, when implemented as a framework of principles and not merely as a set of techniques, can lead to the production of good buildings, neighborhoods, and towns. In his many works, Alexander was definitely not addressing curriculum design. But consider just this one principle: a city or a building needs to have an appropriate entrance. What might some courses and units look like—and feel like to students—if they had clearly defined and inviting entrances? Granted, it would take time and effort for teachers to develop such entrances, but those entrances would help students know that they had begun a new section of their course.

A middle-school colleague's first day of a Social Studies unit on France illustrates Alexander's point. She set the classroom desks in rows similar to those on a jetliner. She dressed in a powder blue outfit like those worn by Air France cabin personnel. In both English and French, she welcomed the class on a borrowed public address system to flight 624, non-stop service to Paris, and she then handed out the unit outlines. Imagine the students in this classroom for a moment. After just two minutes, not one of them would think they were still working on the Japan unit that (actually) ended the previous Friday. Such is the effect of a grand entrance.

Teachers who adopt design language and work design principles into their curriculum and unit planning begin to think differently. When they do, students become more engaged and their teachers flourish.

Teaching as Improvisational Theater

What if teachers viewed instruction less like speaking and more like improv? In her autobiography, *Yes, Please*,[7] Amy Poehler claims that one of the keys to success in improv is being able, in effect, to say yes to what one's fellow and sister actors have said. That is, if another actor has put the scene in a store or on a bus, then that is where you are. If another actor has turned the scene into a robbery or a love scene, then that is where the scene needs to keep going. In short, an improv actor needs to hear and understand what was just said and needs to say yes.

Suggesting improv as a metaphor for teaching does not imply that teachers come to class without plans. It does imply that they be open to where students' comments and ideas might lead. Teachers know, of course, that their job is to lead the class toward and through the curriculum materials and instruction planned for that day. But the periodic yes in response to a student comment shows students that they and their views matter and that the teachers' knowledge is not the only knowledge valued in the room. Such improv moments help build the kind of invitational classroom climate described in Chapter 3, the kind of climate that ultimately helps teachers thrive.

A colleague who teaches in a French immersion classroom illustrates this point well with her story about a third-grade student's answer to her question, "Who are you?" His answer, "Je suis un poisson rouge" ("I am a red fish") could have led the class down a rabbit trail. Or the classroom teacher could have made some corrective comment or given the student a mild reprimand for joking in class. But, because that sentence is a running joke among French students, the teacher used the obviously wrong answer to open up a short discussion about the key elements of language jokes. To use Amy Poehler's language, this teacher said yes to her clever student, with the result that her students engaged in a discussion of language well beyond the learning standards of third grade. At the end of the class's discussion of language jokes, she repeated her question to the same student. He answered her second query by claiming to be a blue notebook ("Je suis un cahier bleu"), another running joke among French students and one that, in this case, fed directly into the content of the class's discussion.

Teaching as Accompaniment

The metaphor of accompaniment offers riches to anyone thinking about how to build classroom community. The French origins of the word *companion* are interesting: *with + bread* . . . being with a person with whom someone eats bread. Without suggesting that teachers eat bread with their students (although bringing food to the classroom helps build community), what might accompanying students mean? The idea of accompanying students may not be a common part of teachers' thinking, but the related ideas of caring and being care-givers are.[8] Were accompaniment or caring to become as central to educational talk as backwards by design, for example, classroom practices might change dramatically, especially in the higher grades.

The survey of the language educators use to talk about their work in Chapter 2 did not include accompaniment. But imagine some of the ways teachers might reframe their daily work and their approach to students if accompaniment were more prominent in the educational lexicon. Kindergarten pupils are trying to understand school itself, as well as learning to read and count; they need someone to walk alongside them. Middle-school students are sorting through their identity questions; they need someone to walk alongside them. Secondary students worry about what's next and what life will hold for them. With professional boundaries solidly in place, it is still possible for their teachers to walk alongside them. The word *companion* has been in the language for 750 years; perhaps it should figure a little more prominently in the educational lexicon.

Teaching as Adventure

Chapter 12 introduces a type of teacher I call an adventurer. The most common image of an adventurer is simple: people who go on an adventure do not know in advance or have control over how things are going to turn out. At other points in this volume, I mention Lockheed Aerospace's Skunk Works and ask whether, with the support of students, a teacher could build a classroom culture that reflected the culture of the Skunk Works. To me, the Skunk Works smacks of adventure, of being perhaps a bit subversive; it is not the kind of classroom culture most teachers envision when they think about their classroom ideals.

Obviously, teachers must satisfy the curriculum requirements of a school and likely a larger educational authority. In many jurisdictions, teachers legally stand in as parents during the school day, and therefore have responsibility for their students, not just to their students. And in many jurisdictions, school-wide student performance—on standardized tests at least—becomes public information. For several reasons then, teachers do not have the freedom to run off in any direction they please with their class time; almost universally, they are motivated to get it right. So yes, teachers have many reasons to act cautiously as they carry out their day-to-day tasks.

With all those conditions and cautions in view, I will argue that the beauty of the Skunk Works is that it produced aircraft that were literally unthinkable until engineers at the Skunk Works thought of them. For example, the U2 spy plane, named long before the band formed, was designed and built in less than a year and could fly higher than any Russian anti-aircraft missile at the time of its introduction. The U2 was unthinkable . . . until someone thought of it. And the U2 airplane met what we might call the school jurisdiction's standards; that is, it could do what the US government told Lockheed it had to do. What effect might the language and thinking of the Skunk Works have on teachers and students as they approach the work of teaching and learning? More contemporary examples abound; teachers could imagine with their students what a classroom would look like if it were fashioned after Google or SpaceX. Rather than running off in every direction, students in such rooms might produce amazing work in the very direction the prescribed curriculum expected them to go. Attempting to launch a Skunk Works, Google, or SpaceX culture in a classroom certainly qualifies as an adventure; no one knows how it might turn out. But curiosity leads to inquiry and inquiry often leads to good results.

Recall that in the *nice* view of metaphors, people understand complex ideas and objects better than they otherwise would. According to the strong view, metaphors shape how people think. If the strong view of metaphors is correct and metaphors actually shape human cognition, then introducing the idea of a Skunk Works classroom would indeed work its way into a teacher's practice, and it would eventually affect the thinking and practice of that teacher's students as well. Teachers and students alike might start to produce amazingly high-quality work. Watching their students produce such work would lead most teachers to flourish.

Teaching as Craft

Imagine if Chapter 2 in this book had listed teaching as a craft along with the other possible ways to identify the work of teachers. If teaching as a craft does not quite qualify as a metaphor, perhaps we can think of it as a way to frame teaching work. However we classify the idea, consider some of the possible ways teachers might think about their work if their default way of framing it was as a craft.[9]

They might sense that they had more autonomy in their profession, that they could take pleasure in doing many things themselves and in their own way, especially regarding their choices of instructional strategies. They could take pride in the accomplishments of their students, the same way artists, potters, and sculptors take pride in their work. They could take pride in figuring things out, as do carpenters, fabric artists, and other crafters who regularly devise hacks, jigs, and workarounds to aid them in their work. Because they would have control over several aspects of their professional lives, when they got bored with some aspects of their work, they could devise new approaches to that work, finding new ways to assess student learning, for example.

Much of the conversation related to the craft of teaching focuses on the less measurable, less tangible aspects of teaching. In other words, many users of this bit of language are attempting to understand teaching as something that is markedly more artistic than it is scientific or mechanical, as something that cannot all be planned, predicted, controlled, and measured. Most teachers have discovered that teaching has that character, that its shape cannot always be planned and its outcomes cannot always be predicted and assessed. The language of craft seems well suited to designate that dimension of teaching.

Assessment offers an example of how including craft in the teaching lexicon might work. A minuscule fraction of teachers work in truly free schools and therefore carry out few or no formal assessments of student learning. The vast majority of teachers need to assess and report on their students' learning. Teachers who take a craft approach to assessment are more likely to seek innovative ways to make assessment more meaningful for their students, to make it more varied for both their students and for themselves, and to reduce the time required for authentic grading. Teachers who view their own work as craft may recognize that some of their students might view their assignments as craft. Such a view of students' work implies that teachers will give more choice in assignments and thereby enable students more fully to bring their own skills and gifts to demonstrate their learning. More choice in assessments need not imply a paperwork nightmare for teachers. But it typically results in students submitting a greater variety of assignments and therefore grading becomes more interesting. No teacher wanting to flourish would complain about grading becoming more interesting.

Conclusion

If these five metaphors—design, improv, accompaniment, adventure, and craft—figured more prominently in the educational lexicon, they would likely induce teachers to think of new and creative ways to execute the tasks of the core cycle of teaching. They would likely think of new ways to engage their students in the curriculum materials, in the instructional activities they plan day by day, and—dare one suggest it—even in assessment.

Later in this book (Chapter 15), I will offer a metaphor that works in the opposite way from "electricity goes through a wire the way water goes through a hose." To open up the question of school cultures, I will make an extended examination of school cultures using *the angle of repose*, a geological concept related to how a pile of soil, rocks, sugar, or any other granular material eventually stops flattening out and settles, depending on the combined effects of gravity, surface texture, and rainfall. I will apply that geological concept metaphorically to school cultures and will argue that every school finds its angle of repose, that the people in school buildings find ways of settling or being together. This chapter draws to a close, but we are not yet done with metaphors. In fact, we never will be.

The five metaphors I explored briefly in this chapter serve only as examples. Educators are smart people who typically love language and ideas and who typically look for new and creative ways to do their work. Is it too much to suggest that readers of this chapter can think of other creative and life-giving metaphors for schools, classrooms, teachers, teaching, students, curriculum, instruction, and assessment? I believe it is not too much to suggest that. Educators desiring to flourish to the last day of their teaching careers should look for new images—new metaphors—for these aspects of the work of teaching. And then they should give those metaphors legs.

Notes

1 From John Locke, *An Essay Concerning Human Understanding*, ed. Kenneth Winkler (Indianapolis, IN: Hackett, 1996).
2 Regarding the *just nice* view of metaphors, see Andrew Ortony, "Why Metaphors Are Necessary and Not Just Nice," *Educational Theory* 25, no. 1 (April 2007): 45–53.
3 *The Rule of Metaphor: Multi-Disciplinary Studies of the Creation of Meaning in Language*, trans. Robert Czerny, with Kathleen McLaughlin and John Costello (Milton Park: Routledge and Kegan Paul, 1978).
4 The University of Chicago Press, 1980. My colleague Harro Van Brummelen and I paid homage to Lakoff and Johnson in the title of our edited book, *Metaphors We Teach By: How Metaphors Shape What We Do in Classrooms* (Eugene, OR: Wipf and Stock, 2012). We and our contributors attempted to unpack some of the common educational metaphors, including two I mentioned at the start of this part of the chapter: assessment is measurement and curriculum is a map.
5 *Understanding by Design* (Alexandria, VA: ASCD, 1998).
6 See *The Timeless Way of Building* (New York: Oxford University Press, 1979), and the earlier volume he produced with doctoral students Sara Ishikawa, Murray Silverstein, Max Jacobson, Ingrid Fiksdahl-King, and Shlomo Angel, *A Pattern Language: Towns, Buildings, Construction* (New York: Oxford University Press, 1977). My own application of Alexander's work to curriculum and course design appeared as *Curriculum Planning with Design Language: Building Elegant Courses and Units* (New York: Routledge, 2019). In that book, I develop educational applications of a dozen of Alexander's patterns.
7 (New York: Harper, 2014).
8 The work of Nel Noddings is foundational to this conversation. See *Caring: A Feminine Approach to Ethics and Moral Education* (Oakland, CA: University of

California Press, 1984), and *The Challenge to Care in Schools* (New York: Teachers College Press, 1992).

9 See Elliot Eisner's, "From Episteme to Phronesis to Artistry in the Study and Improvement of Teaching," *Teaching and Teacher Education* 18, no. 4 (May 2002): 375–85; and Richard Hickman's, *The Art and Craft of Pedagogy: Portraits of Effective Teachers* (New York: Routledge, 2011).

8 Flourishing in the Induction Years

How do new teachers flourish in their first five or six years of teaching? What do they need to know that their teaching degree did or did not provide them? What mindset do they need? In what circumstances are they most likely to stay teaching? What kind of support do they need? How do they find their place in teaching and in a particular school building? In this chapter, I explore these questions and offer a brief summary of the research into the retention of novice teachers.[1] But retention is not my only concern here. I want to ask what teachers need from others and what they can do for themselves so that they put into place both the habits of thought and the practices that will allow them to flourish long-term in the profession.

Staying: The First Task

That heading may seem obvious, but staying is more complex than many novice teachers realize. Staying is not simply a matter of will. All fresh graduates of teaching licensure programs know the language of grit or persistence.[2] But the grit conversation in university classrooms usually focuses not on teachers but on students and the efforts they must make to succeed in their learning, especially if they come from adverse circumstances. Even those new teachers who do know the grit research may think that simply having grit or persevering will be sufficient to get them through the first five or six years of their teaching career. If they think that, they could well be wrong; perseverance is a necessary condition for staying but is not sufficient.

Besides grit, novice teachers need several other things in place if they wish to remain in their chosen profession for their initial years and beyond. An extensive body of research informs any conversation about the retention of induction teachers. At the time of writing, a search of the string *teacher retention and attrition* (without quotation marks) yielded 151,000 records, all of which I clearly did not read. With that admission out of the way, I note that several factors consistently appear in the research[3] into those who stay in the profession.

First, new teachers who continue in the profession build strong relationships both with colleagues and administrators inside their school buildings and with others outside their school buildings. I continue with this theme in Chapter 13, which deals with supporters inside the school building and the need for teachers to assemble a team from outside their school building who will support them in their work.

Second, most teachers who continue teaching beyond their novice phase enjoy the support of a mentor during their first years.[4] Usually, such mentors come from the same grade level or, in secondary education, from the same subject area. Such mentors do not usually function in a monitorial role and typically do not report to the novice educator's supervisor; rather, they work alongside their novice colleague, giving guidance and encouragement.

Third, teachers who stay tend to be those who view the bumps that come in their professional work as natural parts of the territory. That is, they do not consider a difficulty here and there to be exceptional; rather, they view bumps and glitches as normal, and they understand that they must work through them. This theme reappears in the next chapter on teaching in one's middle years (Chapter 9) and in Chapter 11, where I deal with flourishing through to one's eventual retirement from teaching.

Almost all novice teachers have encountered the work of Albert Bandura on self-efficacy during their teaching degree.[5] Typically, they study the concept with reference mainly to students. As a reminder, by *self-efficacy* Bandura meant that those with high expectations of themselves usually work more effectively than those who have low expectations. His work has been applied in many areas, including education, health care, business, and even politics. With reference specifically to education, Bandura's work usually carries a double meaning: the student is capable of good work and the student believes it. To apply the concept to teaching requires little translation. I list this as the fourth typical condition in place for those teachers who stay rather than leave; they achieve some measure of success and believe that they are being successful.

Self-efficacy implies something important for the novice teacher: no negative self-talk, a fifth element typically associated with staying in teaching. All teachers get instruction or their interactions with students wrong sometimes.

Teachers make more mistakes in these areas in their novice years than they will make in their middle years. Framing mistakes as learning—what some now call *failing forward*—is one key to staying in teaching and, ultimately, to flourishing long term in teaching. Learning how to frame one's failures as opportunities for learning points again to the importance of having a mentor who can admit to having made the same mistake as the novice, perhaps even that morning.

The courage to authorize oneself is the sixth typical condition in place with teachers who stay. Not many teachers have heard of the concept of *self-authorization*.[6] This idea has a connection to self-efficacy but has a more direct connection to the teacher's authority. Obviously, teachers already come to class with some authority; they have a degree, a license, and a contract with a school authority. The challenge for new teachers is that, for students, those three sources of their teacher's classroom authority are essentially out of sight. That those criteria are largely out of students' sight is somewhat irrelevant anyway because extensive research reveals that students judge their teachers on other grounds, such as whether they can teach well and whether they care. To the authority question new teachers must answer, no one is going to introduce them to their students, review their qualifications, and list the reasons students should listen to them. No one does a warm-up monologue before the novice teacher's entrance. They must introduce themselves, what in entertainment venues is called *a cold start*. Like the opera singer who stands up from her chair and begins her song without an introduction, teachers must stand up and begin. And doing that takes courage and pluck. New teachers must authorize themselves. They must stand up and begin teaching.

Finding and Making a Place

Upon graduating from a licensure program and securing a first teaching position, another challenge for new teachers is to find a place—a sense of fit—in teaching. Upon arriving in a new school and a new classroom, new teachers must also create a classroom space in which they and their students both want to work. These twin tasks are obviously intertwined. Success at constructing the kind of space in which students like to learn will contribute to a novice teacher's sense of having found a place in teaching. But both of these tasks bring their challenges.

How to create a classroom space or classroom climate where teachers and students want to teach and learn remains outside the scope of this book, although I do address it here and there. I note it here because it goes hand in hand with developing a clear sense that the teacher belongs in teaching and that teaching fits the teacher.[7]

Finding a place in teaching implies looking for answers to several questions. How do you keep students engaged and motivated? What does good teaching look like? How do you know if students are learning? How do you teach students with learning disabilities and other exceptionalities? How do you build rapport with students? How do you gain their respect? What should I do when I don't know much about a curriculum content area I have been assigned to teach? How will I make myself inviting and approachable while continuing to be an authority figure in the classroom? How do I find the right balance between being serious about accomplishing work and making class fun? Do I, or how do I, take time to connect with my students and learn about who they are as people? This rather intimidating list of questions points to the need for novice teachers to have a mentor who will walk alongside them and remind them that many teachers before them have answered the same questions and have flourished as teachers.

Some of the novice teachers' questions about finding a place focus less on the classroom and more on the person. Is this satisfying work? Am I making a difference? Will the world be better off with or without my teaching? Am I content . . . satisfied . . . happy doing this work? Do I know I'm called to be a teacher? Am I sure about this school? Would a different school work better than this one? Do I have it in me to go until I retire? How would I explain quitting to my friends and family?

Some of these questions reveal a degree of uncertainty not experienced by more senior teachers. And some of these questions never seem to go away. Novice teachers need not be alone in their search for a place in teaching. Supportive colleagues and mentors can help. Also, teachers can learn a great deal from the research on retention and attrition among novice teachers.[8] One almost certain outcome of such reading will be the assurance that one is not alone if one asks deep questions and experiences doubts related to the teaching vocation.

Eight Principles for Flourishing

At this point in the chapter, I turn to the work and words of Jaliene Hollabaugh, an expert on novice teachers who focused her doctoral research on the factors that lead novice teachers to stay. In response to my request, she wrote the following, which I quote without editing or commenting.[9]

Flourishing in Teaching: Eight Principles

Jaliene Hollabaugh

Inductive teachers wanting to thrive value relationships. In fact, the high desire and ability of inductive teachers to build and maintain significant relationships are a principle reason why they enter and remain in the profession.

Inductive teachers wanting to thrive prioritize collegial relationships. The notable presence or noticeable absence of collegial relationships is the most significant difference between inductive teachers who view their professional entry experiences as manageable versus stressful, respectively.

Inductive teachers wanting to thrive understand they are a sum of all their causes. They are a sum of the nature and nurture of their upbringing, as well as the people, places, and experiences that influenced them. They choose a workplace that welcomes them as part of an ecosystem in which all contribute to the teaching, learning, and mentorship within.

Inductive teachers wanting to thrive insist that their teaching assignments are matched to their teacher typology. For example, teachers with narrowly focused résumés regarding their educational backgrounds and content area study, who especially take enjoyment in teaching their content area, and whose empathy is displayed best in the planning of high-quality lesson plans for the varied learning styles of their students, are going to thrive if their teaching assignment is like their résumés and, as such, narrowly focused. Conversely, teachers with diverse résumés regarding their educational backgrounds and content area studies, who especially enjoy being a teacher as well as engaging with colleagues, and whose empathy is displayed best by nurturing the overall growth and

> development of others, can thrive with more diverse teaching assignments and are likely to have an aptitude for future leadership roles.
>
> Inductive teachers wanting to thrive have a strong teacher identity, understanding that being a teacher is who they are all the time. As such, they have a higher level of accountability toward being a mentor not only to students but also to other colleagues and community members. The act of mentoring and being mentored, no matter the context, is the epitome of lifelong learning.
>
> Inductive teachers wanting to thrive will seek educational leaders and environments that protect the integrity of the teaching profession and all the people within it. They will seek to work with others who prioritize relationships, collegiality, mentorship, self-awareness, and personal and professional accountability.
>
> Inductive teachers wanting to thrive will understand that their emotional development and career-stage maturity will evolve over time. This understanding fosters confidence and peace, as it affirms that every phase of a teacher's life cycle is valuable.

The Reflective Retreat

The first section of the chapter and this outline by Jaliene Hollabaugh contain much at the level of principle and some at the level of practice for novice teachers who wish to find their place in teaching and flourish long term. We turn now to some ideas focused more on practice, although some of the ideas I present clearly connect to the larger questions of vocation and one's fit in the profession.

Many educators and, for that matter, people working in other demanding professions take periodic retreats to evaluate their progress, their fit, and their plans for what lies ahead. With full knowledge that teachers in the first years might wonder how they would ever find time to get away for such a retreat, I recommend doing exactly that.[10] Because individuals differ as to how far they want to travel, what their budget is, and what combination they want of quiet and interaction, I will not address those matters. But I suggest a number of activities and offer some lines of inquiry that might help make the time spent on retreat more fruitful for the teacher.

- Could you identify a signature unit or instructional strategy, one with which you have had good success with your students? Is it reasonable to think that you could aim at developing a workshop about it within two or three years that you could present on a professional development day? Alternatively, could you blog about it or post some of your material to Teachers Pay Teachers?
- If you enjoy trying new instructional strategies, could you plan to expand your current repertoire of strategies into an arsenal of strategies and then into an encyclopedia? Perhaps such an encyclopedia could be published by a commercial publisher or by your school board or Department of Education.
- What about latching onto outstanding teachers? If your own jurisdiction has an awards program, contact some of the recipients and ask to meet. Or see larger programs such as that of the National Education Association, identify recipients whose work interests you, and find out more about them.[11] Perhaps they have published or posted videos. If they live close enough, arrange to visit their classrooms or meet for coffee.
- If you are not already part of a professional learning community (PLC), what about joining one or even starting one with colleagues from your own building or from other schools?
- Could you plan ahead for the year you start taking interns from a nearby education program, perhaps the one from which you graduated?
- Could you plan ahead for the year you launch your MEd degree? Most graduate programs in education offer both a thesis track and a coursework + project track. Some offer a straight coursework track. Many such programs use a cohort model, so that participants meet face to face for their first summer course and then take online courses during the academic year. Some school districts will provide you with full or partial tuition reimbursement.
- With or without an advanced degree, could you set a research agenda? You could conduct action research into a question being asked in your own building. For example, does Bring-Your-Own-Device work better than a cart of school laptops for such-and-such assignment? There are ways to answer a research question like that. You could work with other colleagues in your building to answer

such questions, thereby exercising your brain, building professional relationships, and likely leading to improvements in your classroom program.

- Would it help you to develop your own *systems manual* (for lack of a better name)? In such a manual, you would commit to paper every process and routine that you know you need to repeat month by month or term by term. In some cases, you would need to build a system. Examples include term start up, book distribution, attendance, collecting student work, communication with parents, and organization of school email. Systems increase efficiency and efficacy, so why not?
- Could you ask someone to evaluate your teaching using a sophisticated and nuanced instrument, such as that of Charlotte Danielson?[12]

The nine lines of inquiry above hardly exhaust what one might do on a retreat. But they do offer some prompts for thinking about one's profession in specific directions. Next, I offer an extended exercise that in-service teachers and my own education students have enjoyed and found helpful in their efforts to reflect on their vocation as teachers.

The Subway Map

Sometimes taking a different approach from our usual helps us think new thoughts and have new insights as we reflect on important matters such as our vocational journey as teachers. People who have never used a graphic organizer make new discoveries. Those who have never used Venn diagrams find new clarity. Those who have never kept a journal find themselves slowing down. In this exercise, I will ask you to produce a subway or transit map with the station names all replaced by important parts of your own biography, formation, and call into teaching. Maps are a great way to engage those dimensions of our thinking that we might not ordinarily bring to sorting out questions of vocation and our own journeys as educators. This exercise employs graphics to help us discern, remember, or sharpen our call into teaching. Making a map can force those who usually default toward language and critical discourse—that's most teachers—to awaken our aesthetic and artistic selves and engage the affective dimension. By making a map, we use other faculties and abilities than language and reason. This is an intensely personal exercise, requiring that map-makers go slowly, write, read past entries in their journals, look at their bookshelves and Goodreads lists, reflect, and meditate.

The idea of representing something other than subway station routes and stations on a map is not my own. For years, the London Underground has produced tube maps with such names as Engineering Icons, Films, and Paralympic Champions. I am not permitted to show an example here, but I invite you to search the London Underground Museum Shop and type *tube posters* into the search bar on the landing page to see examples.[13]

The map I invite you to make requires you to download a subway or transit map of any large city. Choose one with a number of lines suited to the degree of detail you wish to go into. For example, Prague has three lines, while London has more than a dozen. Using your drawing program, strip the city names from this map and save it as a blank. I invite those who are adept at working in a drawing program to work on screen. Some may want to print an 11x17" paper copy and work on paper. Using the subway lines, add your own station names in response to such questions as the following.

> *Who were my mentors?*
> *Vignettes and moments when I knew I wanted to teach.*
> *What life events have shaped who I am becoming as a teacher?*
> *People, events, and forces that have helped me keep my heart open to teaching.*
> *Teaching moments that helped shape my sense of integrity and identity as a teacher.*
> *How my worldview has influenced my journey into teaching and my philosophy of education.*
> *Brilliant days of teaching and utter flops.*
> *Films, or works of fiction and non-fiction, that have shaped my view of teaching.*
> *Travel or work experiences that shaped my vision of life and teaching.*
> *Surprises that students, colleagues, and family members have given me along the way.*
> *Metaphors and images that enrich and give vision to my teaching self.*
> *Some of the tensions I anticipate facing as a teacher.*[14]

Readers will think of other questions. Part of the value of working and thinking in this way, which most of us do not usually consider, is that readers will also remember other answers, events, and the names of people they had long forgotten. Pre-service and in-service teachers who have carried out this exercise often report gaining confirmation that they have arrived at this point in their journey in teaching for good reasons and not by accident. To me, such confirmation is a satisfactory outcome.

Conclusion

If they are to stay in the teaching profession and flourish there, novice teachers need a great deal of support. My hope is that what I have brought in this chapter has combined with Jaliene Hollabaugh's insights to help induction teachers frame this period in their careers in a positive light. Furthermore, I want readers in the early stages of their careers to be able to envision a positive career trajectory for themselves. In the brief discussion of ambition in Chapter 2, I tried to nuance the difference between the kind of ambition that gets teachers out of bed in the morning and the kind that leads to manipulation and deception (or worse, enter Lady Macbeth, stage right).

May early career teachers take from this chapter a deeper sense that they are called to teach, and may that deeper sense of calling produce in them more of the right kind of ambition.

Notes

1 In this chapter, I use the phrases *induction teacher*, *novice teacher*, and *early career teacher* interchangeably.

2 Angela Duckworth, *Grit: The Power of Passion and Perseverance* (New York: Simon and Schuster, 2016). The word *perseverance* has been in the English language for centuries longer than the word *persistence*; I use them interchangeably here.

3 The first three factors I list were all identified in the doctoral dissertation of Jaliene Hollabaugh, *Exploring the Perceptions and Experiences of Inductive Teachers in Secondary Education: How do Inductive Teachers Find Their Place in the Teaching Profession, and What Motivates Them to Remain in the Field?*, https://digitalcommons.georgefox.edu/edd/1.

4   Cassandra M. Guarino, Lucrecia Santibañez, and Glenn A. Daley, "Teacher Recruitment and Retention: A Review of the Recent Empirical Literature," *Review of Educational* Research 76, no. 2 (2006): 173–208. See also Duane Inman and Leslie Marlow, "Teacher Retention: Why Do Beginning Teachers Remain in the Profession?," *Education* 124, no. 4 (2004): 605–14.

5   Albert Bandura, "Self-Efficacy: Toward a Unifying Theory of Behavioral Change," *The Psychological Review* 84 (1977): 191–215; *Self-Efficacy: The Exercise of Control* (Freeman, 1997). See also Deborah S. Yost, "Reflection and Self-Efficacy: Enhancing the Retention of Qualified Teachers from a Teacher Education Perspective," *Teacher Education Quarterly* 33, no. 4 (Fall 2006): 59–76.

6   *The Complexities of Authority in the Classroom: Fostering Democracy for Student Learning*, eds. Ken Badley and Margie Patrick (New York: Routledge, 2022).

7   See Gillian Storey's comments in Chapter 10 for more about fitting into teaching.

8   A rich body of research literature on those who stay in teaching and those who leave may help those trying to answer some of these questions. See, for example, Ahmet Latifoglu, "Staying or Leaving? An Analysis of Career Trajectories of Beginning Teachers," *International Studies in Educational Administration* 44, no. 1 (2016): 55–70.

9   Her 2012 dissertation at George Fox University.

10   Obviously, searching for *retreat centers* online will produce results. Even Google Maps will list retreat centers nearby.

11   https://www.neafoundation.org/projects-initiatives/awards-for-teaching-excellence/.

12   Charlotte Danielson, *The Framework for Teaching Evaluation Instrument* (Princeton, NJ: The Danielson Group, 2014). Also see her *Teacher Evaluation to Enhance Professional Practice*, with Thomas L. McGreal (Alexandria, VA: ACSD, 2000).

13   London Underground Museum at https://www.ltmuseumshop.co.uk/. Engineering icons tube map at https://www.ltmuseumshop.co.uk/engineering-icons-tube-map. Tube film map at https://www.ltmuseumshop.co.uk/underground-film-map-poster. Paralympic champions tube map poster at https://www.ltmuseumshop.co.uk/paralympics-gb-medallists-map-poster.

14   These questions are adapted from *The Courage to Teach: Exploring the Inner Landscape of a Teacher's Life* (San Francisco, CA: Jossey-Bass, 1998).

9 The Middle Years

The middle years of teaching bring unique rewards, but they also bring their own challenges. Teachers who can see their fortieth birthday from one direction or the other can take steps to maintain their vision for teaching and even to enlarge it. The first of this chapter's three sections focuses on some of the challenges facing mid-career teachers and frames those challenges in what many psychologists call the middle passage.[1] In the second section of the chapter, the focus shifts to what steps teachers in mid-career can take to maintain their vision for teaching and stay vital intellectually. The chapter ends with a number of suggestions for how mid-career teachers can significantly overhaul their teaching program and, by doing so, enlarge their vision for teaching.

The Middle Passage

Most teachers in their middle years have already mastered the routines and strategies needed to run an effective classroom program day to day. With curriculum and instructional routines well in hand, so to speak, the day-to-day tasks of teaching make significantly smaller demands on the cognitive capacity of mid-career teachers than they do on a novice teacher. Those who study boredom note that boredom typically sets in when one is engaged in tasks that require only a fraction of one's cognitive capacity.[2] Standing in line is an obvious example of such a situation; it takes almost no mental effort at all to keep one's place in line. Like standing in line, teaching a unit that one has already taught dozens of times may induce boredom. Mid-career teachers need ways to avoid mixing the ingredients of the recipe for boredom.

A related challenge for many mid-career teachers is the weariness that comes with feeling that one has had—perhaps many times over—the same old difficulties with (different) students, the same old changes to (different) software or administrative procedures, and the same old curriculum revisions. Framed one way, these difficulties and changes may induce boredom for mid-career teachers. For some, the challenge may well be to avoid sighing and asking under their breath, "Ah, ya think maybe we've been here before?"

Framed differently, these changes may actually be opportunities for keeping the mid-career teacher's brain vital. That is, learning new software or developing instruction to accompany a new curriculum initiative implies having to think new thoughts and thereby develop new neural networks.

The mid-career challenges teachers may face at school typically occur in the wider context of middle adulthood. Jungian psychologists view the middle years as a time of examination and possible re-orientation of one's identity. James Hollis, among many others, has written extensively about how people can flourish in their middle years. Hollis believes that the task in these years is to distinguish one's primary identity—what he calls one's *self*—from such secondary identities as teacher or school administrator. Those who enter humanistic professions such as social work and teaching because of their moral commitments may be particularly prone to having their primary identity swallowed up by their professional identity. Though Hollis does not address educators specifically, on his account, one task of mid-career educators would be to distinguish who they are apart from being teachers.

Typically, teachers in mid-life are in relationships with family and friends, with neighbors, and with other members of voluntary organizations. Apart from their relationships, they also have moral commitments, visions of human flourishing and the good life, hobbies and reading interests, and so on. Again, according to Hollis, part of the middle passage is to define one's identity with reference to these parts of one's self that are separate from one's work, in this case as an educator. To anticipate the contents of Chapter 11—about the late career teacher and the transition to retirement—wisdom indicates that completing the task of distinguishing one's self from one's profession during one's middle years would yield benefits for one's remaining teaching years and would also help one avoid a crisis upon one's retirement from teaching. Worded positively, completing that task would likely lead to flourishing.

An aspect of this identification of the self apart from one's profession as an educator relates to one's personal mission statement (treated in Chapter 6 of this book). Gordon T. Smith, who has written extensively on vocation, says that teachers in their middle years need to distinguish between their institutional and personal mission statements. Making such a distinction is a means of vocational rejuvenation. It helps educators avoid disappearing into their institutions, and it allows their social lives to revolve around something other than their work. Teachers need to be careful not to lose their lives in their work. He claims that mid-career teachers need ways to frame their work and, in his own words, "strategies and structures to contain [their] work and to keep it at work. This partly involves rhythms of rest, restoration, and refreshment, as well as structures for encouragement."[3]

Smith's advice leads to the question of how mid-career teachers—and, for that matter, teachers at all stages of their careers—can take intentional steps so that they live in a world larger than their school. Some find venues for service, for example, with a local non-profit focused on housing or food security. Some form or join book clubs or film groups. Some get involved in service trips and work with teachers in other countries (although such trips obviously still relate to one's professional work). Different teachers answer the question of building a life outside of school in different ways, but all teachers must answer the question.

By mid-life, most educators will have experienced professional or personal bumps; as the bumper sticker says, life happens. The ways people process those bumps usually have long-term effects, for good or for bad. One theme that emerged from interviews Gordon Smith and I conducted with several late career educators[4] is that people who remain vital from mid-career forward reframe and even rename the difficulties they encounter and are thereby able to move ahead. One of our participants told us, "I knew I had to go through [a bump] because I couldn't go around it," a comment true of many such experiences. Teachers who accept that some bumps are inevitable give themselves a measure of mental health denied to both the blind optimist who thinks bumps are exceptional and to the cynic who believes that life is all bumps and deception, all the time.

Another participant who contributed to that project spoke about how he processed some of the inevitable bumps. He said, "there's been a lot of pain there, but because I don't live there, it's in isolated moments. Now that you mention it, I can give you a litany, but the [events] don't come to mind." The challenge for all educators who want to flourish into the second half of their teaching careers is not to keep living in those memories of pain, an idea that emerges again in the last three chapters of this book.

Staying Vital in Mid-Career

The quotations above came from a set of nineteen interviews with senior educators regarding what steps they had taken in mid-life so that they flourished into their last decades of teaching. Separately, I asked a number of mid-career teachers what strategies they used and routines they put in place to keep their brains and their ideals alive while teaching. The transcriptions of the nineteen interviews from educators near the end of their careers and the written responses from mid-career educators yielded a great deal of valuable insight into how to navigate this stage of the teaching career. Among the many themes that emerged from these interviews and the written narratives are these: the sheer joy of teaching, making or asking for changes to one's responsibilities, and getting intellectual food outside the school building. In the conclusion of "Voices from Classrooms" (the next chapter), I list several more such themes.

Two comments about the sheer joy of teaching bear quoting here, the first from an educator in Ontario, Canada.

> *What really turns me on is that interchange with students, the debate, the discussing, the wrestling through issues which are sometimes touchy, which sometimes require tact, you know, sometimes touch people in possibly hurtful ways, and try to work that out, and try to help people discover for themselves ways of incorporating what there is out there in the world, in their own life, and find it helpful, rather than destructive, okay.*[5]

The second comment echoes the first.

> *What do I enjoy most? It's not the preparation, of course, it's the giving of the course, I would say. It's being in class with the students, in the course. [They have a] thirst for learning, so I enjoy being with [them].*

These two educators' comments contain something instructive for all educators: the core activities of teaching itself ought to be sources of joy.

Another theme that emerged from both the interviews and the written responses to my question about how teachers keep their brains alive was initiating change in one's own work environment. For any number of reasons within or beyond their control, some teachers teach the same grade in the same room for decades. And for just as many reasons, some teachers teach in several rooms and teach several different grades over the same period of time. The quotations that follow come from educators whose teaching responsibilities remained relatively stable but who initiated change themselves.

> I developed a whole large series of courses, during my early teaching career, and kept on doing new things and branching out, and picking up additional work, always revising my courses every year around, always when you're finishing one course, leave yourself some notes about how I could improve this for the next year, and how I would incorporate things that have developed since then.[6]
>
> it's so important that, to have a different course every year. I mean you have to, the course always has to develop, in keeping where the students are, what kind of student body you have, what group, every year the class is different.
>
> I don't believe in repeating a course, in exactly the same fashion two years in a row. Every course is always, there's always something in the course, different, from one year to the next. That's the way I keep alive.

What does one make of comments such as those above? These mid-career and veteran teachers report that they change a portion of their course content or their overall teaching responsibilities every year. Obviously, new curriculum mandates do not come down from one's respective Department of Education at an annual pace, but on their own initiative, individual teachers can employ new teaching strategies, introduce new lessons within some established units, try some new instructional materials, or even release more responsibility into students' hands for some part or parts of a unit. Making these kinds of moves requires work, but the view of these flourishing teachers is that such changes are a necessity for their own brains; they impose new challenges on themselves. Given the typical lifespan of a school system's mandated curriculum, perhaps all teachers should follow their example.

Second, to keep their own brains alive and their students interested in school, some teachers try imaginative—and apparently crazy—things in their classrooms. Granted, some of those initiatives may, in the short run, turn out to be less successful than anticipated, but they often result in increased student support for their teacher's overall program and possibly more engagement at those other times in classroom life when their teacher needs to push ahead with other, perhaps challenging, curriculum materials.[7]

Teachers who flourish through their middle years and into late career focus on the positive when inside their school buildings. They avoid conversations where people criticize their school, and they structure their classes so that students can blossom in ways that encourage not only themselves but also their teachers. These teachers avoid getting pulled into institutional spheres that don't give life. They tend to deal quickly with the interpersonal and institutional conflicts that inevitably arise, so they don't end up arguing in absentia and thereby wasting energy. Many teachers record good things about teaching every day in a gratitude journal, starting their entries with a heading along the lines of "What Went Well Today."[8]

Teachers who stay vital through their middle years stay on top of the baseline tasks of teaching. They keep up with their planning and preparation, their grading, and their record-keeping. Without shame, most teachers use other teachers' materials to save themselves time and to improve the quality of their classroom program. The success of Teachers Pay Teachers (TPT)[9] is in part due to the great number of teachers who have accepted the twin truths that their teacher colleagues in faraway places have developed great instructional materials and that there is no shame in using those materials. While I have no immediate need to teach a unit on the water cycle, I looked it up just now and was offered 2,200 resources. Is it not a no-brainer that if I needed to start teaching that unit next week and had never taught it before, it would make sense to adapt someone else's work in my classroom? Even if I had taught the water cycle many times, why would I not look there to see what creative approaches my colleagues have taken in so many other classrooms?

Flourishing teachers typically seek intellectual food outside their school building. That strategy implies gathering with people who feed each other ideas. It implies reading challenging books. It implies digging in while attending teachers' conventions and professional development days and following up on what one learns in those venues.[10] It implies soaking up every professional conversation one can find. For many, it implies starting an advanced education degree, which many do because they wish to enter educational administration, but some do simply to sharpen their own classroom teaching. One colleague reported starting a teacher film group. One Friday night per month, these colleagues gather with each other (and with any partners willing to talk about teaching) to eat dinner together, watch a teacher film, and discuss. Arguably, this qualifies as a social gathering as much as it does a professional gathering, but the colleague who reported this views it as a source of professional growth.

In Chapter 13, I claim that flourishing long term usually entails identifying one's supporters and friends so that one does not feel alone in one's building. Among those supporters will be our institutional neighbors—administrators and colleagues—but I will argue in Chapter 13 that we can invite our students to support us in our work. And later in that chapter, I suggest that teachers should intentionally gather a team of people, largely from outside their building, who will support them in their day-to-day work, as well as celebrate their joys and carry their sorrows with them.

Teachers who thrive through their middle years habitually attend to their outside-of-school, life-giving activities. Doing so can remind teachers that they do have time for things other than teaching and that their demanding work has not sucked the goodness out of their lives. Whether those activities involve hobbies, faith, family, sports and exercise, music and the arts, or one of a hundred other possible interests, vital teachers make such patterns and activities a habit.

Rejuvenation and Renaissance

The previous section of this chapter focused on maintaining one's vitality through the middle years of one's teaching career. This section consists of an invitation for teachers to take dramatic steps to rejuvenate their teaching, in part by bringing new levels of innovation and creativity to their classroom program.

Certainly, in the middle-school and secondary grades, teachers can actually invite their students into a process of experimentation with curriculum, instruction, and even assessment. The teacher can invite middle-school students to experiment with different structures of class time for two weeks. "Help me here, let's try this change for two weeks and then evaluate it and see how it went." Or a teacher can ask about incorporating a novel into the next unit in a class where students would not ordinarily expect a novel study. These are relatively safe examples of the kind of experimentation some teachers have tried. Other simple but satisfying steps include these

- pilot-teaching new curriculum materials for a textbook publisher through the respective subject-area council or the relevant officers at the Department of Education,
- serving on district or provincial and state curriculum committees,
- building a personal encyclopedia of instructional strategies for distribution on a platform such as Teachers Pay Teachers,
- writing articles or book reviews in your teacher association's magazine. A one-page article usually runs about 750–800 words and brings a

measure of satisfaction to its author (and possibly enough money for a modest meal in a restaurant),

- leading a professional learning community (PLC) with grade-level or subject-area colleagues in one's own school or with colleagues from more than one building,
- implementing a metacognition stream in one instructional unit and reflecting with students to find out in what ways attending to metacognition influenced their learning in that unit as well as how it affected their disposition toward the subject matter,
- beginning some action research with one or two colleagues, examining just one of the puzzles in the teaching program, and
- developing a workshop based on one signature unit or instructional strategy and presenting it on a professional day in one's school or school district.

Recognizably, the above ideas imply work for the teacher. But my point is that taking on such challenges forces teachers to think new thoughts and to create new neural pathways. Those new pathways are key to long-term flourishing in this demanding profession called teaching.

Bolder moves than those listed are available. One such move would involve reading with one's students the Wikipedia article about Building 20 at MIT—especially the "Occupants" section—and asking students what it would be like to study in a classroom that functioned like Building 20.[11] Building 20, torn down some decades ago, became famous during its five-decade life as a center of great invention, interdisciplinarity, and creativity. How would one create a classroom with some of those characteristics? And what kind of work might students in that classroom produce?

In a similar vein, a teacher and a group of students could read about the Skunk Works, the Advanced Development Projects division at Lockheed Aerospace, and think about ways to create a Skunk Works classroom.[12] One cannot read about the Skunk Works without getting a strong sense that the people who worked and work there have fun. Surely, there were and are times of frustration, tension, and the office politics characteristic of all workplaces. But from its origins, everyone in the Skunk Works has known that they were part of something special and their mandate was to think the unthinkable. Do our students ever get the sense that our classrooms are places to imagine the unimaginable? Do they ever think they have permission to suggest ideas that the educational social codes ordinarily prevent them from thinking they should suggest aloud?

To illustrate, what people call *stealth aircraft* were first developed at Lockheed's Skunk Works. Teachers might find it interesting that the Lockheed engineer who first proposed it did so because he read an article about radar in a mathematics journal that he suspected might contain the key to stealth. He wondered if Lockheed could build the unthinkable, an airplane that could not be seen on radar. Of course, there was no such thing as an airplane that could not be seen on radar. That was literally unthinkable. What kind of excellence and what kind of creativity might be unleashed in classrooms if students thought they had this kind of license or even mandate to work, and read, write, and think in unexpected ways?

Another possibility, albeit less bold than trying to create a Building 20 or a Lockheed Skunk Works type of classroom, would be to read about the slow movement with students and ask what a slow classroom would look like and how it might function.[13] Students' responses to that question would likely be all over the map, but some of their ideas would probably be worth trying. And asking about slow would also be an interesting exercise in metacognition. Teachers who explored slow in this way could talk with—rather than to—their students about the pace of learning and what societies and schools expect of students and their teachers. And they could ask their students how they read and how time spent online has influenced them and the culture as a whole.

These are just a few ideas. Presumably, there are many more good ideas to be found among the 103,000,000 hits I got just now by searching *classroom creativity* on Google. Teachers wishing to flourish until their last decade in the classroom need to take bold steps. Certainly, such steps make life more interesting for students. But to the point of this book, such steps make life more interesting for those students' teachers as well.

Conclusion

Teachers who thrive in mid-career—and into late career—take a wide variety of approaches to the questions of remaining vital intellectually and socially. They do so while recognizing the intensity, complexity, and frustrations characteristic of educational work. That is, they do not ignore the demands of teaching. Rather, they implement the strategies they do, and they build the routines they do because of the demands. And, in conclusion, they thrive and flourish into their last decades of teaching and even to retirement.

Notes

1. For example, see these two titles by James Hollis, an American psychologist who works in the Jungian tradition. These titles have overlaps but both warrant reading by anyone who celebrated their fortieth birthday but not their fiftieth: *The Middle Passage: From Misery to Meaning in Mid-Life* (Toronto: Inner-City Books, 1993), and *Finding Meaning in the Second Half of Life* (New York: Gotham/Penguin, 2005).
2. Peter Toohey, *Boredom: A Lively History* (New Haven, CT: Yale University Press, 2011); James Danckert and John Eastwood, *Out of My Skull: The Psychology of Boredom* (Cambridge, MA: Harvard University Press, 2020).
3. Gordon T. Smith, author of *Consider Your Calling: Six Questions for Discerning Your Vocation* (Downers Grove, IL: InterVarsity Press, 2015), in personal conversation, April 2020.
4. Research conducted by Gordon T. Smith and me published as "Called to Teach," *Teaching Theology and Religion* 1, no. 3 (October 1998): 171–6.
5. Quoted from an interview with an educator from Ontario, Canada. The comment below is quoted from an educator in British Columbia, Canada. Both wish to remain anonymous.
6. These quotations come, respectively, from educators in Nova Scotia, Saskatchewan, and Alberta, Canada, all of whom wish to remain anonymous.
7. Elsewhere, I have offered a highly detailed description of a student-friendly approach to term-long scheduling and course planning. See my *Curriculum Planning with Design Language: Building Elegant Courses and Units* (New York: Routledge, 2018). I have also written at length about instructional strategies for higher education, many of which are suited to secondary or even middle grades. See *Engaging College and University Students: Effective Instructional Strategies* (New York: Routledge, 2022).
8. We return to gratitude practices in Chapter 14.
9. https://www.teacherspayteachers.com/.
10. See Tiana Tucker's doctoral dissertation, *Bridging the Research-to-Practice Gap: Factors Affecting Teachers' Efficacy about Instruction* (Newberg, OR: George Fox University, 2015). She concluded that the usefulness of professional

development sessions is reduced dramatically if participants do not put their learning into practice within two weeks. https://digitalcommons.georgefox.edu/edd/55/.

11 https://en.wikipedia.org/wiki/Building_20.

12 I described the Skunk Works in Chapter 7. See https://www.lockheedmartin.com/en-us/who-we-are/business-areas/aeronautics/skunkworks.html. Also see Ben Rich (with Leo Janos), *Skunk Works: A Personal Memoir of My Years at Lockheed* (Boston, MA: Little-Brown, 1994); Kelly Johnson (with Maggie Smith), *Kelly: More than My Share of It All* (Washington, DC: Smithsonian, 1985). With my colleague Amy Dee, I have written about possible applications of the Skunk Works to educational settings. See "Creating an Educational Ethos where Innovation and Accountability Flourish: A New Model for Transparency in Educational Organizations," *Journal of the National Council of Professors of Educational Administration* 5, no. 4 (October–December 2010), https://digitalcommons.georgefox.edu/soe_faculty/52/. Also see the Wikipedia article on the Skunk Works at https://en.wikipedia.org/wiki/Skunk_Works.

13 Elizabeth Hauke, "Make Classroom Connections by Drawing from the Slow Movement," *Times Higher Education*, August 25, 2022. https://www.timeshighereducation.com/campus/make-classroom-connections-drawing-slow-movement.

10 Voices from the Classroom

The ideas and comments of various educators appear throughout this volume. But this chapter clusters together the responses of thirteen teachers to two rather blunt questions: How do you keep your brain alive? How do you keep your classroom ideals alive? The respondents to those two questions all were serving as classroom teachers in the 2024–2025 academic year, and they wrote their responses after the beginning of the academic year; that is, they made their contribution while carrying out their professional duties.[1]

Some of the voices in this chapter are those of colleagues with whom I have never taught. Most of those whose words follow come from teachers whom I met because they enrolled in a university course taught by me. An explanation is in order regarding the question about these teachers: How have they kept their ideals alive? Many of my education students were required to complete an assignment that required them to identify ten characteristics of their ideal classroom. Of course, as pre-service teachers, they had not yet dealt with the challenges of keeping their ideals alive long-term. But the assignment was meant to get them thinking about how they would realize their philosophy of education in their future classrooms. Below is a condensed description of that assignment from a course syllabus:

> Write 600–800 words in which you list and briefly describe the ten most important qualities you hope characterize your future classroom. A detailed description and examples are attached to the rubric, and the rubric and exemplars both will be posted to the course wiki. Format of this assignment can be either introduction plus 10 short paragraphs or introduction plus 3-4 paragraphs where you cluster several ideals together under each of a few themes.
>
> These ideals are to be deeply your own—the reasons you plan to get up in the morning for the next 30 years—but you should describe them with full awareness that you will be realizing them in actual school settings, not in utopia.

Important note: You are NOT to include the baseline ideals or conditions expected (or even required legally) in classrooms: respect, safety, organization, inclusivity, differentiation. These are given. This assignment asks you to focus on the qualities that will make your classroom unique.[2]

The three paragraphs above or paragraphs very much like them appeared in my syllabi for philosophy of education courses in the four-year, undergraduate teacher-education program at Mount Royal University in Calgary and the four-semester, after-degree licensure programs at St. Mary's University in Calgary and Tyndale University in Toronto. In fact, the composite list of ideals in Chapter 6 represents a portion of the many ideals listed by pre-service teachers in these courses over the last decade. Some items on the list in Chapter 6 came from in-service teachers whom I met through graduate courses and workshops. I provide this explanation to help frame the responses that comprise the rest of this chapter; the language of classroom ideals and realizing those ideals is not new language for many of the respondents to my two questions.

Some of the respondents whose words appear below wished to remain anonymous because some of what they have written might compromise them within their work settings. Some of the teachers whose words comprise the remainder of this chapter wrote directly to readers, as if you were sitting down together. Others wrote in a more narrative style, simply recounting what they have done and continue to do to sustain their vision for teaching.

The two questions to which the contributors to this chapter responded appear here as they were worded in the email I sent out:

Question 1: Teaching is hard work. You've just gone back to school and but you know that in this school year, as in every school year, you will have grading, reporting, other admin, curriculum, preparation, instruction, and on and on. So, in the midst of those kinds of work and that typical amount of work, how have you stayed alive intellectually? What steps have you taken, what habits have you developed, what practices have you followed to keep your brain from turning to mush?

Question 2: In the most general terms, I expect that when you got your teaching degree you wanted to leave the world a better place than you found it. You wanted a classroom characterized by curiosity, joy, learning, safety, inclusion, etc. If you had me for a professor in the last decade, you likely did an assignment where you listed and briefly explained your top ten classroom ideals. Again, in the face of the kind of work and the amount of work you have done over your teaching years—and in light of the inevitable bumps and disappointments—what you have done to avoid becoming jaded and cynical, and to keep on envisioning and working toward your classroom ideals? What steps, practices, dispositions, and habits have helped you keep going back to work day after day and year after year . . . and aiming at those ideals?

In workshops and classes and at conferences, I have listened to hundreds of in-service teachers describe the challenges they have faced in their efforts to flourish long term as they fulfilled their vocation as teachers. These questions arise out of those conversations.

Some reasons for asking classroom teachers to answer these two questions are more obvious than others. First, they represent a variety of perspectives, backgrounds, and grade levels, whereas my own perspective is that of a secondary teacher who last worked in a K-12 classroom in 2006 and has worked only as an education professor since then. My firsthand knowledge of K-12 classrooms is therefore somewhat dated. Second, my own memories of secondary teaching have almost certainly become rosier with the passage of time. Third, having served as an education professor for the last two decades, I have worked primarily with pre-service and in-service teachers; my knowledge of K-12 classrooms is thus not only dated but somewhat secondhand. Finally, and in my view most importantly, the book is stronger because these teachers' ideas and practices are expressed in their words, rather than in mine.

The chapter closes with a brief discussion of some of the themes that emerge in these teachers' remarks. What follows may contain a few surprises, but it will certainly confirm that some readers are already on the right track to sustain their vocational trajectories in life-giving ways.

Alex Schmidt

We begin with comments from Alex Schmidt, an elementary teacher from Regina, Saskatchewan.

As a teacher in Saskatchewan, at this time we have been involved in bargaining with a government that strategically de-professionalizes teachers. A substantial way I have felt I am keeping my brain and ideals alive has been to get involved with my local and provincial union. It has not only helped me feel active in changing the issues teachers face, but it has built community among myself and the teachers around me. This work has also given me professional development opportunities. Recently, I went to a session at a conference put on by my union on how to include hip-hop into a classroom setting (as a way to combat systemic racism and oppression). Even as a primary teacher, this conference had my mind spinning with all the potential that existed in this idea. While there are parts of my involvement in the union that have been challenging, time-consuming, and frustrating, I am now much better informed about what to accept within my workplace and also about the resources accessible to me to support my well-being. Teaching is hard; however, the commitment of involvement in a union can vary, and it has been a rewarding experience for me.

Jennifer

The next two paragraphs come from a Calgary elementary and middle-school teacher who wishes to remain anonymous. She wrote the following comments while in her fifth year of teaching in special education classrooms.

I think it is really important to pursue your interests outside the classroom. That being said, it can feel overwhelming considering the amount of work teachers have inside and outside the classroom. When you pursue those interests, it is important to remind yourself that it is a form of self-care. Being able to learn a new skill or new information helps us to continue that lifelong learning that we hope our students will desire. This will improve our practice as we are able to share a different perspective and insight with our students.

Personally, I love to read the news, *National Geographic*, or other informative articles written by journalists. I am able to learn new information and keep up to date with current events and scientific discoveries around me. When teachers learn alongside their students, this creates a classroom environment and culture that is relatable and understanding. Students can see that their teachers are human and learning just like them. It allows students to potentially feel more comfortable and to be able to take risks in a safe environment.

Jessica Maye

Jessica teaches a grade two and three split classroom in Calgary, Alberta. At the time of writing, she was in her seventh year of teaching.

The first word that comes to mind when I think about my career in education thus far is collaboration. I have had the pleasure of being a part of a highly collaborative teaching team, and it has proven, time and time again, to be an essential component for battling compassion fatigue and burnout. It has provided me with a positive and productive outlet for managing the ever-changing and increasing expectations placed on educators. To stay engaged and positive, collaboratively planning lessons, experiences, and assessments for students has proven to keep the spark alive. From the induction years, it has allowed me to ask for support, learn from my peers, dive deep into assessment, and think about how we can change the world within our classroom's four walls with excitement and just a little sprinkle of hope that we are making a difference.

Gillian Storey

Gillian Storey is currently in her seventh year of teaching. She teaches in the upper elementary grades in Calgary, Alberta.

Regarding keeping my brain alive, team planning has made a huge difference for me when it comes to teaching. Not only has it cut down on the amount of work each teacher on the team needs to do, but it also allows each person to concentrate their time and energy on one or two subject areas that they are really passionate about. Whether planning as a pair or in a larger group, I have gleaned so many wonderful new ideas and strategies that I had never thought of or considered. Team planning has also taught me to be more open-minded about my approach to teaching and learning. Less work and fresh ideas—it's been a win-win!

Regarding my ideals, finding my "sweet spot" in terms of the age and grade I teach has been a huge part of my continued love of this profession. While I enjoyed teaching the little ones during my first few years, I have discovered that I have more passion for teaching older elementary students. I have witnessed this concept in other teachers as well.

> Watching our kindergarten teachers' faces light up when they speak about their students' learning, or seeing how animated a colleague became while sharing about being back in a sixth-grade class this year reminded me that sometimes specific grades just feel like a perfect fit. Finding this sweet spot has helped me form deeper connections with my students, has driven my passion as an educator, and makes me excited to go to school each day.

Manuel Philippe

A French immersion teacher, Manuel Philippe teaches secondary students in Airdrie, Alberta, a suburb of Calgary. He is in his fifth year of teaching.

What have I done to stay alive intellectually?

I teach French immersion, so that means that as a native French speaker I routinely read assignments in what can be considered broken French. After twenty to thirty essays, the level of French takes a toll and affects your own fluency level. In order to manage this, I am reading French novels at home.

Another good way to stay active intellectually is through professional development. I have recently started to pursue a Master's degree in Modern Languages and have learned a lot that I can bring into the classroom.

Lastly, to continue functioning and not be burned out, pursuing a hobby will not only stimulate you but will also have the added advantage of being able to de-stress. I personally play guitar and garden.

What have I done to avoid becoming jaded?

It is important to take good care of your physical self. Some of my coworkers do, but most of those who do not, routinely complain about their job or their students. Eating well and being physically active will help mold a positive mindset about yourself and your environment.

Don't take things personally. Let's be honest, sometimes kids are rude; they make mistakes, and that's normal. Always remember that they are learning, and it's not because of you but rather because of something outside of your control. I mean, the alternative would be to assume that little Timmy's outburst was a personal attack and maintain a vendetta against him. Holding a grudge is infuriating and exhausting, and we, as teachers, have no time for it. This also goes for difficult parents (easier said than done, I know).

Make clear boundaries. This applies to students, parents, and to coworkers. Setting boundaries for how much you can take on, how people address you, and so forth will do wonders in creating a positive environment for you.

Don't forget to laugh. Sometimes our jobs get overwhelming, stressful, and just simply too much. It is wonderful how a laugh can make your day better.

It is okay to be selfish sometimes. This is one of the most important ones but also one of the most difficult to realize. When I was beginning my teaching career, I wanted to help everyone and do as many things as possible. Coaching soccer, leading clubs all while teaching. It is okay to NOT take on extra responsibilities. We also have a sort of guilt that sometimes demands we stay after the school day to mark and plan. In my experience, there really is no getting out of that as a beginning teacher. One thing that I have recently adopted is leaving the school at around 4:00–4:30 p.m. instead of the much later time of 6:00 p.m. Teaching is a job where it is easy to work all the time. You have to stay on top of it to make sure that is not the case.

Elisabeth Wendl

Elisabeth, who has taught for five years, teaches in the third and fourth grades near Munich, Germany.

How did I learn about work-life balance?

As a young teacher, the workload seems infinite. You´re the young new teacher who needs to have a lot of energy and knows all the new methods, but also can´t benefit from a lot of teaching materials.

In Germany, you do two years of "Referendariat" [apprenticeship] after university. This is the time you no longer sit in front of many books but learn all the practical stuff and gain real experience in working with children directly. Unfortunately, this is also the most challenging time since the expectations are pretty high, and you feel a lot of pressure to deliver perfect lessons. These lessons are only for show and are way too intense to prepare. You invest three to four weeks' time for only forty-five minutes. A significant number quit due to attrition because it's too intense, but my thought was, "this is only two years; I can do it." Two years of working way too many hours and not having much more on my mind than school. But it's okay for two years . . . I thought. Then, after those two special years, you stand in front of another challenge: you have all those intense lessons prepared and have learned to work way too long to always achieve the most perfect outcome. This doesn't reflect reality. What now?

For me, the most important thing to learn was setting boundaries—boundaries for myself and for others. My first boundary was my workplace. At first, I was pretty comfortable; after school I went home and made lunch. I got tired from the food and had a little nap. It didn't take long before I found myself on the couch in front of the laptop. This was not only a bad choice for my back but also for my daily routine. So, I changed my workplace and started working only at my school. It did take some time to get everything organized and was kind of awkward at first (I was alone in a big school since none of my colleagues worked there). This change of scenery helps me to spatially delimit from work. I can leave school and really leave my school stuff behind and not be tempted to do more at home.

The second boundary was having working hours. A huge plus of being responsible for your own work is setting your own work hours in a way they fit best for your day. However, I always tend to work late in the evening and also on weekends. So, I set myself the work hours I would have in a more regular job. Of course, sometimes it's not enough time, but as teachers, it seems that we can always do even more. I tell myself that even if everything is not ready for the next day, I will do it anyway. I'm there for my students; I hear them out and I think it's much more important to see their needs than to always be doing the perfect class. Also, which students don't love some minutes of free time or play while you quickly look into something to do? The thing I implement consistently is not working on weekends!

With my working hours came another boundary, but this one is more for other people. With digitization also came the constant availability—also for teachers. So I told my colleagues that I would be reachable until 5:00 p.m. After that, they can't expect an answer from me. The same availability hours apply to students and parents. Of course, I will get online messages after 5:00 p.m., but I strictly won't answer these until the next day. Turning off notifications helps. This also applies to social media in the form of just seeing the many amazing ideas other teachers seem to have. Remember: they only show the great stuff!

Besides setting boundaries, another thing that helped my work-life balance was not working alone. It can get pretty lonely being a teacher, and a lot of the time I was confronted with people not wanting to share. I found myself a pretty amazing colleague—now friend. We complement each other quite well: she has a lot of experience in teaching and working with parents, and she has a lot of materials. I can help her with all the new digital stuff and report on new teaching methods. We started to meet once a week and work out the plan for the next week. It helped that we teach the same grade and could do the same things. We split the work into subjects, so one of us would be responsible for math and the other one for arts and crafts. That not only meant half of the work for each of us but also having a second person looking over our teaching materials and finding possible difficulties. We can rely on each other, and it helped me a lot to know I can always call my colleague and not have to be responsible alone.

Last I try to tell myself that I am a passionate teacher—not a perfect one. It's not about doing the most amazing lessons and having the prettiest materials; for me it's about seeing your students for who they are, hearing their needs, and creating a place they want to come to every day.

Amanda

Amanda teaches students from grades one to six in a special education classroom. She is in her seventh year of teaching.

The main reason that I decided to go into the teaching profession was to help less privileged students, whether that be based on socioeconomics, abilities, or any other factors. On the tough days, this is an ideal I try to come back to. It has taken the first six years of my career, in a variety of different positions, to land in a position that involves my working with students of varying abilities. I have dug deep down into my ideals to decide what it is that really matters to me as a teacher, and it is this: everyone deserves the same start in life, and to me, that is ultimately the reason why teachers should teach.

Switching around positions and trying to serve students of varying privileges and communities has also forced me to keep my post-degree brain alive by getting to work alongside different colleagues and learning different techniques based on what my students need to be successful. I have complemented this by going back to university to take my MEd degree, where my own learning is further infused with colleagues from different divisions and instructors with different experiences. I have stayed motivated through some hard years of teaching, including the first five years of my career, which is—statistically—when teachers are most likely to quit, as well as the Covid-19 pandemic, by constantly coming back to the ideal that I teach to serve the underprivileged.

Angela Thompson

Angela, from Toronto, Ontario, has taught grades four and five and also serves as a specialist teacher from grades one to eight. She is in her twelfth year of teaching. Her comments clearly reflect her religious perspective, recalling the discussion of worldviews in Chapter 5.

Regarding keeping my brain alive, sometimes it feels as if the choice to teach is one long pouring out of ourselves, with little in the way of filling up. But if I advocate for the cultivation of critical thinking, the asking of good questions, and the reality that learning is a joyful, lifelong process, then it follows that I need to engage with that process myself. For me, reading is the key way I do this. Sometimes the book will be connected to upcoming lessons, so that I might add to what the textbook says, present alternative viewpoints, or simply flesh out the story that I am delivering. At other times, I read purely to let my mind explore a place, time, or situation beyond my own. I also find creative outlets helpful. Currently, I am watercolor painting and cultivating a sketchbook practice. Creative pursuits provide an opportunity for reflection, refine artistic skills, and help me find new ways in which art can be incorporated into my teaching.

Podcasts and audiobooks on the way to work and on the way home also allow me to explore new ideas, acquaint myself with new discoveries, and expand my world. Ongoing learning fills me with enthusiasm that overflows into the classroom. It reminds me that my role as a teacher is first and foremost to model what it means to seek truth, desire wisdom, and be fed by beauty—to become all I was intended to be.

How have I kept my ideals alive? My experiences in the classroom have not dampened my ideals! However, my perspective on what I do has expanded. I no longer see what I do as a profession, but as a ministry. If the purpose of education is to encourage and cultivate virtuous, well-rounded human beings who think well, communicate well, and are equipped to seek out wisdom and serve others with their gifts—indeed, to become all their Creator intended them to be—then the measuring rod for success is transformed. Ultimately, I may not see the full fruit of what I strive to do each day. But my faith allows me to invest in each child with care and intentionality, and to trust that good things will come from my labor—whether I have the opportunity to fully see the outcome or not.

Tough days are inevitable. But when I feel discouraged, or when steps forward are offset with two steps back, I remember the patience with which Christ teaches me. He knows all about seeds planted that go awry! Still, He sows, waits, corrects, and loves. He fosters fertile soil in me and coaxes growth. My goal each day is to reach one. To see the light in the eyes of one student, and to celebrate even the smallest victories when they happen. This practice lets me go to bed joyful and grateful for the privilege of doing what I do, and satisfied that I am where He intends me to be. When my ideals are grounded in Him, they not only survive; they flourish!

Shelby Kleinsasser

Shelby teaches grade two in Calgary, Alberta. At the time of writing, she is teaching in her seventh year.

When I first began teaching in 2018, I was eager to dive right in and ensure that everyone (students, parents, colleagues, etc.) was tended to as soon as anything arose. Teachers wear all the hats, and I was determined to wear them well. However, within the first couple of years, I became exhausted both mentally and emotionally. I couldn't figure out why. Wasn't this how teachers were supposed to do it? Aren't we supposed to teach all day and then come home and be available for parents or colleagues by email? Simply put, no. By doing this, I was missing out on the life I was building at home. The little things that I enjoyed the most were being pushed to the side.

One way to diminish some of that exhaustion was to delete the school email account from my phone. At first, this was a scary feeling. What if a parent or colleague needs my response? What will my principal think? However, it is now a freeing feeling. In this job, there is nothing that can't wait until the morning. I can now spend quality time with my loved ones in the evening and give myself a fresh start each day, allowing me to be my best self for the most important people—my students. Do I still occasionally check my email in the evenings/weekends? Absolutely. But this way, I have control over the load I am placing on myself.

David Cloutier

David teaches technology courses from grades four through nine and physical education from grades seven through nine. He is in his eighth year of teaching at Calgary Academy.

How have I kept my brain alive? The best practices I've employed to keep my mind sharp and vibrant have been embracing variety, trying new things, and engaging in activities beyond work. I've had the unique privilege of never repeating the same experience in my teaching career—each year has been different from the last. I once had an administrator say that they appreciated I could work just about anywhere. Additionally, pursuing educational opportunities (such as a Master's degree and LQS) and volunteering (like running for the Alberta NDP) have helped me build my network and find meaning beyond my time at school.

How have I kept my ideals alive? My teaching philosophy has kept me from leaving the profession more than once. I remember a particularly dark day during the Covid pandemic when a colleague, in a non-confrontational manner, asked me why I was there—they wanted to know about my teaching philosophy. Revisiting and reflecting on it in that moment not only helped me gain clarity during those tough times but also illuminated how my perspective had evolved; more importantly, helped me stop just "going through the motions" and reconnect with the reasons for my being in the work. Eventually, it became clear that it was time for a career shift into a leadership role, especially when I found one where the organization's philosophy resonated so deeply with my own.

Colin Young

Colin has taught grades four through seven and is located in North Vancouver, British Columbia. Including his years as an educator at the Vancouver Aquarium, Colin is in his fourteenth year of teaching.

Regarding keeping my brain alive, I've been lucky, living in Vancouver, to have a lot of weekend warrior activities available, like hiking and kayaking to help my brain refresh. Doing things just for my own enjoyment, such as cooking or going to the theater, is important. Keeping a strong set of personal interests alive, with folks I love outside of work, remains essential.

Professionally, having those best teacher friends that you can sit and talk shop with over an adult beverage has been pretty key. Colleagues to kvetch with, plan with, share resources with, and enjoy time with to get into it all really have made a world of difference. In the rare years I have not had that, I've gone out of my way to connect with networks of educators, taken on mentees in union support programs, or gotten more actively involved with university training programs to take on student teachers. More work seems to happen when you're in it together rather than feeling you have to be alone in your class as the only adult. You bring a bit of your adult connections with you as you create lessons and engage with the kids.

About keeping my ideals alive, honestly, the education system as it is tends to be Grey Hat territory. Not a true evil (though it has done that and still does a lot of that), but not a universal good either (though there is a lot of good that can come out of this process too). I was a social worker before teaching, so seeing how a system fails vulnerable people, such as children, disabled people, gender non-conforming people, and so on, was something I had experienced going into the school system.

Doing your best with the kids in front of you, and their families behind them, is all you can do. Mantras such as "I've done what I can" and "I may not have been the teacher to make this change for them this year" or "It wasn't what I could have hoped for, but I've seen some progress" have been helpful. In rare cases, some students keep coming around years down the road to check in and update me on how they are, even if they're not well at that moment, knowing I can still support them, and that makes it really worth slogging through the morass of the system.

I guess the summary is that I didn't think I would be entirely a force for good going into this, but the effort to keep being so is worth it.

Payge

This last contribution comes from Payge, a grade three teacher in her eighth year of teaching in Alberta. She wishes to remain anonymous.

Keeping my brain alive has been an immense amount of trial and error. I have been fortunate enough to have been given a wide array of advice on what I should or shouldn't do, but ultimately I had to try it out firsthand to see if it worked within my capabilities and priorities. For me, it is not realistic to give this profession all of me. That means there is nothing left for my family, my interests, and my health. I think there is a notion that if you are not wholly identifying and encompassing yourself as a teacher, then you must not be working very hard or caring about education. I believe the opposite. It is because I care about my students that I want to show up as my best self for them. That means only staying late one or two nights a week, not having my work email on my phone, and not working on the weekends (unless it's report card season). When I can mindfully and presently show up for the parts of my life outside of teaching, I am in a much better frame of mind when I am with my students in the classroom.

As to how I keep my ideals alive, let me start by saying that I love teaching. When I am in the classroom, my heart and soul feel like this is where I am meant to be. Over the past few years, I have noticed (and maybe become more aware of) the amount of expected work placed on educators that extends beyond the classroom. I have to shift my thinking away from negativity when I am asked to administer another standardized assessment or work with fewer supports, etc. This has been permeating into the parts I love most about my career and vocation. I wanted to know what I could do and how I could learn more to support my students on a broader scale. I started to become more involved in my union to understand the processes of how and why things felt like they were changing. This helps me feel that as I learn about how certain ideals and shifts come into place, I can also advocate for the profession and the students.

Another practice that helps me to find the light in a job that can have its darker moments is to surround myself with a solid support system. It sounds cliché and it's advice I have heard many times over, but I am so much stronger person because of the wonderful, empathetic, and resilient people in my life. This encompasses my family, friends, and trusted colleagues.

Carey Wegner

Carey and I taught in the same Alberta secondary school for several years. We traveled together to work with teacher colleagues in Machakos, Kenya. Carey is now a veteran teacher, working in Calgary, Alberta.

I have kept my brain alive in two ways. I have taken advantage of many opportunities within the educational realm, and I have invested energy in interests outside the educational realm. Very briefly, my work history divides into four parts. I began my career as a senior high math and physics teacher, but I taught a variety of other courses, including math, at my second school. At my third school, I shifted to middle-school math and then returned to teaching only high school math at my current school.

Within the educational realm, I have done the following:

- From years three to fifteen, I graded government math exams in both British Columbia and Alberta. Doing so led to great conversations with teacher colleagues about effective teaching practices, what we value in learning, and how we assess what we value.
- In year 6, I changed schools, moving from a regular public school of 2,200+ students (grades 8–12) to a publicly funded, alternative

Christian school of less than 800 students (grades K-12). This led me to rethink my philosophy of education, the value of educational choice, and how to manage a classroom where the students all knew each other.

- In year ten, I traveled to Kenya to work with Kenyan teacher colleagues. Doing so helped me understand that I had something to offer other educators, and it sparked my interest in helping other teachers improve in their craft.

- In year twelve, I participated with teams of colleagues to develop questions for provincial assessments, refining my understanding of what makes a good assessment question.

- From years eleven to fourteen and in year twenty-four, I worked with teams of teachers and district leaders to update, refine, motivate, and communicate new assessment policies. Doing so further clarified my understanding of what comprises good assessment.

- In years sixteen and seventeen, I represented math teachers in my school by collaborating with lead teachers from other secondary schools on a project meant to increase students' achievement in mathematics by improving teacher competence. In the second year of this district project, I left the classroom to work as a math consultant, leading my district's team of lead teachers in our pursuit of excellence in teaching mathematics. This was a spectacular year of learning because I had time to read, think, discuss ideas with colleagues, and lead many professional development sessions for math teachers.

- As part of that initiative, I reviewed curriculum updates and helped write standards documents meant to clarify curriculum expectations. Doing so deepened my understanding of those expectations and my understanding of the curriculum-writing process.

- At the end of year seventeen, I moved to Nairobi, Kenya, to teach seventh and eighth grade students in an international school. Teaching was still teaching, and the skills that I had developed over the previous seventeen years were still effective, but I felt more freedom to explore what I thought was important in teaching, learning, and assessing mathematics. Even though this school was

- accredited by the Middle States Association (USA), I felt less bound by government and district expectations and directives.
- When I left Nairobi after year twenty-one and thought that it might be a good time to transition out of teaching and try something else. When I finally said this out loud, my wife responded by purchasing, at Heathrow airport, the book, *Cakes, Custard + Category Theory: Easy Recipes for Understanding Complex Maths*.[3] Reading the book reminded me of why I love math and reignited my desire to continue teaching this beautiful subject.
- I then moved to my current position. I now teach senior high mathematics in a charter school with the most supportive and engaged administrators and staff I have ever worked with. There is great diversity among the staff, but there is unity related to the school's purposes, most importantly regarding the character development of students. This unity leads to consistent behavior expectations in both the halls and in the classrooms. In the week-long orientation for new teachers, a full day is spent addressing classroom management. What I have learned about classroom management that began that day has been critical to my ongoing desire to teach.
- Finally, in year twenty-nine, I took on the five-month challenge of working as an "Inclusive Intervention Numeracy Teacher." In this position, I worked with elementary teachers and students to explore ways to help students experience greater success in mathematics. It was wonderful to experience the world of elementary education and to investigate, with elementary teachers, how young students can come to understand the ideas of mathematics. If the position had not shifted to include literacy, I would still be doing it.

I have had amazing professional development opportunities throughout my career, but I would argue that the hands-on experiences I have listed above have had a greater impact on why I have continued in the profession.

    I have found that developing, refining, and maintaining a classroom management plan that fits who I am is central to my longevity as a teacher. My plan begins with the question, "What makes me happy when I am teaching?" The answer to that question begins with discovering where my teaching sweet spot is on the order-chaos spectrum for the students in my classroom. As much as I love teaching in a conversational, playful style, I have learned that too much play leads my class toward a level of chaos that makes me grumpy and makes it harder for me to love my students. I continue to answer the sweet-spot question by imagining the student behavior that will make me happy in scenarios such as these:

- students enter the classroom
- the bell rings
- I am recording attendance
- I am speaking to the class
- I have asked a question
- when a student is answering a question
- when I am distributing handouts.

My actual list is much longer, but working through it has helped me clarify my expectations.

Related to these scenarios, I have also found it very beneficial to answer the question, "Why are these expectations important?" Sometimes, the answer is simply "for efficiency," but often my expectations are tied to student character: it is my job not only to teach mathematical ideas and skills to students, but also to help them grow in character. I am prepared to discuss the character-based rationale for my classroom expectations and to negotiate different expectations that will support their character development. It is my job to communicate my expectations clearly and consistently to the students and to help them learn to work with me. If I am not happy with something that is happening in my class, it is my job to do something about it. It helps to have supportive administrators who will back me up if I need it.

In my first paragraph, I said that the second answer to the question of keeping my brain alive had to do with investing energy in interests outside the educational realm. Very briefly, I have given my energy to two major kinds of activities. First, I have been actively involved in my church, with music, teaching, and leading. Second, I have taken time for exercise almost every day. Mountain biking has been one of the most beneficial activities for my brain. I am a slow, methodical thinker; my brain does not like to be rushed. A brain on a mountain bike cannot be slow and methodical. On a mountain bike, my brain has to make quick decisions in response to unexpected circumstances. Somehow, mountain biking

> frees my brain to be more responsive to situations beyond mountain biking as well. My brain benefits from being pushed outside its comfort zone.
>
> What I have done to keep my brain alive might not be for everyone. But I strongly recommend that teachers take advantage of opportunities for growth and service within the educational realm and that they give energy to those parts of their lives outside their classrooms.
>
> Eugenia Cheng, *Cakes, Custard + Category Theory: Easy Recipes for Understanding Complex Maths* (London: Profile, 2015).

Conclusion

What to make of these responses to the two questions I asked these thirteen teachers? Several noteworthy themes appear, as well as many practices or ways of thinking reported by only one of the contributors to the chapter.

Several of these colleagues note how their involvement with their unions has benefited them. This involvement has take several forms: involvement in bargaining, mentoring younger colleagues through a program run by the teachers' union, and taking advantage of professional development opportunities offered by the teachers' association. Professional development is not restricted to teachers' unions; some report having begun or completed an advanced education degree.

Maintaining boundaries around work emerges clearly. Some wrote about limiting contact to certain hours, working in the school building to prevent taking work home, and preventing their phones from becoming channels for doing school-related work.

The importance of recreation appears several times in these comments, whether it be physical activity, attending events, or engaging in the arts.

Two themes fill out this brief summary. A few of the teachers represented here note the importance of taking satisfaction in as much as one has the capacity to accomplish. That is, teachers cannot do it all, a theme I return to in Chapter 14 where I discuss dispositions. Also, a number stress the benefits they gained from collaboration with colleagues, a matter I return to in "Supporters," Chapter 13. Beyond this summary, I will not repeat what our teaching colleagues have written. Their powerful words speak for themselves. In important ways, their powerful words speak for all of us.

Notes

1. Out of a desire to let my contributors speak for themselves, I have done only the lightest editing of their words. Post editing, all the contributors to this chapter approved the final wording that appears here.
2. From the syllabus for a Philosophy of Education course (EDUC 4321) at Mount Royal University in Calgary, Alberta, September semester, 2019. The official description reads this way: This course examines basic beliefs concerning what is "sensible," "right," and "good" in promoting learning. Participants will critically reflect upon significant issues and experiences and will develop their philosophy of teaching and learning. https://catalog.mtroyal.ca/preview_course_nopop.php?catoid=7&coid=9449.
3. Eugenia Cheng, *Cakes, Custard + Category Theory: Easy Recipes for Understanding Complex Maths* (London: Profile Books, 2015).

11 The Summit Push

In previous chapters, I looked at the novice and middle years of the teaching career. We turn now to the last decade of teaching—a period during which even good teachers are at risk of losing momentum and the encouragement they need. My singular goal in this chapter is to offer life-giving ways to approach the last years of the teaching career so that my readers do not find themselves merely limping toward retirement. As was the case with the contents of previous chapters, the material in this chapter on late career vitality is compiled from years of shared stories as well as the experiences of fellow and sister researchers and teacher colleagues. The chapter focuses on the salient themes that surface in reports from teachers who have continued flourishing in their classrooms into and through the final years of their careers. This chapter is neither the last word nor a dour word on a teacher's final decade in the field.

All the chapters that follow also contain material that applies to the third part of the teacher's career. The dispositions teachers grow into (Chapter 14) and the strategies teachers use to stay focused on teaching (Chapter 15), for example, apply to all teachers but especially to those who, despite their long experience keeping a classroom program humming, need to remain diligent and intentional about taking care of themselves.

Preparing for the Push

This chapter begins metaphorically with the idea of the summit push, the final leg of any major climb. While never more than a recreational climber myself, I have been an avid reader of books about big-wall climbing, especially the Himalayan giants such as Everest and the world's second-tallest mountain, K2. From written accounts of ascents of those peaks, I shamelessly appropriate the concept of the summit push to frame the last years of the teaching career and to cast this era in a light that reveals its demands, its efforts, and its ultimate rewards.

The imagery of the final push on a climb suits the last years of teaching, highlighting as it does the kinds of physical, emotional, and psychological effort and focus a teacher must summon to finish well. At this juncture, as teachers venture into the last decade, physical energy has declined. Some parts of the teaching job have inevitably become routine. Veteran teachers recognize these realities but sometimes do not view their final years of teaching as a time of either hard work or great inspiration. And the summit push is typically both. On big mountains—like Everest or K2—how do climbers prepare for the summit day? And, of great interest to those who track mountaineering accidents, how do they get back to base camp in one piece?

Preparation for a big wall includes both extensive climbing experience and intensive physical training. The Everest books record how those who come only with big-wall ambitions and plenty of money often end up in trouble, even after hiring the best guides. Long experience on mountains teaches the climber the habits, skills, and systems needed for safety and ultimate success. Long experience teaches climbers about the need for food, drink, calm, and rest before the final push. And long experience helps climbers develop the dispositions needed to succeed on a big wall. Long experience in education teaches parallel lessons to all these things that climbers learn.

Preparing for the summit push on a big mountain involves several components. Obviously, long in advance, climbers must have obtained permits and, in many cases, hired a professional guide. With the help of the guide, climbers must have planned the route. Map and compass have now been replaced by GPS, but climbers still must know how to navigate. Again, with the help of their guide, climbers must have acquired the needed equipment and supplies. Teachers know the parallels to this kind of preparation as well.

On the night before the summit push, climbers carefully separate everything in their backpack into two categories: what they definitely need for the final push and what they could leave in their tent while they attempt the summit. It seems like a simple enough distinction, but for obvious reasons, it's a distinction with a fuzzy middle. "I might need this item, but it's more weight . . . and it's only one day." A flashlight is a good example of such an item. Those who have read accounts of disasters on big mountains know that wrong decisions about items in that fuzzy middle can cost climbers their lives. What should the emergency kit include? Given the lack of support on the summit day, one may have to support oneself. Where is that sweet spot between safety and comfort? Or is there such a thing? What food? What clothing? Pencil? Journal? Flag? Camera? These are the questions élite climbers must answer because every gram counts.

Veteran teachers who flourish to the end go through the same kind of checklists, differentiating the essentials from the nonessentials as they approach each new school year and, for that matter, each new teaching day.

Big-wall climbers report that psychological preparation for the summit push is another matter altogether. After days of slogging at high altitude to get to the last camp, does the climber still have the will to put one leg in front of the other? Climbers know that the temptations to abandon the climb will be persistent and strong. At altitude, attitude isn't everything, but it is an important thing. And while teachers do not work at the same altitudes as big-wall climbers, the right attitude remains a necessity for success for teachers as they commence their own summit push.

Climbers abandon climbs on summit day for a variety of reasons. Obviously, accidents and physical injuries force their own logic on climbers. The climber must make a decision: is what happened inconvenient and painful but bearable, or is it unquestionably a climb-stopping injury? The weather may cooperate, and it may not. Climbers regularly experience equipment and clothing failures that force them to stop climbing and turn around. Team dynamics sometimes become so toxic that one or more members abandon the climb, or the guide calls a halt. Sometimes the chosen route simply will not yield, forcing the climbers to retreat and attempt another route or give up altogether. Obviously, exhaustion can overtake a climber, so much so that it becomes literally impossible to do anything other than sit down. Not to make light of the energy required in a teacher's day, but teachers also have their moments when they run out of energy and wonder . . . "if I could only sit down!" And teachers in their final decade recognize other parallels to the kinds of conditions climbers face.

The books about big-wall climbing record how some have had to abandon climbs because they no longer had the energy or will to put one foot in front of the other. Others gave up because they had misinformation or incorrect estimates regarding route, required equipment, terrain, or conditions. Perhaps they became lost. And, on Everest especially, some climb for bragging rights, but on summit day discover those rights to be an insufficient motivation to push through the slow, high-altitude traffic jam that now characterizes the final day on the world's tallest peak.

The Teacher's Summit Push

What can this extended metaphor offer teachers? For teachers, the long-term preparation for the summit push characteristic of big climbs is already done. Teachers at this point already have the training, experience, habits, and systems needed to execute a successful classroom program. That is, they know the ins and outs of curriculum, instruction, assessment, and building classroom culture. And they likely have the dispositions needed to flourish (Chapter 14). These teachers do not need a guide and, as I will argue in the next chapter, are more likely to be a guide to younger colleagues and to pre-service teachers. There is likely no metaphoric equivalent need for a GPS device at this point in the teaching career. If teachers at this point in their careers do not need a guide, what do they need?

Teachers making the final push do need to know what is essential to their work and what is extraneous. Most already know what they definitely need and what they can most likely do without as they prepare for and navigate the summit push. For teachers, unlike climbers, failing to make good distinctions at this point will not lead to fatalities, but it can impose costs in student learning and in teachers' own joy and satisfaction. On the last day of work in their careers, teachers need to know that they did a good job and that their students succeeded.

Arguably, while the summit push is a visibly and concretely physical feat, for teachers in their final years of teaching, the challenge makes unseen but mounting psychological demands. Teachers in the throes of the summit push need to recognize and prepare for the temptations to give up or to give in. Other conditions may lead teachers to abandon their profession during the summit push, as many veteran teachers did because of Covid. Changes in the political climate and increased levels of criticism of schools, teachers, and education in general lead some to give up. Dynamics inside a school building lead some to retire sooner than they expected. Not that teachers should become cynical, but a teacher's psychological preparation for the summit push should include accepting the facts that the political climate does change, that there will be criticism, that there will be new software and reporting structures, that there will be changes in curriculum and policy, and that there will be toxic colleagues.

Research on the Last Years of Teaching

A wealth of research exists in areas such as teacher disillusionment and burnout, teacher job satisfaction and dissatisfaction, and teachers' commitments to their institutional mission statements.[1] Dozens of master's theses and doctoral dissertations are added annually to the subfield of teacher attrition. The gist of much of this research is that teaching is hard work; it wears people out, and many leave the profession. I note the abundance of research into these aspects of teaching to point to a relative shortage of research on self-care, joy in teaching, and especially, late career vitality. Counting book titles on Amazon or in WorldCat and references in major educational databases reveals that material on burnout, attrition, and related concepts outnumbers material related to flourishing in teaching about five to one.

Rather than attempting to review the masses of research available, I comment on the work of a few scholars—work that has been particularly helpful to me and my colleagues in our own efforts to flourish as veteran teachers. These researchers' work and words have helped many educators navigate today's choppy educational waters and flourish in their last decade of teaching.

To begin, I note the work of Doris Santoro, who, in her attempt to understand what lies beneath the surveys and numbers about burnout and attrition, has identified what she calls *moral depression*. By this phrase, she implies a kind of heaviness suffered by educators who enter the profession with high ideals but find that the moral rewards of teaching remain somewhat out of reach. She concludes that these rewards remain out of reach in part because the ways teaching is structured often do not foster moral rewards.[2]

Santoro's work implies something quite important for thriving long-term: teachers need to attend to what one might call the emotional and intellectual contexts of their work. They need to find conversation partners who will remind them of the nobility of their work. The corollary of that claim is that they need to avoid conversations with toxic colleagues and exposure to the criticisms that seem to come at teachers from all sides in this cultural moment. They need to attend to their professional reading because doing so broadens their framework and perspective.[3] Periodically reviewing their list of classroom ideals (Chapter 6) will help teachers remember why they go to work every morning.

Next, we turn to the work of the developmentalist, Erik Erikson.[4] Most educators first encounter Erikson early in their undergraduate work, perhaps in an educational psychology or child development course. For most, if only one phrase remains in memory it is likely that Erikson identified what he called a *developmental task* for each stage in life. Erikson assigned those in their middle years the task of *generativity*, of helping the next generation or two get on their feet as adults who contribute to the common good. He assigned the task of wisdom to those in their senior years.

Readers can decide for themselves where they fit in Erikson's schema. For many educators, generativity within their professional orbit implies mentoring pre-service teachers in their classrooms or inducting teachers in their school building. Some take on leadership roles in their schools or districts, as department heads, grade-level team leaders, instructional coaches, or members of school district (or provincial or state) curriculum committees. Of course, such realizations or expressions of generativity help the larger cause. But, to Erikson's point and to the question of flourishing to the end of one's teaching career, these generative tasks also help the educator who takes them on. They enlarge that educator's sense of the educational world beyond the single classroom and the hard work needed to sustain a classroom program day to day. In other words, taking generativity seriously helps sustain the educator's vision through to the end.

A number of teachers have found the concept of *tempered radicalism* to contribute to their goal of flourishing into late career.[5] In a short article, Meyerson and Scully describe the conflict that professionals in many kinds of organizations experience. That conflict usually arises out of the apparent gap between the individual's vocational ideals and the combination of the challenges of their day-to-day work and the climate of the organization in which they do that work. Teachers are as prone as anyone to draw the conclusion that they and their ideals do not fit well in the school buildings in which they work. Budgets, public expectations of schools, necessary administrative details, stacks of grading, resistant students, and other realities can easily lead educators to feel that they don't belong, even leading to their asking deep vocational questions and wondering if they somehow ended up in the wrong profession. In just fifteen pages, Meyerson and Scully offer both a cognitive framework and several workplace strategies for educators to maintain both their ideals and their mental health while working in settings in which they sometimes feel like outsiders. Educators who have read this article consistently report finding it liberating and sanity-producing.

Other insights come from research Gordon Smith and I conducted with nineteen flourishing educators in their last decade of teaching.[6] Based on recorded interviews with these educators, aged fifty-seven to sixty-seven, we concluded that educators who remained vital into late career had adopted several noteworthy postures by the mid-point in their career and that they carried those postures into their final decade of teaching. First, they had an institutional orientation. That is, while not being enmeshed in or married to the places they worked, they recognized that they were part of something larger than themselves. They needed to fulfill their teaching vocations in institutional settings. We noted that our participants all used the pronoun *we* rather than *they* when they spoke of their work colleagues. To our participants, this careful pronoun usage reflected an essential sense of belonging and purpose, as well as an energizing collective morale.

Second, all but one of our participants had navigated the stormy waters in which they found themselves in mid-career or early career. These stormy waters ranged from losing employment to the death of a child. All of our participants recognized that they had to go through those waters because they could not go around them. One participant noted that when we asked about a difficult chapter in his life, he could think of several sources of pain but that he moved through that and no longer dwelt on what had transpired. This perspective on such life events contains a clear lesson for the educator who wants to finish well: one does not begin finishing well five years before retirement; rather, one starts in mid-career or earlier, giving real effort to navigating the difficulties that inevitably arise when they arise. Big-wall climbers also encounter difficulties; they may not know in advance what precise difficulties they will face, but they start a climb and they prepare for the summit push knowing that, even if the mountain they are attempting to climb is located in a park, climbing it will not be a walk in the park.

Third, all participants were members of meaningful communities. In some cases, those communities consisted mainly of colleagues, and in other cases of friends and supporters from outside the institution. From our interviews with these educators, we concluded that flourishing into late career is a phenomenon that does not and likely cannot occur in isolation.[7] I return to this matter in a discussion of finding supporters and gathering a team in Chapter 13. Being part of a team also connects to climbing; ultra-élite climbers may climb big walls alone, but in almost all cases, climbers of the highest mountains go as members of a team.

What Experienced Teachers Say

Teachers who have flourished have reported on the activities and habits they believe have kept them fresh into their final decades of teaching. Recall the thirteen educators who contributed to the previous chapter. They maintained boundaries so that school did not take over their personal lives. They participated in the arts and recreation. They became involved in their professional associations. They took advantage of professional development opportunities, and they began advanced degrees. They mentored younger colleagues. As it happens, none of the teachers who contributed to Chapter 10 was over fifty. They were all somewhere in mid-career.

On the other hand, the nineteen educators who contributed to Gordon Smith's and my project on late career vitality were all fifty-seven or older. And my correspondence with others in their middle years or in their final decades reveals some themes that overlap with those whose words appear in the previous chapter and some other themes that do not overlap.

The theme of leadership runs through these reports. Some became involved in their teachers' associations and unions, at all levels: building, district, and province or state. In a couple of cases, these educators were seconded from their classrooms to serve for a year or more. Some served on subject-area committees for their respective school district or their state or provincial Department of Education. Responsibilities on subject-area committees typically include making decisions about new curriculum or revising curriculum already in place, overseeing centralized examination programs, and working with publishers to develop new textbooks. Some teachers become members of their state or provincial Teacher Standards Commission. Such commissions, usually a branch of the Department of Education or at least reporting to that Department, give oversight to the teacher training programs and portions of the Schools Act or Education Act relating to teachers.[8] Most of these leadership roles are unpaid, but they all offer those who assume such roles a wider view of teaching than teachers typically enjoy if they work only in their own classrooms.

Forcing oneself to learn new things runs as a second theme through the reports of vital late career teachers, as it did in the reports of those who contributed to Chapter 10. Some teachers consistently ask for a change in their teaching responsibilities, for example, to teach a new course or switch to a different grade. Making such changes obviously requires that such teachers understand curriculum materials they have not taught before and expand their instructional program accordingly. When asked why he would voluntarily take on new work in this way, one educator answered that it was how he had kept his brain alive. Blunt language perhaps, but instructive. A number of late career teachers report that continuing to read professionally helps keep them vital, even if they are not working on a second or third education degree.

As do some mid-career teachers, a few late career teachers register with their respective Department of Education that they would like to teach new textbooks still in development. Pilot teaching implies a degree of cooperation between teachers and students; together, they work through a new spiral-bound textbook, reporting back to the Department and the educational publisher what works well, what does not work so well, what is missing, and so on. Students typically enjoy being asked to bring their expertise to the task of developing the next generation of curriculum in a given school subject. Although textbook authors rarely meet the pilot teachers who work on their books, they view such teachers—and their students—as partners in the writing process.[9]

In the next chapter, I argue that many teachers have the knowledge and experience to become guides, helping younger colleagues and pre-service teachers find their way in teaching. Many senior teachers do take pre-service teachers in their classrooms, thereby connecting with college and university teacher-education programs. A theme running consistently through their reports relates to pedagogy: they learn new instructional strategies from their interns. A few such teachers also end up teaching courses at a local university, usually a course in an area specialty such as elementary mathematics or reading. Squeezing a university course into a teacher's work week can be challenging, but those who do it say the intellectual rewards compensate for the increased work.

In Chapter 16, which deals with nurturing the teacher's core, I offer more ideas about staying alive into one's final decade of teaching. To conclude this short section, however, let me point out the theme that seems to run through all these reports from the field: late career teachers flourished and thrived in their classrooms, in some sense, by getting *out of* their classrooms. In the major internship I completed as part of my own BEd degree, I had two mentor teachers, one of whom was what Westmont College education professor Andrew Mullen calls a *counter-mentor*. This teacher was in his final semester of teaching before retirement. I was to teach his grade eleven English literature class during block five of a five-block teaching day. The first day I entered his room, he said to his class, "This is Mr. Badley; he'll be teaching you until mid-April." With those words, he walked out of the room and never returned.

When I asked another member of that school's staff what had happened to my mentor teacher, I learned that he sat in the staff room every day while I taught in his classroom. It was the last semester of his career and he did not feel like exerting himself too much. His exit from that classroom is obviously *not* what I mean by getting out of the classroom. To twist a common phrase, he was not even phoning it in. He served as a counter-mentor because he modeled for me exactly the opposite of what thriving in one's final decade means. In Erik Erikson's terms, he had no interest in generativity. In fact, to consider the task that Erikson assigns to the next age, neither did he show wisdom. I end the chapter with this account of someone who did not thrive or flourish because it points to the potential for senior teachers to settle so completely that they lose the vision for teaching altogether. To use Erikson's language again, they stagnate. To frame the account positively, it points to the need for late career educators to engage inside and outside their classrooms in constructive ways so they flourish until the day they retire.

A colleague said to me that teachers in their last decades of teaching need to make a *truly revolutionary choice*. Teachers wanting to flourish until the day of their retirement need to take that phrase to heart. Knowing all they do about curriculum, instruction, assessment, and classroom climate, senior teachers can easily settle into a work mode that, while easy, ultimately will not lead to their flourishing. Thriving until the day of retirement requires that teachers make truly revolutionary choices.

As it does in big-wall mountaineering, the summit push in teaching requires psychological preparation. Part of the preparation that teachers who would thrive must do is to reflect on what a truly revolutionary choice might be for them.

Notes

1 Portions of this chapter are adapted from "Self-Care in the Transition Decade," from *Self Care for Educators: Soul-Nourishing Practices to Promote Well Being*, eds. Cathy E. Freytag and Paul Shotsberger (Central, SC: Freedom's Hill Press, 2022), 172–91. It appears with permission from the editors and publisher. Recent examples of research into the final decade include Janne Pietarinen, Kirsi Pyhältöb, Tiina Soini, and Katariina Salmela-Aro, "Reducing Teacher Burnout: A Socio-contextual Approach," *Teaching and Teacher Education* 35 (October 2013): 62–72; and Jennifer D. Walker, Kimberly M. Johnson, and Kathleen M. Randolph, "Teacher Self-Advocacy for the Shared Responsibility of Classroom and Behavior Management," *Teaching Exceptional Children* 53, no. 3 (2021): 216–25.

2 Doris A. Santoro, "Good Teaching in Difficult Times: Demoralization in the Pursuit of Good Work," *American Journal of Education* 118, no. 1 (2011): 1–23.

3 The value of reading and staying alive intellectually into late career and retirement is borne out in the research reported in David Snowdon, *Aging with Grace: The Nun Study* (New York: Bantam, 2001).

4 Erikson's works most closely related to this project are these: *The Life Cycle Completed, with* Joan Mowat Erikson (New York: W.W. Norton, 1998); *Adulthood* (New York: W.W. Norton, 1978); and *Identity and the Life Cycle* (New York: W.W. Norton, 1974).

5 Debra E. Meyerson and Maureen A. Scully, "Tempered Radicalism and the Politics of Ambivalence and Change," *Organizational Science* 6, no. 5 (1995): 585–99. At the time of writing, this article was available at https://pubsonline.informs.org/doi/abs/10.1287/orsc.6.5.585.

6 Gordon T. Smith and Ken Badley, "Called to Teach," *Teaching Theology and Religion* 1, no. 3 (October 1998): 171–6.

7 I return to this matter in Chapters 13 and 14 in my treatments of supporters and dispositions.

8 I met the two teachers I mentioned in the Introduction to this book during my own service on the Council on Alberta Teacher Standards. I served as one of three teacher representatives from across the province, along with colleagues representing the colleges of education, the Department of Education, the School Boards Association, and the teachers' association.

9 As an author of several secondary textbooks, I speak personally here. I have always enjoyed seeing the marked-up spiral-bound copies of my books when they came back from schools with teachers' and students' comments written on the pages.

12 Six Kinds of People One Meets on the Road

On actual journeys, one meets many kinds of people. One draws conclusions about those people based on their luggage, their clothing, their behavior, and even their tone of voice. Are they traveling for work or are they on vacation? Are they part of a school tour or a sports team? Do they seem stressed or do they seem to be enjoying themselves? How experienced are they with the typical details of travel? In this chapter, I introduce six kinds of people one might meet while traveling: tourists, travelers, adventurers, refugees, pilgrims, and guides. Speaking metaphorically, one might meet these same six kinds of teachers. Thinking about the six kinds of people one might meet on actual journeys can yield valuable insights into teachers and the vital question of career-long flourishing in the teaching profession.

Tourists

Most people have been tourists at some point in their lives. At their best, tourists want to see and experience the particular nuances of the places they visit. They want to meet local people and learn more about what those local people do and how they live. At their worst, tourists want to be told what to eat, what to photograph, and maybe even what to think. The lines, "If this is Belgium it must be Tuesday" and "I will never travel there again because I need a good steak every night," likely capture tourists at their worst. Residents of the Canadian province of Alberta have a joke about tourists that goes, "Well, that's Banff and Lake Louise, let's check off Jasper today too." Albertans know that tourism is a significant part of the provincial economy, but those Albertans who enjoy the Rocky Mountains also tire of the crowds of people who exit their vehicles, line up for selfies at the spots with the most internet-worthy backdrops, and climb back into their vehicles.

As I write, the tourist season of 2024 has just drawn to its close in the northern hemisphere. Many will remember 2024 as the year when locals in several European cities such as Venice and Barcelona looked for ways to ask tourists simply to go away. Residents of Barcelona fired toy water guns at tourists, a relatively harmless action but one they hoped would send the message that this was their city, their home. Venice began charging visitors five euros simply to enter the city. The Alberta Rockies, Venice, and Barcelona have suffered the effects of what some now call the Instagram effect on popular travel destinations.[1]

Perhaps no one should fault tourists for wanting to enjoy the views at the places they visit. But many tourists insist on staying clean and dry; they like to have all their travel details arranged, they want someone to carry their bags for them, and everything must be convenient. At their worst, they simply want someone to show them what they are supposed to see and, certainly, to avoid the dodgy sides of town. They typically leave the places they visit largely untouched by their circumstances. Some tourists simply look for the lady holding up the flag, and they follow her. To the worst kind of tourist—what some call Duke and Duchess tourists—the various sights and sounds become a blur in which Paris, London, and Amsterdam all seem the same.

Likewise, some teachers want the teaching journey to leave them clean and dry. They want all their students, colleagues, and administrators to be above average, an obvious statistical impossibility (and a running joke in many workplaces). They expect their teaching days to go smoothly, with no hiccups or hitches. Just as, inevitably, the tourist's luggage will be lost if they take enough trips, teachers will inevitably experience disappointment, in part because teaching is simply not set up for tourists. As Chapter 4 made clear, teaching is both complex and intense, and anyone just passing through will not find the teaching profession that comfortable or convenient.

We have all heard the criticism that teachers are just in it for the holidays. While good teachers find this criticism frustrating, it likely still applies to some of those who fit the category of tourist teachers. They tend to demarcate each school year by paydays, breaks (big and small), and the end of the academic year. By doing so, they likely miss some of the joy that their more engaged colleagues take in the teaching moments when students' eyes light up. Over the long haul, missing the joy of those moments reduces tourist teachers' likelihood of flourishing in the profession.

Constantly looking forward to Friday at 3:30 p.m. or to the next break can cloud a teacher's ability to see the good things going on in one's classroom at the moment. A student is concentrating on reading. Another student is smiling because she just finished a report. A group of students is congratulating each other because their experiment worked the way the textbook said it should. Teachers who want to thrive throughout their whole career witness and enjoy these moments. Tourist teachers tend to miss them.

Travelers

Initially, the traveler might be thought of as someone who likes to visit many places, but lots of tourists have that same desire; thus, the desire to visit multiple destinations does not set travelers apart from tourists. The traveler is more likely someone with a kind of humble, hands-on posture—a learning posture—toward those places, toward the people who live in them, toward how to get to them, and toward what to do upon arrival.

In airports, bus depots, and train stations, travelers are usually easy to spot. Their clothing and their luggage may show signs of wear and tear. Experience has taught them to be patient with both customs officials and airline staff. They know that trains and planes sometimes run late, and that some taxi drivers take an indirect route to their passengers' destination simply to increase their own income. Their travels have taught them both about the kindness of strangers and that not everyone can be trusted. Many travelers know that the English words *travel* and *travail* are etymologically connected and that both have their roots in the French word for *work*. That is, they expect travel to be work.

No doubt, many teachers qualify as traveler teachers. They know that teaching is work, perhaps some of the hardest work one can find. They know that things don't always go as planned. They know that not all their students will love being in class all the time and, their classroom ideals notwithstanding, that not all their students will succeed. But they also know that most students will succeed and that most students will come to class gladly and with a measure of gratitude. They know that the hard work of teaching is among the most rewarding work one can find. They expect the world to become a better place because of their work. And it often does just that.

Travel will involve some misplaced bags, some unexpected walking, perhaps some linguistic difficulties, and perhaps the sounds of small creatures while one is trying to get to sleep. In all this, though, travelers know that the work—the travail—will be worth it. They know that at the end of the day they will have seen some interesting things and met some people they would likely not have met had they signed on for the package tour.

As do many, I like to think of myself as a traveler. I have hiked, canoed, climbed, and flown on tiny airplanes. I have even had a Kenyan say to me, "No *wazungu* (*foreigner* in Swahili) has walked from Machakos to Mitaboni since the road was built decades ago. Why would you want to do that?" I've gone thirsty on the English-Scottish border because I stuffed my daypack with Gore-Tex and fleece instead of with water. I've slept in some very inconvenient and sometimes dangerous places in the Rocky Mountains. But this is travel. These things I've learned and seen, these little mistakes, and these mini-adventures have taught me about the importance of the unknown and about creating room for unforeseen opportunities.

At minimum, teachers must be travelers. Not that they must hike in the Rockies, paddle in Canada's Yukon, or work with teachers in Kenya, but that they must approach their teaching vocation as travel and as travelers. They must start each day knowing that by the end of the school day they will be tired. They will start their days knowing that while there in fact is a road running from Machakos to Mitaboni, they want to walk through the range of hills because that's where they will meet Kenyans. They know that only in their real encounters with students, only in their real tangles with curriculum, instruction, and assessment, and only in their real efforts day to day and year to year, will they construct a learning and teaching space that reflects their highest ideals as educators and that they hope to actually fulfill their vocation as teachers.

At their best, teachers know these truths. Inevitably, teachers get tired from preparation and grading. Teachers get frustrated by toxic people in their workplaces. Teachers' heads sometimes spin at the speed with which they are supposed to respond to new initiatives. And teachers feel insulted when people who have never managed a classroom for two minutes explain in a letter to the editor or claim in an online comment all that teachers or schools get wrong. In these circumstances, a teacher's vision for teaching may dim temporarily, but traveller teachers know they can continue to thrive even at those times when the wind seems to blow the wrong way.

Adventurers

You have likely met a few adventurers or been on a few adventures yourself, some of them planned and some of them perhaps unplanned. For some of us, the word *adventure* takes us back to Winnie the Pooh and his friend Christopher Robin, Huckleberry Finn, Indiana Jones, or perhaps to the characters in the great road trip story some simply can't get enough of, Tolkien's trilogy. Those characters from literature (and film) actually fit well with what we understand to be an adventure, for they went out exploring without knowing what they would find or how the trip would turn out. If an adventure is a trip with an unknown outcome, then perhaps adventurers may be simply travelers with less defined plans and more openness to what comes.

Likewise, the adventurer teacher may simply be the teacher who admits that everything cannot be predicted or planned in advance. After all, none of us can control how it will turn out, not even tomorrow's instruction, let alone a whole academic year or, for that matter, a whole career. Nonetheless, the adventurer teacher looks forward to trying new ideas in class and watching how students respond to new learning strategies or assignments. Adventurer teachers get excited to teach the new curriculum or embrace the new software because it might work better than what they have used before. Perhaps not all teachers should become adventurers, but—to some degree—viewing teaching as an adventure will give teachers more health and satisfaction, and those who adopt an adventurer posture will flourish long-term in the teaching profession and derive the most joy from the ride.

Adventurer teachers are aware from the start that they cannot plan or predict all the details, so they simply launch out. Adventurer teachers know that they don't know how their own teaching careers will turn out. Simply put, too many factors affect the outcome, among them educational budgets, their own health and other personal circumstances, demographic trends they cannot control, which students they will teach from one year to the next, and even when to expect a pandemic.

Honest adventurer teachers admit that they don't even know how the current school year will end. It is not that they have heard the apocalyptic hoofbeats, but simply that they cannot yet finish writing the current year's story. With Yogi Berra, they know it ain't over till it's over. With reasonable accuracy, of course, most teachers can predict the main contours of their teaching work and other responsibilities for the rest of the current year and possibly the next. They should go ahead and make the adjustments to their instruction that they thought of in the last few months. They would be irresponsible—perhaps tourist teachers—if they decided that everything they did this year should work fine again next year. But knowing that they ultimately can't control all the factors that give shape to their work, they might do well to adopt the mindset of the adventurer.

Like travelers, adventurers set out with a plan. Perhaps like some travelers, they have a kind of "let's see how this goes" approach to the realization of their plan. Certainly, that's how mountain climbing works. Climbers try a route to see if it will work. They try this hold and see if it holds, to use climbing language. The parallel in teaching is obvious. Adventurer teachers try an approach and they see if it works. They constantly assess their own work, recalibrating what needs to change before they teach a given bit of material again, and adjusting their theories about instruction or curriculum when needed.

Teachers who accept the fact that they cannot control all the outcomes of their work might find themselves less stressed when their work does not go as they hoped or planned. They will find themselves more open to the pedagogical surprises that pop up in the daily work of teaching. They may find themselves in a bit of difficulty from time to time, but if they have prepared responsibly for their adventure—as wise adventurers and professional teachers do—then, barring a natural catastrophe, things usually work out.

Pilgrims

On two different occasions, I have walked as a pilgrim on the Camino de Santiago de Compostela in southern France and northern Spain. My walks on the Camino have similarities to, and some dramatic differences from, other walks and hikes I have undertaken. A major difference is the great variety of reasons pilgrims walk on the Camino. Like some pilgrims I've met, Martin Sheen's character in the feature film *The Way*[2] walked to try to understand a significant event in his own family: the death of his son on the Camino. I walked and met people processing the natural transitions that come with aging. Others walked with religious motives. Some pilgrims wanted a break from the busyness of urban life. Some simply wanted to see if they could do it.

As I met pilgrims with these varied reasons for walking, I could not help but think of the parallels to those one might consider pilgrim teachers. Teachers who are not counting down to Friday or to the next break or to retirement may qualify as pilgrim teachers. They know that this teaching moment and this teaching day are the priority, and they attempt to live in those moments and in those days.

Pilgrims acknowledge the significance of every footstep, every bend in the path, and every new vista that greets them as they walk. They also know that creaky knees, blisters on their feet, and exhaustion come with the territory. Wherever pilgrims can learn a lesson, they learn it. And pilgrim teachers are willing to learn the lessons that come their way, not only from their colleagues and supervisors but also from their students (as I argue in Chapter 13). They treat teaching as an opportunity for their own transformation as individuals. As was the case with the pilgrims in John Bunyan's *Pilgrim's Progress*,[3] they view their interactions with their travel companions as opportunities to learn and grow.

Before my first walk on the Camino, I memorized a French saying given to me by one of the friends with whom I would be walking: "this is what the path asks of each of us, that we finish the journey." What might this saying mean for teachers? Pilgrim teachers know that when they help their students learn to read, write, and count, they are taking steps toward finishing the journey. They know that when they introduce their fifth-grade students to the electricity and magnetism unit, they are taking steps toward completing the journey. They know that when they help their students understand the differences between Hamlet's tragedy and Macbeth's tragedy, they are taking steps toward finishing the journey. These teachers—these pilgrim teachers—are all doing what the teaching path has asked of them.

In the discussion of adventure, I noted the definition of an adventure as a trip where no one knows how it will turn out. Many pilgrims take that approach too. Though they may have a goal, they don't know how far they will get that day, how their feet and legs will hold up, whether they will find drinkable water, or perhaps what their accommodations might be that night. But more to the point, they don't know what changes will take place inside them as they journey along the path. Likewise, pilgrim teachers do not know how they will change by the end of a given academic year or by the end of their careers. For such teachers, that is part of the meaning of their vocation—and even part of the fun; they do what the path asks of them.

We all know what changes have taken place inside us as we have worked in service to our students and thereby to the world thus far. What can my French saying mean to us as educators about the years ahead? What does it mean to say that the path demands of us that we journey to the end? The obvious and defensible literal interpretation—that we work through to retirement—comes to mind. But I want to argue that the teacher as pilgrim implies more. I think we experience more meaning as teachers and more health as individuals who teach if we approach each teaching year with some interior goals.

At minimum, I have argued that we need to come to teaching as travelers, more likely as adventurers. If we approached teaching as pilgrims, I believe we would, in a sense, treat ourselves to a health-giving perspective on our teaching work. This perspective would help us frame our classroom work within a much wider context than the immediate instructional priorities of our classroom program or of the policies of the building we work in or the jurisdiction of which it may be a part. Our work is part of the healing of the world inasmuch as we are contributing to the growth and wholeness of the people in our charge who live in that world. Furthermore, viewing ourselves as pilgrims raises the importance of our work to ourselves. We do not become selfish or focus only on what our teaching can do in us or for us. But, viewed this way, we recognize that our work nevertheless does something in and for us. Approaching our work as pilgrims, we can become more intentional about what those internal changes might be.

Guides

At one point or another, some travelers will have hired a guide for their travels or inadvertently found one, perhaps a helpful local. At other points, readers perhaps wish they had hired a guide. People use paper and video guides as well—for understanding new software, for walking the Camino, for learning how to lay tile, for getting stains out of upholstery, or for setting up an escape room activity in a middle-school science unit. Indeed, guides are a part of life. Real-life guides can range from overbearing to barely present.

But somewhere on that continuum—different for each person, perhaps—is the guide suited perfectly for each of us. At its simplest, a guide is someone who helps another person find their way. Beyond that bare definition, guides may contribute to the traveler's cost savings, convenience, and safety. And guides possess information about such matters as accommodations and local traditions.

In Kenya, a guide named Patrick drove some teacher colleagues and me on a safari in the Maasai Mara National Reserve in Kenya after we had worked for two weeks with Kenyan teachers. I recall Patrick talking on his radio to other safari drivers because they were wondering where the lions were.[4] We looked at each other in amazement as he spoke these exact words into his radio: "just east of that big tree on the top of that hill." My Canadian colleagues and I listened in amazement in part because the Maasai basin is comprised of hundreds of square kilometers of plains and hills, and, as visitors, we found it amazing that guides would know the precise meaning of "that big tree on the top of that hill." Obviously, Patrick had vast knowledge of the Maasai Basin and the animals living there.

As it turns out, guides, like Patrick, do a lot of different things, such as help Canadian teachers find lions in Kenyan national parks. And what about guide teachers? What do they do? They probably do the metaphorical equivalents of safari guides, and perhaps even the lady with the flag I mentioned in the opening section about tourists. Some veteran teachers help new teachers with some of the most basic tasks. For example, think about how easy it is for the veteran teacher to manage taking attendance compared to the emerging teacher. Regarding this simple but essential matter, the guide teacher might help the induction teacher by offering any number of suggestions about how to remember to do it, or about how to simplify the process, or about how to make it part of the ritual of welcoming students into the classroom. In helping a new teacher sort out this daily routine, a guide teacher is acting as a senior partner or mentor.

New teachers need guides who can draw on years of experience and who can therefore say calmly,

> Sure, this didn't go that well, but I messed up a few times too when I was just getting started. You'll get through this. I can already see that you're going to become a great teacher, in part because you can tell when you didn't get it right... you're a learner. In fact, I still make mistakes every day.

We tell our students to adopt the posture of failing forward—of learning from their mistakes—and we need to adopt the same posture.

What might be the educational equivalent of a big Himalayan mountain? And how would someone guide a teacher who decided to take on such a challenge? For some teachers, it might mean applying for a classroom in a different grade or at a different school with all the challenges implied in that. For others, it might be applying for an administrative post or launching an advanced degree. Many teachers start to think about another degree or some other new professional challenge late in their first decade of teaching. To whom do they turn when they start to consider these kinds of challenges? In my view, they turn to a guide, to a veteran teacher colleague, or to a mentor from their own school or another school.

And what about Patrick, the Kenyan guide who found the lions and, a few days later, helped my colleagues and me avoid an unwanted encounter with some elephants? To be precise, Patrick guided my colleagues and me for several days. We were his clients. He learned about the work we had been doing with teachers, and we learned about his family and the work he did in Nairobi when he was not driving clients on safari. At the end of our days together, I felt like Patrick had taken care of us, not just guided us. What is the equivalent of this in teaching? When I think about Patrick as a metaphor, I realize that all teachers need people to encourage them, but teachers in the first years of their careers especially need mentors who will walk with them and encourage them in their day-to-day work.

Veteran teachers have their own deep knowledge of how classrooms work and are uniquely situated to act as mentors to their colleagues and to pre-service teachers completing an in-school practicum. To return for a moment to the work of Erik Erikson, guides who support the next generation engage in generativity instead of stagnating.[5] If he is correct in offering those two options, educators who become guides and help others also help themselves.

This book began with two vignettes of award-winning Alberta teachers. One thread ran through almost all the nomination packages I read in the three years I served in that program: the outstanding teachers who had reached the appropriate stage in their careers were acting as guides. When teachers choose generativity—choose to be guides—they thrive and they flourish.

Refugees

Most teachers are more likely to help a non-profit organization care for newcomers to their country or refugees halfway around the world than they are to meet actual refugees on the road. On the other hand, a minority of teachers will have traveled to one or more of the world's troubled spots and will have met actual refugees. Because we so regularly see images of migrants and refugees, we all know something about the ongoing plight of refugees and internally displaced persons in the world. While I use the metaphor of the teacher as refugee here, I clearly do not want to diminish the genuine fears and struggles that actual refugees endure in their journey from what was once home to somewhere else.

Still, to write metaphorically, there are refugee teachers who, for any number of reasons, left the place they once worked for somewhere else, perhaps simply to a different school building in the same city, or perhaps to another city and district for higher pay, but one that nevertheless seemed to offer a better context to fulfill their vocations as teachers. Perhaps like refugees in general, such teachers may prefer not to talk about the situations from which they came or their reasons for leaving. They may have floundered in their first post and never recovered from the bumps. They may have offended a previous administrator and found themselves in what they viewed as an educational Siberia. Some may even have left another school to work elsewhere but nevertheless feel like they do not belong in the setting to which they came.

At times, I have felt like a refugee teacher myself. During that time, I faced regular reminders of my status. In the course of writing this chapter, I reread a desperate email I wrote to my principal at one point in my career because I felt my refugee status so powerfully. This rereading reminded me that many teachers feel like they do not fit in the place where they have found themselves. Many teachers wish things could have been different than they were before, or where they are now. That is, we all likely have refugee teachers among us; they may be our colleagues, and they may be us.

Given that all teachers know or have known a colleague who fits the category of refugee teacher or have felt like refugees themselves, what might be the non-refugee teacher's responsibility to such a colleague? Obviously, the classroom teacher's central task is to execute a classroom program, not to carry a wounded colleague. Still, like guides, those who support another usually find themselves receiving as well as giving. Supporting a wounded colleague strengthens not just that colleague but also strengthens a whole school. Helping to dress the wounds of another teacher can ultimately contribute to one's own flourishing as an educator.

For example, I recall a conversation with a teacher in a school parking lot. I had served on an accreditation team and spent the day visiting that school, observing classes, and meeting with staff. In my view, my 4:30 p.m. conversation with one teacher was nothing more than a friendly chat between two educators. If anything, this teacher was seeing me off the school grounds politely by engaging in a conversation about the challenges of teaching in general and about the ways wise teachers respond to their school environments. A few days after that conversation, the school's principal phoned me to tell me that her staff member's sense of vocation had been completely reawakened by that conversation. In her words, he was now "totally pumped" about his teaching. Having been wounded by several prior events, he had followed me to the parking lot seeking the advice of someone older than himself. When the phone call with this principal ended, I exclaimed to my empty office, "No way I could have that effect on another teacher!" My own sense of vocation had been sharpened. I was reminded again of the truth that guides receive when they give, even at those times when they may not recognize what they have given.

Conclusion

Recall the discussion of metaphors in Chapter 7 of this book. Metaphors are not just helpful ways to explain a complex process or concept by framing it in the terms of something simpler. While they do compare—in both helpful and unhelpful ways—metaphors actually shape cognition.

Recognizing the potential of metaphors, including these six images of teachers, wise teachers may want to view what I have offered in this chapter as a possible way to frame some deep reflection on their own posture toward their teaching career and their vocation as teachers. Such reflection could well be life-giving. Teachers who would thrive to the last day they teach might use the six categories offered here as a framework for that reflection. They might ask what steps they could take or moves they could make to become more like travelers or adventurers. If they are of a certain age, they might ask whom they could serve as guides. Those who have been refugee teachers or perhaps remain so should identify what conversations or supports would help them heal from their wounds.

A further invitation is in order. With or without the six categories in mind, teachers should find and spend their time with colleagues who will inspire them rather than drag them down. I return to this idea in the last chapter of the book where I discuss caring for what I call the teacher's core or interior. Teachers who thrive to the end of their careers consistently report intentionally avoiding toxic colleagues and spending time with positive colleagues. This theme accords with the research into educational workplaces.[6] Give to and get from the colleagues who are clear about their vocation as teachers.

Certainly, as teacher travelers, one might meet other kinds of teachers in a school building than the six I have identified here. I hope this schema helps teachers think about the variety of postures we may hold with regard to our work.

One of these approaches—tourism—seems to arise out of cynicism and perhaps boredom, and it likely leads to more of both. Tourist teachers, whether they like it or not or admit it or not, are in a spiral that may be characterized by convenience but does not produce joy.

Another of these categories recognizes the wounds that some teachers carry from, and to, their work settings. Four of these postures—travelers, adventurers, pilgrims, and guides—foster life, joy in teaching, and long-term flourishing.

Notes

1   Matthew Voyage, "How Is Instagram Changing the Way We Travel?," November 29, 2023, https://medium.com/@matthieuvoyage/how-is-instagram-changing-the-way-we-travel-a406a1841cd3. Obviously, after the Covid pandemic, many more people than usual traveled to compensate for what they missed in 2020 and 2021. See Doug Gollan, "Inside the Challenges of the Post-Covid Travel Industry's Soaring Demand," *Forbes*, August 18, 2023, https://www.forbes.com/sites/douggollan/2023/08/18/inside-the-challenges-of-the-post-covid-travel-industrys-soaring-demand/.

2 Emilio Estevez, director (Elixir Films; Filmax; Icon Entertainment, 2010).

3 (London: Nathaniel Ponder, 1677, 1684).

4 An obvious reference to Bruce Cockburn's song, *Wondering Where the Lions Are* (Toronto: True North Records, 1979).

5 *Identity and the Life Cycle* (New York: W.W. Norton, 1994); *Life Cycle Completed* (New York: W.W. Norton, 1998).

6 Brandy Yee and Diane Yee, *International Perspectives on Ethical Educational Leadership: Lessons from Workplace Cultures That Have Lost (and Found) Their Way* (London: Palgrave Macmillan, 2024).

13 Supporters

Teachers need supporters. I write this declaration as a short sentence with a period because it needs to be read, processed, and even digested. It is easy to assume that my readers, who are educators in varying capacities, find this statement to be obvious. However, the teaching role is the role of the supporter: the champion, the hero, the mentor, the instructor, and the sage guide of the classroom. Many teachers who enter into this calling may forget or fail to recognize the extent to which their work in the classroom must be fueled by the presence and voices of their own supporters. In this chapter, I propose two possible kinds of supporters beyond the usual suspects, those being their administrators and colleagues. The first of these is students themselves. The second is a semi-formal team that a teacher intentionally assembles.

A typical phrase in many teachers' lexicons is *supportive administrator*, usually shortened to *supportive admin*. Teachers should expect such support, and school administrators should expect to give it, and they usually do. The immense volume of easily available research and writing on this topic, ranging from extended ethical perspectives to short, how-to articles, reduces the need to repeat here what educators already know and expect.[1]

Most teachers expect the same of their colleagues and expect to give support to their colleagues. Those colleagues may be close, inasmuch as they teach the same grade or subject area. Or they may be literally closer, because they teach nearby in the same hallway. Explaining the idea of supporting one's teaching colleagues and gaining support from those colleagues is as unnecessary as going on at length about the role of school administrators in supporting teachers.[2] I noted in the previous chapter that guide teachers see the mentoring of younger colleagues as a natural part of their work. But veteran and senior teachers are not the only ones who should support their colleagues; all teachers need to do so and need to be able to receive such support. Without wanting to seem glib about the two groups of people from whom a teacher might ordinarily expect to receive support, I will move on to those two possible sources of support that teachers might not ordinarily think of.

Students as Teachers' Allies

Some readers may find this title and the idea that students could be their teachers' allies surprising. After all, teachers are professionals, and they must carefully maintain the boundaries between themselves and the students who come to their classrooms day after day. They are to treat their students in a friendly manner but are not to become friends with them. To one degree or another, Professional Codes of Conduct and Ethical Codes of Conduct in every school jurisdiction stress that teachers are to recognize and work carefully within these boundaries (some teacher films notwithstanding).

Recognizing and honoring such boundaries, in what sense can students become supporters of a teacher's classroom program or even become a teacher's allies? The answer to that question divides into two sections. The first section suggests that teachers who gain such support typically approach the core cycle of teaching activities identified in the model of teaching presented earlier (Chapter 3), and notes how they approach the three larger contextual matters that inform teachers' work within the core cycle: teaching who their students are, teaching who they are themselves, and teaching where they are. The second answer to this question comes as a brief survey of the forms such support takes, indicating what it looks like when students become the allies of their teachers.

Approaching the Core Cycle Invitationally

Students become a teacher's allies when they are invited to do so, both through teachers' effective and inviting execution of the core tasks of curriculum, instruction, and assessment, and by way of a classroom culture that emphasizes inclusion and agency—a culture built collaboratively between teachers and students.

We begin with curriculum. Teachers can bring curriculum and students together in ways that lead those students to become their teachers' allies. Recall that John Dewey said to start where students are, with what interests them.[3] Dewey did not say to end there, which clearly would not be in students' ultimate interests, a matter many of his critics seem to miss. Rather, he asked educators to start by finding connecting points between the curriculum materials and students' lives. Ultimately, Dewey's approach hinges on knowing the particularities of individual learners that cause them to come alive in response to new moments of learning.

To illustrate Dewey's point, one colleague[4] wrote about starting a Social Studies unit on Hitler and Stalin by having students write a short, autobiographical assignment entitled "The Bully I Knew." Although this assignment carried little course weight, it required students to recall their own experiences of being bullied, and it served as a means of framing one of the central ideas in the unit: the authoritarian bullying of Hitler and Stalin. To support Dewey's point, this colleague's Social Studies class did not become a group therapy session. The unit began with a topic close to students' hearts, but it moved from there into the prescribed curriculum materials. This teacher also made clear to students that the comparison of a schoolyard bully to Hitler or Stalin fell short in deeply significant ways.

In *To Know as We Are Known*, Parker Palmer argues for a view of the relationship between classroom knowledge and teachers' expertise that places both the student and the teacher in front of and, in a sense, below what he calls *the big subject*.[5] In his telling, traditional instruction often requires that students go through their instructor—who possesses the knowledge of the expert— to get to the curriculum materials the educator has planned. In the model Palmer envisions, teachers stand with their students in submission to the subject. That is, even though teachers come to the classroom as experts, they adopt a posture of humility with regard to classroom knowledge.

Some teachers in the upper grades demonstrate this posture by inviting their students, on the first or second day of the course, to identify their own course objectives. Doing so does not constitute a denial of their own subject-area or pedagogical expertise. Nor does it imply that the jurisdiction's specified learning outcomes are of no consequence. But teachers who practice this demonstrate that they care about the ideas and learning desires their students bring to class. By doing so, they send a strong message to students about the kind of learning community in which they themselves want to work and in which they want their students to work.

One secondary colleague reports using a short written assignment in which students identify their own course objectives after their teacher has worked through the course outline on the first day of class. This teacher attaches 3 percent course weight to this simple assignment. Students' lists of their objectives inform the revised course outline, which invariably reflects some of the language and priorities that appeared in the students' submissions. While shaping the course is the obvious purpose in inviting students to list their objectives, it is only one purpose; this teacher also wants to send the message that he and his students are working on the course together and that he wants his courses to work for everyone.

Palmer's argument in *To Know as We Are Known* is consistent with that of psychologist Carl Rogers, who wrote decades before Palmer about the need for educators to be what he called *co-learners* with their students.[6] In short, Palmer and Rogers both argue for humility in how teachers approach classroom knowledge and when they judge whose knowledge counts in their classrooms.

The Shapes of Student Support

To the second part of the answer, what does student support look like? What does it mean for students to become their teachers' allies? First, it implies that they have granted their teacher the authority to teach them, what sociologists call *consent*. That is, because their teachers have earned the right—the social capital or moral authority—to teach them, students grant those teachers more room to carry out their instructional program than they otherwise might.[7] Recognizably, most teachers come to class with three important symbols of authority already in hand: a teaching degree, some kind of license or teaching certificate from the appropriate government authority, and a contract with the local school authority. That is, they have already been authorized to teach by authorities outside their classroom. But if they rely only on those official authorizations to execute their classroom program, they may end up with a group of resistant students whose attention may be focused on the fact that they are required to attend class in that particular room rather than on the educational content. In effect, authority granted by outside entities does not sustain or guarantee the realization of classroom teachers' larger epistemological endeavors. That power lies in the hands of the learners in the desks.

Thus, teachers need more than their students' required attendance to execute their classroom program successfully. Teachers who have gained their students' consent or goodwill enjoy the opposite of compulsory attendance by resentful children or young people. Moment to moment, students may not understand why their teachers do everything they do or why the curriculum includes these particular contents, but they trust their teachers enough to go along with what those teachers have planned. They actually want their teachers to succeed.

This kind of consistent and felt trust or consent has a twin: respect. It is not the job of this chapter to settle the question of which one is born first; however (and importantly), when teachers have constructed an engaging classroom program and created an inviting classroom climate, their students usually show them respect. They respect their character. They respect their expertise. They especially show this respect when their teachers give them an appropriate measure of authority over their own education.

Students also demonstrate that their allyship takes the form of genuine care. In a collaborative culture, students care that their teachers do well in executing their instructional plans and that they succeed in creating the classroom environment they want to create. Most teachers have received emails, cards, mugs, and other swag because students and their families want to show care and express gratitude for their classroom work. Sometimes, when things do not go as well as they might in class, students even offer apologies along the lines of, "Sorry we weren't with you this morning," or "It wasn't your teaching, it was us." Those apologies demonstrate that some days, when classes do not go as planned, students have the capacity to recognize that the lack of pedagogical fireworks is not entirely their teacher's fault. Such apologies and confessions illustrate that when a teacher has built the right classroom culture, students will want that teacher to succeed. They express their care by making clear their desire for their teachers' success.

Students also care about their teachers' lives outside the classroom, even though in some sense it is none of their business. As we know, news spreads, and our students inevitably hear things. Often, from a posture of care or concern, they will ask after this or that aspect of their teachers' personal lives. Perhaps with no specific issue in mind, a student may ask privately if a teacher is okay, noting that they "looked a bit tired in class" or "seemed a little distracted or down." More often than we probably realize, students see the humanity of their teachers and seek to dignify it, particularly when they have internalized a sense of participatory belonging in the classroom community.

The Sources of Students' Support

Instruction

Most readers of this chapter already know the degree to which various instructional strategies engage students. That simplifies my job immensely. My thesis here, though, is that varied instruction not only engages learners, but it also helps to produce an invitational classroom culture. When students feel invited to class and see their teacher working hard to keep class interesting, they will support their teacher. At the best of times, they become completely engrossed in their work, entering what Mihaly Csikszentmihalyi calls a flow state (which I mentioned in passing in both Chapters 3 and 6).

Csikszentmihalyi deals at length with the qualities or characteristics of a flow state, which athletes typically call *the zone* and jazz musicians have historically referred to as *the groove*.[8] I will not discuss those qualities but will simply list them here as they apply to classroom work: the student finds the activity inherently worth doing; the student does not want to stop (even for a bell); the student loses awareness of the passage of time; the student loses self-consciousness. I recognize that applying Csikszentmihalyi's conditions to a classroom will likely will sound utopian to some, but some years back, a colleague and I collected narratives from teachers who described classes where students became so engaged they did not want to stop what they were doing. Most of the stories these colleagues provided us described classroom settings where students exhibited all four of the qualities listed above.[9]

In Chapter 12, I argued that adventurers were one of the six kinds of teachers whom teachers meet along the way. One characteristic of adventurer teachers is their willingness to try new approaches to curriculum and instruction. In a class where students and teachers share trust, students will still enjoy working with their teachers, even when an instructional strategy doesn't work.

Assessment

Some readers may be skeptical about any claim that assessment can be a means of drawing students into a teacher's classroom program. Teachers' experience with assessment and their knowledge of most students' feelings about it reduce my need to list the reasons for such skepticism. However, teachers have found ways to frame assessment that destigmatize it for their students and make assessment less of a barrier to their becoming supporters of their classroom program.

What one colleague calls *co-determining the rubric* with students increases their understanding of what their teacher expects them to accomplish in a given assignment. This colleague reports that her students have an increased sense that she cares about what they think and that she takes into consideration their conceptions of what a good assignment looks like. Very simply, she has the students work in small groups to evaluate the rubric for an upcoming assignment. She invites her students, if they wish, to suggest different weights for the rows already in the rubric, to suggest new rows (new criteria) that should be added to the rubric, or to suggest different wording for some of the cells. She reports that she does not negotiate the number of columns or their labels because her secondary school uses the same four columns and labels across all classes. Groups turn their work back in to her, and she comes back the next day with a revised rubric.

This strategy serves as the transition from assessment to classroom climate. This colleague uses the word *miracle* when she describes how well this strategy works. She rarely has to make substantive changes to a rubric. Students sometimes suggest clearer language for one or more cells. She reports that she almost always has students say to her, "Now I really understand this assignment." And she reports that students tell her privately that they were honored that she wanted to know how they thought a given assignment should be assessed. To summarize, she devises a means of engaging them in the assessment of their work that helps them understand their assignment better and, by doing so in this particular way, she helps build the kind of classroom ethos within which she wants to work with her students.

Classroom climate

A consistently positive classroom climate is a necessary condition for students to support a teacher's instructional program. When students think of a given teacher's classroom as engaging and invitational, they will care about that teacher's success.

Thousands of researchers have studied the components of quality teaching in both K-12 and higher education, revealing that students and educators themselves use dozens of different criteria to judge what is good teaching.

Among the dozens of criteria, four show up consistently: that a teacher is caring, is prepared, has subject-area expertise, and has pedagogical expertise.

In recent years, *mattering*, a subfield of psychology and first cousin of caring, has begun to show up in research.[10] The research on mattering has revealed what most teachers perhaps already know: people—in our case, students—engage more readily when they think they matter to other people. Again, most teachers know this; the obvious takeaway from this emerging field of research is that teachers need to show that their students matter. Specifically, teachers wanting to demonstrate that their students matter will incorporate their students' interests and viewpoints into classroom life. Teachers will engage in more individual conversations with their students. They tell students who return from an absence that the class was not the same without them. In short, teachers show their students that they matter by telling them they are important. Students who believe they matter are more likely to become the allies of their teachers.

Mattering can make a major contribution to a positive classroom climate. Chapter 3 included a graphic of my own model of classroom work. Here, I want to expand on the idea that teachers do their classroom work—with curriculum, instruction, and assessment—in a classroom ethos or climate constructed by themselves and their students over time. Building classroom climate works as a cycle. With reference to Figure 3.1, when teachers repeatedly structure class time and employ instructional strategies that allow their students to get into a flow state, their inclination to engage with their teachers in future activities and classes increases. At its simplest, they enjoy the class they're in, and they look forward to what future classes might hold. As they form the habit of engaging, they increase their trust in their teacher. On their side, teachers come to trust their students more because they know about their students' increasing desire to learn. As engagement and trust grow, teachers gain more room for instructional experimentation; they can try more things.

The pronouns *we* and *our* can also have a powerful effect on classroom climate. A colleague reported to me how he uses this language as part of his effort to build classroom community. He told me that his students feel more like their knowledge and their purposes are important because when they consistently hear the class referred to as "our class" instead of "my class," they come to feel like they and their teacher are indeed on the same team. This is obviously not a stand-alone strategy; it functions in concert with a number of other consistent practices. But, according to this colleague's account, these pronouns have an important effect on students' attitudes toward both the work that their teacher is trying to do and their own work.

Teachers who communicate to their students that they expect amazing things sometimes get just that. Three stories illustrate this claim and the wisdom of treating students as if they know much more than they are often given credit for knowing.

The first story comes from a secondary school in Sheffield, England. Miles Solomon, at seventeen years of age, identified an error in data recorded by NASA at the International Space Station on the effects of radiation on humans. NASA experts had not noticed the mistaken data that Solomon spotted. "It's pretty cool," Miles said, "You can tell your friends, I just emailed NASA and they're looking at the graphs that I've made."[11] A question arising out of this story for all educators might be how to create classroom conditions where students consider such discoveries as that made by Miles Solomon to be within their reach, that they also might make a discovery or have an insight into something newsworthy.

Another such story involves a group of six Tennessee secondary students who solved a decades-old cold-case murder. Their sociology teacher, Alex Campbell, was leading them in a unit on profiling. The link provides far more detail than I provide here, but in short, at the conclusion of their assignment, these students held a press conference attended by police and others involved in law enforcement. With the students' findings in hand, officers made an arrest within days, and the arrest led to a conviction.[12] Again, a question all educators might ask is how to structure assessment so that students' work aligns with the motto "real work for a real audience in the real world."[13] Or we might ask what kind of expectations we communicate to our students.

The third such story also involves death, but this time of turtles. Hawaiian secondary student, Maddux Springer, wanted to understand why the sea turtles near his home were dying. Through hundreds of hours of research, including diving, he concluded that the turtles were eating an algae containing a lethal virus. Like Miles Solomon and the six students in Tennessee, Maddux Springer did real work for a real audience in the real world.[14]

Recognizably, these three cases are exceptional. Every student will not find errors in NASA's data from the International Space Station or solve cold-case murders. But it is within the reach of every teacher to create a classroom climate where exceptional work does not surprise and where students know that they and their work matter. Sometimes, in their weary moments, teachers may be inclined to ask this question about their students: "What can they know."[15] Stories like these should remind us all that the answer should be, "More than we sometimes think."

Teams

Having argued that teachers, administrators, and colleagues normally want teachers to succeed, and if teachers create the right kind of classroom ethos their students will likewise become their allies, I now turn to the claim that all teachers need a team.

Although the idea of a supportive network to encourage people to carry on working is not new, the origins of the team idea as I describe it here are quite specific. At a conference some years ago, a colleague informed me that I needed to gather with some others in a pub that evening because she needed some advice about a vocational decision she needed to make. I will anonymize her as Andrea in this telling because she wishes not to be identified. When Andrea, her other colleagues, and I met that evening, she told us about her dissatisfaction with her current position and asked if we thought it wise for her to take another post she had been invited to consider. For me, the kicker sentence in that conversation was this: "You're all on Team Andrea and that is why I am asking you." The idea that there was actually a Team Andrea or that I might be a member of that team had never occurred to me. Membership on that team felt like an honor, but it came with a sense of responsibility. She was actually asking me and her other colleagues what to do. She wanted to know what we thought.

Upon arriving home from that conference, I spent some time reflecting on the question of who might agree to serve on Team Ken. That is, very simply, I wanted to be assured that there were specific people who cared week to week about me and my work. By the word *care,* I don't mean care in some general or fuzzy way. I mean that they would know specifically what my work involved that week and would ask with interest whether I had finished my work and how well it went. I identified several people whom I thought I could ask to serve in this way, and all those I asked agreed. The composition of Team Ken has changed slightly over the years as my own circumstances or other people's circumstances have changed. Some original members remain.

Over time, my relationships with some of the members of Team Ken have become more two-directional. I have become a member of their teams in a mutual and reciprocal relationship, implying that I consistently ask how their teaching is going and how they are doing with other projects.[16] One is a college president; I promised him I would sell several of my car dealerships and send him the money. More seriously, one is a young professor whom I do my best to encourage as new semesters and new publication deadlines approach.

Conduct an online search for images with the word *team* and your own given name, and you will see that the idea of a team did not originate with my colleague Andrea. Clearly, the idea of gathering a team—of declaring one's support for others—has become part of our cultural moment. Although its popularity may not be a sufficient reason in itself for teachers to assemble a team, it may indicate something about the human need for support.

Typically, educators who gather teams evolve a pattern for their communication. In my own case, I send an email early in the work week providing some detail about my planned work for that week. Late in the week, I tell my team members how the week went. Different teams develop different mixes of support and accountability. Team membership implies a baseline responsibility to encourage one's colleagues to keep showing up and keep doing a good job. Different members will have different levels of comfort with the idea of accountability and asking how it went. The person who gathered the team must be willing to tell the truth.

Most teachers, for most of their teaching week, work as the only professional in their classrooms.[17] If you do have a conversation with colleagues at lunch or after the school day, you may talk about how the day went but will not likely get the kind of ongoing support you need to address the specific challenges of teaching in a given week. In light of the intensity of the typical teacher's actual workday, this section ends with an obvious recommendation: assemble a team. Do so with intention, care, and the expectation for meaningful reciprocity.

Conclusion

In normal circumstances, teachers expect their colleagues and administrators to support their work. This chapter began by treating that claim as a given. However, in the two major parts of the chapter, I have attempted to build two other cases. First, I argued that if teachers get their instructional program right and build the right kind of classroom ethos their students will support their work and even care about them as people, apart from their being their teachers. Second, while recognizing the wisdom of knowing in a general way who one's supporters are, I argued that educators should act intentionally to assemble a team of supporters who agree to take on specific week-to-week responsibilities. Those responsibilities range on a continuum that runs from something like warm support to hard-nosed accountability. And those responsibilities imply corollary responsibilities for teachers pulling such teams together; those assembling such teams must be specific about their upcoming work, and they must be honest when they report in. In both the treatment of staying focused in Chapter 15 and the treatment of what I call nurturing the core in Chapter 16, I return briefly to the idea of teams.

Notes

1. At the time of writing, a Google search of "administrators supporting teachers" yielded 188,000,000 hits.
2. A Google search of "teachers supporting colleagues" yielded 371,000,000 hits, implying that there is more about this topic than there are teachers in the world.
3. John Dewey, *The Child and the Curriculum* (Chicago, IL: The University of Chicago Press, 1902). Dewey returned to this claim in *Experience and Education* (New York: Macmillan, 1938), in part to address critics who were claiming that he was more concerned about children's interests than he was about the curriculum. Obviously, if teachers taught only what children found interesting, the kindergarten curriculum would feature dinosaurs almost all the time.
4. This colleague wishes to remain anonymous.
5. (New York: Harper, 1983).
6. Carl Rogers, *Freedom to Learn: A View of What Education Might Become* (Columbus, OH: Charles Merrill, 1969).

7   See *The Complexities of Authority in the Classroom: Fostering Democracy for Student Learning*, which I edited with Margaretta Patrick (New York: Routledge, 2022). We and our contributors explore such topics as consent or authorization at length. Notably, teachers who share a measure of classroom authority with their students typically gain their students' support more quickly than those teachers who retain all the classroom authority for themselves.

8   Mihalyi Csikszentmihalyi, *The Psychology of Optimal Experience* (New York: Harper and Row, 1990).

9   Susanna Steeg Thornhill and Ken Badley, *Generating Tact and Flow for Effective Teaching and Learning* (New York: Routledge, 2020).

10 For example, see Gordon L. Flett, *The Psychology of Mattering: Understanding the Human Need to be Significant* (Boston, MA: Academic Press/Elsevier, 2018).

11 "UK Schoolboy Corrects NASA Data Error," *BBC*, March 22, 2017, https://www.bbc.com/news/uk-39351833.

12 Andy Corbley, "How a High School Class Solved Six Murders and Identified the Bible Belt Strangler," *Good News Network*, May 29, 2024, https://www.goodnewsnetwork.org/how-a-us-high-school-class-solved-six-murders-and-identified-the-bible-belt-strangler/.

13 A slogan originating from Justin Cook, director of Learning for Edvance Christian Schools Association, Ontario, Canada.

14 See https://www.goodnewsnetwork.org/high-schooler-wins-10000-for-discovery-solution-to-mysterious-outbreak-killing-sea-turtles-in-his-hawaii-hometown/.

15 This question is meant to honor Lorraine Code's 1991 book title *What Can She Know?: Feminist Theory and the Construction of Knowledge* (Ithaca, NY: Cornell University Press, 1991).

16 The initials of Team Ken's members appear in the acknowledgments in the front matter of this book.

17 Recognizably, they may have an educational assistant for part or all of a teaching day.

14 Dispositions That Foster Flourishing

Teachers who thrive to the last day of their teaching career typically possess a variety of dispositions. That is, they are disposed toward certain ways of thinking, feeling, and acting. These dispositions are not mysterious. Lists of dispositions include such ordinary words as humility, contentment, openness to surprise, grit, and gratitude. Teachers who thrive to their last day of teaching typically have the capacity to wonder, to laugh, and to listen. They typically know how to forget those events in their biography that are best forgotten and to remember rightly, by which I mean not to produce an image of themselves either as victims or as superstars. This list could have been shorter, and it obviously could be longer. For reasons that will become apparent as the chapter unfolds, we will work with the list the way it is for now. In Kentopia, that place I dream of where everything works perfectly, I plan to grow into all the health-giving dispositions, keep all my resolutions, and then write the last word on how to be good.

A robust literature has developed related to teacher dispositions. Michelle Hughes, for example, has written at length about the dispositions she believes teachers need. In her framing of dispositions, not only do teachers need these dispositions, but, with Aristotle, she believes they can be cultivated; we can grow into them. In her 2025 book, *Dispositions are a Teacher's Greatest Strength*, she gives separate chapters to curiosity, reflection, empathy, resilience, gratitude, encouragement, collaboration, courage, hope, and joy.[1] I recommend her book without reservation and, where possible, will avoid repeating work that she has already done.

New research on a variety of dispositions derives in part from the growing concern for teacher self-care and in part because of the recent growth of research on gratitude in education. Clearly, a chapter focused on the dispositions that lead to long-term flourishing is a chapter about teacher self-care. But I also want to frame this chapter with reference to student learning and the construction of a positive classroom climate.

This chapter serves as a corollary or perhaps antidote to Chapter 4. If teaching is as complex and intense as I described it in that chapter, and if some of the external and objective conditions of teaching are not within the control of educators themselves, then we should likely address the internal conditions that are within our control. How can our state of mind influence how we function and how well we function while doing this complex and intense work? Some of us are naturally disposed to respond to complexity and intensity in health-giving ways. Others of us are not. My thesis here is simple: we can develop health-giving ways to frame and handle the complexity and intensity of our work. We can practice health-giving dispositions and incorporate them into our posture toward our work and our lives.

Ordinary language has in it sentences implying that one is born with certain personality traits or dispositions and that those dispositions remain fixed for life. For example, "She's a born optimist." To some degree, this common belief is true; people do tend to live with certain dispositions or postures throughout their lives. However, long before teaching became as complex as it now is, Aristotle presented another view in his book, *The Nicomachean Ethics*[2] and that view offers an important perspective for everyone interested in finding more joy in life, especially for teachers. In short, Aristotle's claim is that if we act as if we already possess a given disposition, what he called a virtue, we can actually learn that disposition; by acting the way we would act if we already possessed a disposition, we will grow into it; it will grow on us. For example, habitually doing things that would ordinarily flow out of gratitude—thanking people who work in stores, for example—will ultimately lead to an internal state of gratitude for those people who serve us.

If Aristotle is correct in suggesting this approach, a teacher could even come to see and appreciate the gifts that a troublesome student brings to the classroom. Regarding the dispositions most needed by teachers, Aristotle distinctly brings hope. Educators can develop the dispositions they need to flourish over the long haul in the teaching vocation. The short treatments in the first pages of this chapter represent only a fraction of what one could write about dispositions. Nevertheless, these dispositions are among those that seem most likely to contribute to long-term flourishing in the teaching profession. Later in the chapter, two longer sections deal with two specific dispositions: gratitude and remembering.

Key Dispositions for Long-Term Flourishing

Among the many dispositions one might recommend that teachers strive to develop, I will very briefly treat seven in the pages that follow: humility, surprise, awe and wonder, persistence, humor, contentment, and hope. Following those brief treatments, I will consider two more at some length: gratitude and remembering rightly. Readers should not conclude that the brevity of my treatments of the first seven dispositions indicates anything about my views of their relative importance. Book chapters and entire books have appeared on all of these seven topics, and I have written elsewhere about some of them.

Humility

Several of the preceding chapters in this book include comments about classroom knowledge and the degree to which students' knowledge is valued in the classroom. Some of these comments included references to the work of Parker Palmer and his book, *To Know as We Are Known*.[3] There, he argues that teachers and students stand before the big subject and they learn together. Such a posture toward classroom knowledge requires a degree of humility on the part of the teacher. Some teachers might think students would consider such humility a sign of weakness or perhaps see it as an indicator of a lack of subject-area expertise or pedagogical authority. However, when students see their teacher demonstrate such humility, they actually see classroom community being built before their eyes, and they accord their teacher greater authority.

Listening

The willingness to listen obviously connects to humility, and it also connects to being open to surprise, the next disposition I treat in this section of the chapter. The model of knowing Palmer proposes in *To Know as We are Known* implies not only that we learn with our students but that we can learn from them as well. Depending on the tone with which it is pronounced, the question, "What can they know?" can serve derogatory purposes or it can express humility and a willingness to listen. The previous chapter contained at least three interesting answers to the question, "What can they know?" A student in England knew something was amiss with radiation data NASA was receiving from the International Space Station. A student researched and came to understand why turtles were dying on a beach in Hawaii. Students in Tennessee solved a cold-case murder. Granted, these stories made international news because they were exceptional. But as I claimed in the previous chapter, stories like these should remind us all that the answer to "What can they know?" might well be, "More than we sometimes think." Let us develop the disposition of listening to our students more than we might be naturally inclined to do.

Openness to Surprise

Being open to surprise is related to humility and is a typical expression of it. After all, the person who knows everything will never be surprised. To be open to surprise both requires humility and demonstrates humility. Without wanting to reduce openness to surprise to the status of an instructional strategy, such openness nevertheless fosters student engagement in the curriculum materials at hand and helps build classroom community. The teacher willing to take time for further exploration of a student's question or a comment—even if that comment seems off the wall—may discover a gem in the moments that follow. Barring the discovery of gems, taking that time still demonstrates that a teacher values student contributions and thereby raises their interest in the remainder of that day's class.

Awe and Wonder

After four or five centuries of advances in our scientific understanding of the world around us, people living in the twenty-first century may be excused for their lack of wonder. Yet wonder, like the willingness to be surprised, is essential for people such as teachers who do hard work. Occasions of wonder lift people beyond the day-to-day and possibly mundane details of their lives and remind them that their lives are part of something bigger. Given the complexity, intensity, and mixed rewards of teaching, teachers might be wise to make a habit of putting themselves in the path of wonder. Awe and wonder have the capacity to lighten a teacher's load. Of course, seeing the Aurora Borealis induces wonder. But what about that mundane activity of grading a stack of assignments? Can teachers actually reframe the pedestrian parts of our work so that even grading allows us to see something bigger . . . for example, that teaching changes students' lives.

A teacher's disposition to stand in awe or to be struck by wonder is infectious. In fact, Eleanor Duckworth argues on the first page of her 2006 book, *The Having of Wonderful Ideas* that the essence of good pedagogy is to provide opportunities for students to have wonderful ideas.[4] That is, teachers should facilitate their students having experiences of wonder. Students who are regularly struck with wonder in a classroom are more likely to like coming to that classroom and to engage with the teacher in that classroom. Such student engagement will contribute to teacher flourishing. That is, while teachers who are disposed to wonder feed their own souls directly, they also create a feedback loop wherein the increased levels of student engagement also nourish them.

Persistence

Since her 2007 TED Talk on grit, Angela Duckworth's work on grit has become widely known among educators.[5] Of course, grit is not a novel concept; persistence—or, as it was historically called, perseverance—has been considered a virtue for millennia. The discussion of persistence among educators has tended to focus on the importance of helping students—rather than teachers—develop grit. Given the nature of teaching work, especially the complexity, intensity, and mixed rewards described in Chapter 4, teachers should apply these lessons on grit to their own teaching practice.

Laughter

Older readers may recall that one of the humor sections in *The Reader's Digest* magazine used to be called "Laughter: The Best Medicine." Neurologists and medical scientists who study the brain have confirmed this age-old claim.[6] In short, laughter causes the secretion of endorphins in several areas of the brain. In general, endorphins lead to an increase in awareness and they foster social connection. In classrooms, this translates to student engagement and a stronger classroom community.

Some researchers have concluded that the right amounts of classroom laughter lead to improvements in student achievement.[7] The experience of many teachers bears out the conclusions of these researchers. One colleague reported to me that his students' exceptional grades on standardized tests were a direct result of the class spending as much time as it did laughing. Even if we presume that he spoke somewhat hyperbolically, we can still safely conclude that the laughter must not have harmed his classroom program. To end this brief treatment of laughter, let me point readers to the endnote at the beginning of this paragraph. It leads to one of the most interesting doctoral dissertations I have seen on any topic, and I recommend it without reservation to my readers.

Contentment, Satisfaction, and Joyful

These three dispositions or tendencies are not the same, despite being treated together here. If you recall the description of teaching in Chapter 4 as complex, intense, and delivering mixed rewards, then treating these three dispositions together makes sense. It is commonplace knowledge that teachers, admittedly along with professionals in many other fields, rarely finish everything on their to-do lists. Given that their school day will not suddenly shrink or the cat in the hat suddenly show up to help with the grading backlog, teachers need strategies to find satisfaction in what they succeeded in checking off their to-do lists.

Being able to take satisfaction and joy in what one has been able to accomplish is essential for those who literally can never can do all they might do.[8] One colleague described what she called a *contentment practice*. To counteract the nagging effect her never-finished to-do list has on her thinking, this teacher notes in her journal every evening what she *did* get done. She points out that as much as she loves writing that she finished grading a set of papers or that she really got through to this one student, many days her list includes such ordinary tasks as getting groceries or taking her daughter to soccer. Such tasks are obviously no less important than grading, but the point of her practice is to focus on what she has accomplished rather than on what remains undone. She notes that producing this brief list before bedtime helps her fall asleep because her brain enters a resting mode more easily when one of its last tasks of the day does not connect with undone work.

Almost all teachers have a to-do list somewhere: in their brain, in an app, or in a pile of papers. Would that all teachers could develop a disposition toward and a practice of taking satisfaction and joy in what they had accomplished. Most teachers do amazing work, and much of it is unrecognized in the daily bustle of teaching. May we develop the skill of recognizing our amazing work ourselves and of taking satisfaction in or even joy in what we accomplish day to day.

Hope

As is the case for all the dispositions, hope has seen its share of research.[9] Psychologists, theologians, philosophers, self-help gurus, and even some climatologists have all addressed hope, as have educational researchers. To the point of this chapter, over four decades of research into the connections between health and hope have made it clear that hope strengthens the immune system and that people are more likely to heal from various illnesses, including cancer, if they are hopeful.[10]

Physiological responses aside for the moment, hope also helps teachers with the practical matter of returning to work each day. Yes, their work is challenging, but teachers who locate that challenging work in a hopeful frame are continually reminded of the larger context of their work. Children are learning to read and count. Children are developing physical and artistic skills. And children are learning civil behaviors and the dispositions that undergird those behaviors. These larger realities mean that teachers can remain hopeful that their work is much more than curriculum, instruction, and assessment; it creates change in the world.

In preparation for a public lecture some years ago, I asked dozens of teachers how their work contributed to human flourishing. One of the teachers responded to my question with these words: "Education is by definition work for the future. That means education is always about hope. Teaching basically says no to despair." This quotation serves as an inspiring reminder that teaching is ultimately about hope, and teachers who can remind themselves of that daily are more likely to flourish long term.

Gratitude

More than perhaps any other disposition discussed in this chapter, gratitude in education has become a significant subfield in educational research. Although the gratitude conversation has gone on for decades, Kerry Howells' 2012 book, *Gratitude in Education: A Radical View*,[11] had a significant impact on the conversation and, notably, on the role of gratitude practices in classrooms.

To complete her doctoral project, Howells worked with a number of Australian teachers who implemented gratitude practices in their own classrooms. They observed the effects of implementing these practices and reported these effects back to her. Effects included increased student engagement with the curriculum and instruction and decreased feelings of teacher burnout. Such findings may not surprise educators now, but Howells completed her work when gratitude practices in education were in their relative infancy, at the beginning of the shift toward morning and closing circles.

For teachers, recognizing privilege can be an important expression of gratitude. Many teachers are aware that, while challenging, their work is less physically demanding and less dangerous than the work of many other people. Teachers get to work with people and with ideas. Teachers from immigrant families and working-class backgrounds—referred to by sociologists as *class migrants*—are typically more keenly aware than some others that their work is good work and that they are privileged to do that work.

The quotation about hope preceding the *Gratitude* heading above was only one of about fifty responses I received in answer to my question about the contribution teachers make to human flourishing. Many of the responses I received focused on gratitude. Note some of the themes in the seven comments below.

> *I believe my work as a teacher increases human flourishing because I aim to create a classroom culture in which students feel comfortable, safe, and included, and that aims for students to reach their highest potential.*
>
> *As a teacher, I share my lived experiences, my passions, my curiosity, and my love of our awe-inspiring world. The privilege of sparking joy, empathy, and curiosity in a child is why I teach.*
>
> *As a teacher, it is thrilling to witness how young minds interact, learn, and grow with one another. Being the gentle guiding hand makes it even more rewarding and exciting.*
>
> *Teaching, what an honor it is to host a classroom that is warm, welcoming, and safe. In such a space my students flourish in their physical, cognitive, and social emotional development and experience self-actualization. . . . I suppose I do as well.*
>
> *I believe that my teaching makes the world a better place because I get to be a role model for my students.*
>
> *It's a privilege to be in the position that I'm in, and to be entrusted, however ineptly or inelegantly I perform the task, with helping to shape . . . the next generation.*

> *I believe my work as an educator contributes to human flourishing because I get to be a part and play a role in every child's life. The years I get to spend with each student allow me to motivate and inspire a generation of changemakers.*

The comments above represent both elementary and secondary teachers. They provide a taste of the gratitude response of teachers who love to see their students learn and grow. Recall that I asked about how their work fostered human flourishing, not about gratitude. Their focus on helping other people flourish gave them rewards in return.

A number of teachers have expressed the sense that they owe debts of gratitude to those who supported and helped them along the way. One teacher told how she gathered small pictures of a dozen such people and hung those pictures on her home office wall near her desk. She wrote, "these pictures are of people to whom I consider myself in debt. But these are debts of gratitude, not of money. If I wrote an homage to the people pictured on my wall, it would be called *Big Debts, Big Gratitude*." This colleague spoke of how these pictures not only make her grateful; they also help her carry on when she feels overwhelmed with work.

Another recounted how she had written letters to all her elementary teachers to thank them for their work. She permitted me to include this portion of one of those letters.

> *Thank you for teaching me in Kindergarten; I know that it was in your classroom that I learned to read. You should know that I'm still doing that! I admit to being shocked years later when we bumped into each other at an event and you came up to me and introduced yourself to me as my Kindergarten teacher. The shock at the time was that you could remember me, and when I suggested that I must have been a trouble-maker you said, no, you remembered all your students. That inspired me. Kindergarten was 36 years ago. Please know that I have taken concrete steps since that day to remember my own students, even digging up class lists from my first years of teaching.*

The author of that paragraph, a third-grade teacher, said that writing letters to her elementary teachers changed how she viewed her own pupils. She started to see that her work with them would last well beyond the end of whatever school year she taught them and that what they learned in her class would equip them for a lifetime. She ended her email to me by noting that she had even begun to view the curriculum in new ways, one of which was her gratitude for all the people who had worked to produce the materials she used day to day.

Early in the chapter, I noted Aristotle's claim that by practicing a disposition—by living as if we already were disposed toward a given virtue—we would actually grow into that disposition. The concept of human agency may not have been part of the conversation when Aristotle wrote his *Ethics*, but he clearly was granting us the agency to grow into postures we would not naturally adopt. We can develop dispositions.

Remembering Rightly and Forgetting

All teachers have experienced wonderful days of teaching when they felt like they had come home, like they truly belonged where they were. And all teachers have experienced bumps and disappointments along the way. How does one remember those great teaching days? And how does one reframe some of those bumps and the memories of them?

These two questions drive this section of the chapter. Along with everyone else, teachers need to develop strategies and rituals to help themselves remember their great days. The demands of teaching day to day can easily drive the landmark days from memory. And along with everyone else, teachers need to develop ways to reframe and ultimately minimize the bumps and disappointments.

In his book, *The End of Memory*,[12] Miroslav Volf addresses this reframing; he calls it *remembering rightly*. Teachers who want to thrive and flourish may need to follow Volf's approach and ask some probing questions about the bumps: Am I remembering correctly what happened? Might other people have a different perspective on these events than my own? How much free rent am I giving these bumps and episodes in my brain? And how could I evict some of the people who are living rent-free in my brain?

In his book, Volf recounts being interrogated while in prison during the Balkan wars in the 1990s. Over the course of several chapters, he recounts interrogation sessions with one particular officer, and he admits, on reflection, that he likely does not remember the traumatic events accurately. Volf admits recalling that officer as an even worse human being than the officer probably was because doing so allowed him to feel more like a victim. Perhaps the lesson in Volf's book is to realize that we tend to color our memories to suit our own psychological needs. One of those needs might be to believe that none of the fault for what happened ever lies with ourselves.

Remembering rightly and reframing sometimes requires that individuals find a new language for or rename the people and events that seem so firmly lodged in their memory. One former colleague kept a sign on his home desk that read, "You are someone else's idiot colleague."[13] He reported that the sign helped him remember that some of his colleagues might view him as less a contributor to the school's life than he thought he was. In their view, an ideal photograph of the school staff would not have him in it. Of course, his own fantasy photograph of the staff had him in it, but two of his colleagues were absent.

A parallel to this kind of renaming and reframing is available in the moves made by First Nations people in several countries to restore their pre-colonial names to places of historical importance to them. For example, what were once called the Queen Charlotte Islands in British Columbia are now called Haida Gwaii. With this change, the Haida people recovered part of their history and identity. Similarly, by finding new language, teachers may be able to reappropriate some of the harder chapters of their own biographies and thereby contribute to their own flourishing.

Some teachers report that their practice of recalling their mentors and landmarks helps them remember rightly the bumps and disappointments and, ultimately, helps sustain their sense that they are at home in teaching. In our day-to-day navigation, we use landmarks. For example, spoken directions might include something along the lines of ". . . just a block north of the traffic light by IKEA." In fact, a whole genre of rather unsympathetic jokes has developed involving city people asking rural people for directions. The directions typically include such information as "take a right where Young's barn used to be and then a left at that tree." More seriously, tourists and travelers to a foreign city want to see the landmarks—the museums, galleries, parks, castles, bridges, theaters, and cathedrals for which that city is famous. Not incidentally, a hotel chain has named itself The Landmark Group, presumably to imply its solidity and staying power; it is a point from which one can orient oneself.

In Chapter 12, I mentioned that I have paddled in Canada's north. While a wilderness canoe trip is no place to get in a rush, one still wants to know where one is and one wants to measure one's progress toward a goal.

Landmarks figure centrally in my own efforts to orient myself while paddling on the Yukon River. Hootalinqua is two or three days' paddle before Carmacks. Minto has road access. Meacham Creek has a good camping spot with a bench overlooking the river. These are the Yukon River landmarks by which paddlers measure their progress. In Alberta, where I live, thousands of people travel every day between Calgary and Edmonton, stopping halfway between in the city of Red Deer for gas and food. For Albertans on Highway 2, the Tim Horton's coffee shop and Peter's Drive-In serve as landmarks, as important waypoints on this three-hour trip. For most travelers, these sources of food are more important than any of the cultural or civic landmarks in downtown Red Deer.

What are the landmarks for educators? Although we know that, all things being equal, we will continue teaching, we cannot know for certain where, what, or whom we might be teaching five or ten years hence. Mapping the future in one's teaching vocation is not as simple as paddling on the Yukon River or driving from Edmonton to Calgary. However, we can map how we arrived at the point where we are. We can reflect on our professional landmarks, and we can remember those mentors who helped us get to where we are now. Graduation from one's licensure program is an obvious landmark. Most new teachers view their permanent certificate or permanent license as a landmark ("I got a job!!"). Completing an advanced degree in education, an administrator's license, or an advanced qualification in a subject area can serve as a major turning point in the direction of an educator's work. We may not know the future, but we can look back at such landmarks as these.

What landmarks can teachers return to when they feel lost or wonder about their progress? To the coursework in their teaching degree? To their best days teaching? To some positive evaluations from former students and supervisors? To their first round of report cards and parent interviews? To the first 100 students they taught, or the first 500? To the first students they taught who have now finished university? To their first curriculum revision? In Chapter 8, I suggested that readers produce a subway map to help them remember how they got to where they are professionally. Such maps can serve as powerful navigation tools for those who might feel lost. The metaphorical stations on a personal subway map can help someone go back toward home. In a teacher's case, the meanings of *going back toward home* might range from important fiction and non-fiction books to teacher films to one's mentors and those who called that teacher into teaching.

Many in-service teachers who complete the subway map exercise I described in Chapter 8 discover that the reflection—the remembering—and the artwork required to produce the map help them rediscover some of the deep reasons they became teachers. In that chapter, I suggested several questions to guide the production of a personal subway map. Several more suggestions appear below. For the teacher wanting to remember correctly or wanting to find the way back home, producing a personal map can be a great help. To supplement the suggested questions (subway lines) listed in Chapter 8, here are eight more questions that might prove worthwhile in the production of a subway map.

- who are the people who have sustained me?
- who are the people who called me into teaching?
- what moves might I make to return to my teaching home?
- what strengths and resources do I bring to teaching?
- what are the characteristics of my desired teaching spaces?
- what are some of the great things in my own experience of education?
- what were some of the numinous moments when teaching worked perfectly?
- what were the strong currents in my own training to become a teacher?

Reflecting on questions like these on paper or on screen will bring back memories that will increase a teacher's feeling of being at home vocationally and thereby contribute to long-term flourishing. Taking the additional step of producing a map requires that one engage one's aesthetic capacities and will thereby deepen the impact of that reflection.[14] In the subway map instructions and rubric I provide to my university students, I note that transit systems often use a dashed line to show projected (future) subway lines. Many of my students will use this option, including a projected line to indicate that they envision teaching in another country for a year or completing an advanced qualification.

Envisioning such future steps should not be the preserve of education students. In-service teachers can contribute to their own nourishment by giving even half a subway line over to a projected future. In the real world, not all projected subway lines get built. And not all teachers' dreams come to fulfillment. But look at this reality from another side. No subway lines are built that are not first projected, planned, budgeted, and contracted. And very few professional ventures—or adventures—become reality unless someone envisions them first.

When I first drove the Alaska Highway from Dawson Creek, British Columbia to Whitehorse, Yukon, Canada still measured road distances using the imperial system. When the US military built that road during the Second World War, they placed wooden signposts to mark every successive mile of the 918 miles between these two places. Some Yukon locals still refer to various settlements on the Alaska Highway by their milepost number, rather than their name (1083, 1216, etc.). In the years between my first trip to the Yukon as an undergraduate wanting to work in construction and the year I am writing these words, Canada has converted to the metric system. The Alaska Highway now has kilometer posts spaced ten kilometers apart. For travelers—with or without the convenience of a navigation system in their car—these posts help mark one's progress toward one's goal. They contain information. But they also encourage.

The teaching journey has its own mileposts. My treating them in this volume arises out of my concern that the day-to-day labor of teaching—being behind on grading and preparation, for example—may cause teachers to forget about their overall progress. As do landmarks of all kinds, visible mileposts have the potential to help teachers remember that they have already come a long way on their journey: the number of years taught, the estimated number of essays graded, the number of pre-service teachers taken as interns . . . these are all mileposts. A question remains: how do we get these kinds of accomplishments into our field of vision more frequently and powerfully?

Conclusion

Dispositions alone will not get teachers from Point A—graduation from their licensure program—to Point B—their retirement party. That is, dispositions are not sufficient for thriving in this challenging profession. But they are necessary, especially for those teachers who want to leave their retirement party knowing they have flourished. Taking our focus off the retirement party for a moment, healthy dispositions are also necessary for teachers who want to leave their school building day to day and week to week knowing that they have made a difference to the students they taught that day and that week. If Aristotle is right that people can grow into dispositions by practicing them, then it is time to start practicing.

Notes

1. Michelle Hughes, *Dispositions Are a Teacher's Greatest Strength: Mindful Pedagogical Practices to Develop Self-Awareness to Flourish in the Classroom* (New York: Routledge, 2025). See also Valerie Hill-Jackson, Nicholas D. Hartlep, and Delia Stafford's, *What Makes a Star Teacher: 7 Dispositions That Support Student Learning* (Alexandria, VA: ASCD, 2019); and Arthur L. Costa and Bena Kallick's, *Dispositions: Reframing Teaching and Learning* (Thousand Oaks, CA: Corwin/Sage, 2014).
2. Aristotle, *The Nicomachean Ethics*, ed. Robert C. Bartlett and Susan D. Collins (Chicago, IL: The University of Chicago Press, 2011).
3. Parker Palmer, *To Know as We Are Known: A Spirituality of Education* (San Francisco, CA: Harper, 1983).
4. Eleanor Duckworth, *The Having of Wonderful Ideas* (New York: Teachers College Press, 2006).
5. Angela Lee Duckworth, "Grit: The Power of Passion and Perseverance" (TED Talk, 2006), https://www.youtube.com/watch?v=H14bBuluwB8. Also see *The Power of Passion and Perseverance* (New York: Simon and Schuster, 2016).
6. Honor Whiteman, "Laughter Releases 'Feel Good Hormones' to Promote Social Bonding," *Medical News Today*, June 3, 2017, https://www.medicalnewstoday.com/articles/317756.
7. For example, see Melissa Lee McCartney Matthews' doctoral dissertation, *A Funny Thing Happened on the Way to the Hippocampus: The Effects of Humor on Student Achievement and Memory Retention* (Arizona State University, 2011). The dissertation is available for free download by searching her title on Google Scholar. Chapters 4 and 5 (beginning on page 74) are especially interesting, but the literature review on pages 11–41 traces decades of research and holds big rewards for the reader.
8. Richard Sima, "Want to Feel Happier? Try Snacking on Joy," *Washington Post*, November 22, 2022, https://www.washingtonpost.com/wellness/2022/11/17/feel-happier-joy-flourishing/.
9. For example, see Elena Aguilar's, *Onward: Cultivating Emotional Resilience in Educators* (San Francisco, CA: Jossey-Bass, 2018); Ezra Stotland, *The Psychology*

of Hope (San Francisco, CA: Jossey-Bass, 1969); and Martin Seligman, *Learned Optimism: How to Change Your Mind and Your Life* (New York: Knopf, 1991).

10 Norman Cousins, *Head First: The Biology of Hope* (New York: Dutton, 1989); Jerome Groopman, *The Anatomy of Hope: How People Prevail in the Face of Illness* (New York: Random House, 1998).

11 Kerry Howells, *Gratitude in Education: A Radical View* (Rotterdam: Sense Publishers, 2011).

12 Miroslav Volf, *The End of Memory: Remembering Rightly in a Violent World* (Grand Rapids, MI: Eerdmans, 2006).

13 The actual language of that sign was rather earthier than reported here.

14 I write in my journal daily and I redraw my own map every couple of years, usually on a full-day retreat. Doing so helps me remember how I got to this point and allows me to project where I might go and what I might do next. Because the maps are never the same, the exercise also helps me see my own progress on my journey as an educator.

15 Staying Focused on the Journey

Throughout *How Good Teachers Thrive*, I have made clear my assumption that most people who become teachers do so out of deep, humanistic ideals. They want to see children flourish. They want to make the world a better place. With such humanistic goals in view, some teachers consider the improvement of their school's culture to be a natural place to invest some of their energy. It makes perfect sense; students learn more in safe and welcoming schools than they do in unsafe and unwelcoming schools. Why would a teacher with humanistic ideals not work to improve school culture?

In this brief chapter, I will argue that teachers should focus primarily on their own students and their own classroom program and only secondarily on changing their school's culture. Although school culture matters a great deal, individual teachers typically cannot change it to the degree they might wish and in proportion to the energy they might end up investing. Borrowing a concept from geology, the angle of repose, I argue here that schools tend to become the way they are for deep-rooted reasons and that individual classroom teachers' chances of significantly changing a school's climate or culture are slim and could possibly distract them from what should be their main focus: their own classroom. The question remains then: How do teachers retain their focus on their own classroom program and their own students' learning?

The Angle of Repose

A quick search of the phrase *angle of repose* will turn up records related to both geology and literature. The geological concept is simple: over time, any pile of sand, gravel, or soil will respond to gravity, weather, shape, and surface friction by settling at its angle of repose—the angle at which it will no longer settle further toward flatness. Large boulders and broken concrete slabs used to protect a pier or seawall will barely settle at all, likely staying in place for decades. A pile of refined white sugar will spread across a flat kitchen counter and find its angle of repose in seconds. Garden soil will take more time and will be affected by rainfall. When we hear of tragedies involving excavation sites caving in and trapping construction workers, or of a sandy cliff giving way and smothering children at a beach, we likely do not consider the geological concept of the angle of repose. Yet, those tragedies happen because this principle is always at work.

As I noted, an online search of the phrase *angle of repose* will likely produce some records related not only to geology but also to literature, specifically to Wallace Stegner's 1971 novel, *Angle of Repose*.[1] In this novel, Stegner explores the long marriage of his protagonists, concluding that married couples reach a kind of agreement or way of being together; they come to terms with each other. Indeed, one could argue that most people achieve a way of being in— of coming to terms with—the world in which they find themselves. To refer to metaphors again, Stegner created this metaphor decades ago and, here, I lift it from his novel into educational contexts.

As far as schools are concerned, the occupants of all but newly opened buildings have already found their angle of repose. In having done so, they differ little from those in government departments, business offices, orchestras, sports teams, and myriad other organizations and gathering places. Sociologists remind us that social groups establish the traditions they do for the simple reason that few of us could cope with the alternative: *anomie,* the Greek word for the absence of law, a situation without rules. Out of psychological need, groups and whole cultures establish formal and informal rules, and their members come to accept the truth of Tevye's claim in *Fiddler on the Roof,*[2] that to a significant degree most people are ruled by tradition, that certain things always happen in certain ways.

The Angle of Repose in Schools

Back to the metaphor, schools—headed by the principal—find their angle of repose; they develop their traditions and put routine practices in place. As teachers, students, and administrative staff inhabit their schools over time, they conform to these traditions and practices. And as they inhabit, they inhibit. They inhibit some practices and accept or promote others. For more than a century, sociologists have studied conformity and deviance, noting how institutions socialize their members. Anthropologists study the same processes in whole cultures. Of course, not everyone in an institution or culture accepts the prescribed socialization. Both sociologists and anthropologists also study how groups attempt to bring deviants,[3] those members who deviate from the group norms, back into line.

A teacher colleague told me about the group norms in a secondary school she had worked in. In this school, the same teacher always moved the adjournment of the monthly staff meeting. When he decided the meeting was done, he would simply make the motion to end it, month after month, year after year, outlasting the tenure of several principals. When my colleague, new to her building, asked another colleague why this continuously happened, he actually quoted Tevye—it was simply the tradition. In fact, this reply to my colleague's query was so much like Tevye's song in *Fiddler* that one wonders if Tevye was a sociologist at heart. This discussion-stifling, meeting-ending practice illustrates how a group of people—in this case, a teaching staff of seventy—achieve and accept an angle of repose.

As it happens, the principal at the school in that anecdote was relatively new to the building. According to my informant, that principal was attempting to change the culture of that school. But he encountered strong resistance from a coterie of teachers—all from one department—who had exercised their power for more than a decade before his arrival. And the meeting-ending staff member was a member of this small but powerful group. Presumably, if this principal could read all the 25,000 records that an online search of the string *changing school culture* would yield, he might have found ways to budge this obstacle to his attempt to build a more collaborative school culture. But this story precedes the internet and so, in some important ways, he was on his own.

To continue with this illustration, the teacher who ended staff meetings almost certainly did not serve the best interests of his school. If school staff meetings ought to be venues for professional educators to discuss important ideas and policies, then granting a cynical, late career teacher the power to end discussion month by month whenever he wishes is the equivalent of voting, month by month, for institutional mediocrity. If excellence in a school building requires a politics of excellence, then permitting mediocrity must require a politics of mediocrity, presumably based on the ideas of the (fictional) ancient philosopher, Mediocrates. And many schools—and many other work settings—have such politics firmly in place. However, no one should be shocked.

Shirley Jackson's short story, "The Lottery,"[4] illustrates in fiction what introductory sociology textbooks have always claimed: that some traditions continue for the most insane reasons. So what should teachers do who want to flourish but who work in buildings where less-than-great cultures are already in place? In the words of one educator in his last decade of teaching, "There was nothing I could do to build a school except do a good job in the classroom and work with my students. The best thing I could do was a good job of teaching."[5] Like that teacher, most teachers who have flourished to the end of their careers in such schools have tended to focus on their classroom work and their own students rather than on changing the culture of their school buildings. The lesson to draw from both the clever saying that culture eats strategy for breakfast[6] and the quotation from this interviewee is obvious and one that culture may have difficulty eating: teachers who flourish typically do not focus on changing their school's culture.

Alternatively, the angle of repose can represent sanity and excellence. One (non-fictional) elementary school principal, at afternoon dismissal, stands in the main school hallway and greets over 400 elementary students—by name—as they leave her building. On the day of my visit to that school, I witnessed this happy afternoon parade. She frequently told one of her students to enjoy the evening, to greet an older sibling who used to attend that school, to take care, or to remember to get their homework done that night. Furthermore, this same principal visited every classroom in that school every instructional day of the entire school year.

This combination of both warmth and high professionalism saturated the routines and practices of that school, illustrating in spades that the angle of repose need not represent cynicism and laziness. Note, however, that this story involves the work not of a classroom teacher but that of a principal who used her personality and the authority of her office to establish those norms. Because of this leader and the environment she created, children wanted to be at that school, and teachers from that school district applied to work there. Such excellence requires a politics—how authority, communication, relationships, and responsibilities are viewed—in the same way that mediocrity does.

Can a classroom teacher create the same kind of culture in one room? Can a teacher create a politics of excellence in a single classroom? Of course. Will students want to be in the classes taught by such a teacher? Of course. Just as the angle of repose in a whole building represents and fosters excellence, so can the angle of repose in individual classrooms.

The possibility that the angle of repose could be renegotiated by a newly arrived principal, by individual teachers, or by groups of teachers varies from school to school. For the purposes of this chapter, consider that schools have quite firmly in place both their culture and their methods of reinforcing and maintaining that culture. That is, as cultures in general, school cultures are powerful.

The illustration about moving adjournment at a school staff meeting is but one example of the angle of repose in an educational setting. One could analyze a school or an individual classroom on dozens of dimensions and consistently discover the set ways in which a school, teacher, or classroom has, in effect, come to function. Consider these examples:

- Inquiry-based learning versus teacher-centered instruction
- Varied learning strategies versus the same strategies every day
- Orderly classroom versus chaotic classroom
- Noisier versus quieter
- Hierarchical authority versus shared authority
- Joy in learning versus learning is a drag
- Democratic decision-making versus top-down decision-making
- Principal rarely visits classrooms versus principal visits regularly
- Students take pride in their school versus lack of school pride
- Striving for excellence versus good enough is good enough

Among teachers themselves, one can also see a range of postures:

- Volunteerism versus I do nothing I'm not paid to do
- Vocational vitality versus vocational resignation and cynicism
- Warm and relational versus coldly professional
- Ongoing professional growth versus professional stagnation
- Collegiality among staff versus closed doors (metaphorically or literally)

These two sets of examples both illustrate that an angle of repose can represent excellence or mediocrity, engagement or disengagement, and, presumably, many points between the pairs of views and practices listed. They illustrate that teachers follow varied teaching philosophies, use different teaching styles, and build different kinds of classroom cultures.

The Angle of Repose in Classrooms: Staying Focused

Given the realities—positive and negative—of the kinds of cultures that those who work in schools develop, how do teachers who want to thrive stay focused on their classroom program and thereby flourish in their profession? Several earlier chapters contain suggestions about staying focused, and so does the next chapter. But briefly, here are several ideas.

As a baseline for retaining a focus on their classroom, teachers must have the materials related to the core cycle of their basic teaching program organized so they neither feel behind nor lose time looking for information. That is, staying on top of classroom routines and administration is essential to staying focused. A few examples of such routines are tracking materials on loan to students, storage of EpiPens, keeping records of phone calls and emails related to students' work, and storage of standing substitute teacher plans. Either these matters can live rent-free (and make a mess) in a teacher's head, or that teacher can develop systems so that they stay in the appropriate places. Such systems allow teachers to focus on the main point of their work: teaching their students.

Launching creative instructional initiatives can help classroom teachers focus on their classroom instead of on their school because such initiatives require attention. For example, it would take energy and focus for a teacher to follow the suggestion in Chapter 9 and read about Building 20 at MIT or Lockheed's Skunk Works and work with students to construct a classroom operating more like one of those two settings. And that focus would be on one's own classroom, not on the school building.

Likewise, purposely seeking new ways to attend to metacognition, differentiation, trauma-informed practice, or flow would all tend to focus a teacher's energy on the classroom instead of on the school. Teachers who do launch initiatives such as these sometimes find that their efforts actually bring about a change in school culture, albeit an incremental change. A whole school building may feel the ripple effects from one classroom's culture. Such efforts in one classroom give students more good reasons to come to that classroom and, perhaps, another reason to come to school. Teachers whose classroom cultures rippled outward in that way would be happy, but my point here is that their goal was to execute their own programs and work with their own students, not to transform their schools.

Most teachers know the phrase *school within a school* and know that it usually means that more than one administrative structure is created inside a larger school building. On rare occasions, a single classroom is recognized administratively as a school within a school. But a single classroom can become a school within a school culturally, and many teachers who have flourished into late career have created such cultures. In doing so, they may not have changed their school's culture in substantial ways, but they have significantly changed the culture in one space and thereby, albeit slightly, the angle of repose of their whole building.

Conclusion

My appeal to you, my teacher colleagues, is therefore to direct your efforts for change toward your students' reading levels, their understanding of mathematics, their ability to be transported into the secondary worlds created by fiction authors, their skill at crafting questions that will lead to deep learning, their ability to reflect and to predict, their skill in using KWL sheets (Know, Would like to know, Learned) effectively, their metacognitive skills, and their ability to wonder at all the amazing things in the world they live in. Focus on those things instead of school culture, and not only will you become a happier and more fulfilled teacher, but your students will be more exceptional people on the day they leave you than they were on the day they arrived. And that would be a good thing. And maybe, just maybe, your efforts in your own classroom with your own students will produce some change in the culture of the school you work in. Whether your school's culture changes or not, your having focused will lead to your own flourishing.

Notes

1 (New York: Vintage Books, 1971). This treatment of the angle of repose is adapted from a book chapter called "The Angle of Repose, or Don't Try to Change the World During Your Placement," in *So, You Have a Teaching Practicum*, which, with eight undergraduate education students, I published on Amazon in 2019. Those interested in reading more about the concept should start with the Wikipedia article on the angle of repose at https://en.wikipedia.org/wiki/Angle_of_repose.

2 Norman Jewison, director (Mirisch; Cartier, 1971).

3 The word originally denoted only deviance from social norms; it accrued the negative connotations it now carries over the decades since.

4 First published in *The New Yorker* on June 26, 1948.

5 From an interview with a teacher who wishes to remain anonymous.

6 A search of the phrase *culture eats strategy for breakfast* will yield dozens of book titles and thousands of records related to changing workplace cultures. The phrase is variously attributed, with many crediting management guru Peter Drucker.

16 Nurturing the Teacher's Core

How can teachers attend to the core of their being so they do not burn out and become cynical? How do they take care of their own teaching souls so that they thrive and flourish, not just survive? How do they frame their daily work so it gives them joy? This book has been driven by these questions and others much like them. We have approached the questions from many angles, and my hope has remained that all my readers will have found ideas here that will help them frame their vocation in new and life-giving ways.

By now, the general answer to the questions above is obvious: teachers who thrive in the final years of their working life do so in part because they have addressed two broad areas essential to flourishing. First, they have built a classroom climate in which they like to work and their students like to learn. Within that classroom, they have executed their instructional program competently and with clear purpose. Second, they have taken steps to nurture their core.

This final chapter focuses on how teachers can nurture their core, their interior. Teacher colleagues who have taught from kindergarten to university have all contributed to my thinking about this matter of nurturing the teacher's interior being. They have used, relied on, and suggested many of the strategies and approaches described in this chapter.

Besides the educators who have shared their approaches with me personally, others have influenced me from a distance. Parker Palmer has served as a powerful influence on my own framing of the question of the teacher's interior. When I first read about his teaching style, I secured permission from my academic dean to ask Palmer to come to the college where I was then teaching and lead professional development sessions for our faculty. He came for two days and, in the words of one colleague, gave the best two days of professional development we had ever had. I read all his books, reviewed several in print, and used *The Courage to Teach*[1] as a course text in university courses for many years.

Readers cannot have missed some of my other influences, among them Mihaly Csikszentmihalyi and his work on flow, Max van Manen and his work on teacher tact, Christopher Alexander and his work on design, Kelly Johnson and his work at the Lockheed Skunk Works, and Erik Erikson's work on the developmental tasks we face at different ages. Along with many others, these people have shaped my thinking about flourishing as a teacher.

The book closes with this chapter, based on my reading and on conversations with dozens of colleagues who have flourished until the day of their retirement party. In what follows, I offer four clusters of suggestions about how good teachers thrive. The first suggestions are grouped under the self-explanatory heading "Inside the School." Following that group, I treat suggested practices and steps teachers can take outside their schools. The third cluster, "Out of the Ordinary," is not extensive but does contain some radical suggestions. The last section deals with Reflection Practices that many educators follow to sustain their own interior lives while carrying on with the complex, intense, and sometimes frustrating work of teaching.

Inside the School

Some of the following suggestions have already appeared in earlier chapters of this book. Some appear for the first time here. This four-part chapter starts inside the school because one of the necessary conditions for flourishing is that one has one's classroom program working well. The first half of this book's title was not incidental: good teachers thrive. Bad teachers do not thrive. Among other things, good teaching implies professional execution of a classroom program.

The To-Do List Refined

A colleague who talked about her feeling of being overwhelmed by her work inbox reported that each day she identifies the one most important thing on her to-do list. When she gets that one thing done, she identifies the next most important thing. She reports that this simple strategy has a calming effect on her and helps her worry less about the length of her to-do list.

The Philosophy of Education Statement

Recall the suggestion in Chapter 6 that teachers write out a brief philosophy of education statement for their classroom wall. Such a statement can have a clarifying effect on the teacher's thinking, especially on those days when teaching seems overwhelming. Even though you might not be able to read it from anywhere in the room, you will be able to see it and, if you have kept it short, you will know what it says. If it is hanging near a doorway where students can see it, it may also lead to some conversations with them about why you went into teaching and what you hope to accomplish day by day in your classes; such conversations build community and increase the likelihood that your students will become your allies.

Mastering the Threshold Tasks of Teaching

Practicing self-care is essential to long-term flourishing in this profession, and some of the simplest practices give life well beyond the required investment. The mastery of threshold tasks may seem like review to some readers, but teachers who stay on top of their planning and preparation, grading, and record-keeping are more likely to flourish. First, the teacher who stays caught up with those daily tasks does not have to listen to that nagging interior voice about what needs to get done. Second, teachers who stay caught up have more time for other life-giving activities and for foci outside their school building.

Get Ambitious

At some point, most teachers learned in an English literature course that Lady Macbeth's kind of ambition was bad. But all ambition is not bad; it is what gets teachers to work day after day. And it is not wrong to plan a growth trajectory and work toward it. In fact, it is essential.

Several ambitious suggestions come to mind, all meant to nurture the teacher's person. Some teachers suggest changing 10–15 percent of your course content per year, even if a new curriculum mandate does not require that you do so. Such revisions might include new lessons, new assignments in several units, or even one completely revised unit annually. A related possibility is to launch a metacognitive layer in one class. Give your students the plain English definition of metacognition—thinking about thinking—and ask them to engage in it with you for a defined number of weeks. At the end of the trial, discuss as a class what effects it had on their approach to the curriculum materials and their learning. One assumes that such changes would enhance student learning, but my interest here is in forcing the development of new neural pathways for teachers and thereby nourishing those teachers' sense of vocation.

Several colleagues have suggested that teachers who want to thrive start a professional learning community with grade-level or subject-area colleagues. Start simply, reflecting on how each other is approaching this or that topic or a particular learning objective. Some PLCs bring lesson plans and ask their colleagues, "How would you teach this?" Related to the idea of a PLC, start some action research alone or with a colleague, examining just one aspect of one of the puzzles in your teaching program, making some changes, and evaluating the results in assessment, personal satisfaction, and student anecdotal reports. Both these suggestions would likely lead to improved instruction, but they also would force those involved to do new thinking, one of the keys to long-term flourishing.

Almost without exception, teachers who take interns from local education licensure programs report learning from the pre-service teachers who come to their classrooms. One colleague worded it bluntly: "I got more than I gave." A number of colleagues report learning new instructional strategies from their interns who, fresh from their university classes, come wanting to try out some of the latest approaches they have learned from their professors and classmates. Colleagues also report being forced to rethink some of the fundamentals of instruction as they meet with their interns and university supervisors to debrief their interns' successes and failures. Again, the brain needs to form new pathways. Taking pre-service teachers in one's classroom typically leads to long-term flourishing.

The last suggestion in this section of the chapter relates to collegial conversation, and it serves as the segue to the following section on things teachers can do outside their school building to strengthen and nourish their sense of vocation. Recall again—fat chance you could forget—that teaching is complex, intense, and sometimes frustrating. With their work characterized by those three qualities, teachers need challenging intellectual conversation with peers. Such conversations sometimes happen inside one's school building, but those conversations can easily slip from larger questions of education into comments about specific students or building policies. Some colleagues report finding peers in their building with whom they can talk about their grand vision, but it's more likely that such colleagues teach at another school or even work in some other profession. The conversations teachers need don't just happen; teachers need to initiate the conversations they want.

Outside the School

Reading

Teachers need intellectual food that moves them out of their classroom work, and those who want to thrive long term keep their brains alive by reading (obviously among other things). Recall that some of those who contributed to Chapter 10 made reference to their reading. Other teachers report the many benefits of reading fiction, professional books, and non-fiction on topics other than education. They report listening to audiobooks and podcasts during their commute. The point is to keep the brain active.

Many teachers start or become members of a book club or reading group. Typically, these groups take one of two forms. The more common form has all the members of the group reading the same book for a month and then gathering to discuss it. One colleague reports being in a group that agrees on a theme for the next month; when they gather, members each report on whatever book they read that month.

Assemble Your Team

Teachers may survive in some minimal way, but they will not flourish unless they find supports throughout their teaching careers. Chapter 13 included an extended argument to this effect. One's friends and loved ones are important sources of support, and I include them here as obvious and important relationships. Besides one's friends and family, most teachers report to a supervisor, and most have supportive colleagues in the same building or at a distance. Many teachers are members of a professional learning community or teacher book club, and many are assigned mentors in the first years of their careers. At various points in their careers, many more teachers seek mentors even when they are not assigned one. Here, I remind but will not repeat in detail what I wrote in Chapter 13: even with all the supportive people you may already have around you, assemble a team.

Social Interaction

The research on aging and longevity is clear: along with physical exercise and intellectual stimulation, social interaction is a key to a long and good life. My readers need no explanation of what I mean here. If, like a lot of educators, arranging for a meal or a night out with friends feels like a challenge when the time comes, then plan in advance. Go online now and book those tickets. Some teachers report that season tickets with friends lead to their actually going out instead of staying home on a weekend night, even after a tiring week at work.

Professional Opportunities

Several kinds of professional opportunities are available outside school buildings, and teachers who take advantage of these almost universally report that such involvements are worth the effort. Examples abound. Present a workshop session at a professional day in your school district or at a teacher convention. This could be a solo workshop or one you develop with a colleague, even one from another school. Get involved in a district, state, or provincial body related to your subject area. Possible involvements include grading standardized essay exams, serving on curriculum committees, reviewing potential textbooks, and pilot-teaching textbooks.

Out of the Ordinary

Take a Once-in-a-Lifetime Trip

With complete seriousness, I suggest taking a once-in-a-lifetime trip. Take a trip you will look back on fondly for years to come and remember that it was good to do. You need not break the budget to do this. Such trips might be available quite close to home but could become once-in-a-lifetime because you walked, or cycled, or paddled instead of driving. Suggesting those alternative means of transport reveals something important about such trips: the geographic endpoint is only part of the fun; how one gets there can be part of what makes it once-in-a-lifetime.

In one recent education class, I suggested to my students that they should consider coming with me to Canada's north, where we would paddle on the Teslin and Yukon Rivers. One student came up to me immediately after class and said, "I'm in." She and her mother—both teachers by then—came a year later and we paddled for a week in the Yukon wilderness. Both still say that for them it truly was a once-in-a-lifetime trip, one that they will never forget. The sub-section ends with language that reads like it's only a suggestion, but I want to make it more urgent than that; start planning that trip.

Start an Advanced Degree

Consistently, teachers who work regularly toward advanced qualifications or who start an advanced degree while teaching full-time report that doing so stretched and thereby benefited their brains. Yes, they may have learned new teaching strategies or engaged in interesting research. Or they may have learned about some of the intricacies of educational administration. But for many, the fact that they had the opportunity—or were compelled by program requirements—simply to learn at all is what they found so enriching, despite how it affected their weekly schedules during the school year as well as their summers when their cohorts met face to face for several weeks.

Staff-room conversations about advanced degrees often shift toward a calculation of tuition costs versus increased salary. In such conversations, one sometimes hears, "It doesn't make economic sense." Not to be rude about staff-room conversations, but intellectual health must have some value beyond a salary increase to someone who spends most of every day doing the hard work of teaching.

Andrea Nelson, a classroom teacher in Oregon, completed her doctoral degree with no ambitions to become a school administrator or to get a position in her school district's central office. She responded with the words below in answer to my request that she tell my readers what her doctorate in education meant to her teaching.

> My time as a doctoral student at George Fox University was integral to my tenure as a classroom teacher. I began the program early in my career, but far enough into it to know that I needed a challenge or a change every few years to keep me engaged and content in the classroom. The program opened the door to explore my academic interests, travel and teach abroad, and teach as an adjunct [at a university] for several years after graduating. It also taught me new ways of looking at education, broadening my perspective on the purpose of education. and helping me define my educational philosophy.

Inasmuch as everyone does not need a doctorate, Andrea's story may also qualify as "out of the ordinary." Still, everyone needs to keep their brain alive, and despite the work and likely financial commitment, an advanced degree is guaranteed to broaden an educator's perspective on the daily work of teaching. Because most master's and doctoral programs in education use a cohort model, one will also meet new colleagues from other settings than one's own, an enriching experience in itself.

Try Writing for Publication

Teachers' association magazines need content, some of which comes month by month from the keyboards of classroom teachers. The question of whether or not your teacher association's magazine pays or does not pay for such content is simply a distraction. The key here for anyone wanting to thrive long term is that writing for publication stretches the brain.

Another possible destination for writing done by classroom teachers is the book review section of academic journals. Specialized journals are published related to every subject in the K-12 curriculum. Although those journals do not pay for content, they still need content. The book review editors of some academic journals and subject-area journals publish lists of recent books they would like to see reviewed. Most of them also accept suggestions from reviewers who have a specific title in mind. Although reviewers are not paid for their content, they do get a free copy of the book they review. The prospect of writing such a review might seem sobering for someone who has never written for publication, but the reward of stimulating the brain cells makes the work more worthwhile than the two additional lines on one's résumé. Reviewing is a distinct and health-giving change from the hard, daily work of teaching.

Go on a Service-Learning Trip

Teaching colleagues in dozens of countries would gladly attend professional development sessions offered by you and some colleagues if you were willing to travel to their country during one of their school breaks. Among the many such volunteers I have spoken to, I have not met anyone who participated in such a trip and regretted doing so. Many teachers who participate in such projects come back surprised at how much they learned from their colleagues, most of whom work with far fewer material and instructional resources. Teacher volunteers learn, for example, that teachers in other countries face many of the same challenges teachers at home face, challenges related to classroom resources and to the levels of assistance available for students with special needs.

To everyone contemplating or about to leave on such a trip, I recommend reading Ivan Illich's essay, "To Hell with Good Intentions" and watching a short video on YouTube called *Saving Africa: Who Wants to be a Volunteer?*[2] Despite making seven trips to work with colleagues in Kenya, I did not save Africa, but working with teachers there dramatically transformed my own understanding of my work as a secondary teacher and professor in Canada. And I believe that kind of transformation is available to anyone willing to commit to the necessary preparation and sheer grunt work of getting involved in such a project.

Explore New Educational Metaphors

Chapter 7 included brief descriptions of five atypical educational metaphors. Working with a new metaphor would require new patterns of thinking and would lead to new patterns of instruction. Read Chapter 7 again and ask how working even one of those metaphors into your classroom program would change your work.

Practicing Reflection

Reflection has already appeared at several points in this book, and the first items appearing below are reminders of suggestions made in earlier chapters. But following those, I present several additional suggestions for reflection and approaches to reflection meant to support educators' efforts to thrive throughout their careers.

Take a Retreat

Most teachers who thrive to the end of their careers regularly step back from their teaching work and go on retreat. Some prefer to go to a retreat center in a natural setting. Others need only a few hours away from their responsibilities and their computer. The commonality here is that these educators get away from the immediate demands of work and family and take time to reflect on the larger questions of their work and their lives.

Several lists of questions that could guide a retreat appear in the book, and a summary of the directions of those will suffice here. Those questions relate to mentors, to those who called us into teaching, and to the days and forces that diminish or sustain our hearts for teaching. I asked about the resources we bring to teaching and the factors that perhaps limit our use of those resources for maximum benefit to our students and ourselves. I also asked about the surprises our students may have given us. At two points, I recommended that my readers take the time to produce a subway map as a graphic way to represent the answers to some of these reflective questions.

Educational Ideals

Recall the discussion of classroom ideals in Chapter 6. Compiling a list of a teacher's educational ideals and revisiting it periodically will help that teacher go back to work day after day.

The Most Rejuvenating Things You Do

What are the most rejuvenating things you do? Answers to the question will range across working in the shop, sewing and weaving, swimming, walking, listening to music, making music, running, having coffee with friends, painting, reading, tinkering, and so on. Some teachers find that even composing such a list has a restorative effect inasmuch as it reminds them that there is life outside teaching. Of course, a bigger challenge than listing those things that rejuvenate us is actually getting to them. I have no interest in inducing guilt in my readers at this point, but I will ask this: would it work for you to ask someone else to encourage you to actually to get to those restoring and rejuvenating activities?

You 5.0 or 8.0 or . . .

One colleague describes taking a weekend-long retreat every couple of years and asking what her next reinvention might look like. Using the language of software, she described her most recent retreat as Sandra 8.0 (not her real name). She reviewed the chapters of her life . . . childhood and youth, undergraduate degree and licensure degree, first teaching job, and so on up to her current position, which she called Sandra 7.0. Using software language again, she asked what features she would like to build into Sandra 8.0. She reflected on both her professional work and her personal life, obviously including friends and family but also such matters as redesigning her garden and re-reading several books she had read years before. She spent a couple of hours reflecting on her work with several interns she had recently hosted from a local university, and she asked how she could revise her approach to serving as a cooperating teacher.

That brief paragraph does not catch the enthusiasm with which she reported how exciting it was actually to think about reinventing herself again. Knowing her report would appear in print, she did add this one rather blunt bit of advice for readers: If you're at that point in your life and career that you feel you must choose between a nineteen-year-old, a sports car, or re-envisioning your life and work, take the retreat.

Being Alive in the Larger World

My readers know how easy it is to get pulled so deeply into school life that you lose a measure of contact with the world outside of school. Reflecting on this tendency can help break the pattern and lead to flourishing. Write out what principles you will try to follow and what patterns you will try to build into your life so you do not get swallowed whole by work. Ask people close to you to remind you of those commitments until you have developed new thought patterns and work patterns.

Your Ten Best Days

List the ten best days of your life.[3] Listing the ten best days of one's life typically produces gratitude and satisfaction. A list of your ten best days will possibly include days on holidays, meals in fine restaurants, accomplishments in various fields, time with friends, and any number of other activities. Another form of this list would be to list your ten best days teaching. Recall those memorable days when everything worked well and students' eyes shone. Several colleagues who have kept this practice for over a decade or two report that they eventually had to change the list to fifteen days and then twenty. As the number of days increased, so did their sense of gratitude.

Keeping a Journal

Those who keep journals report a great variety of benefits, one of which is that the act of writing itself aids memory. Many of my readers already keep journals. I recommend doing so to the rest. Some might say, "But I'm just not the journaling type." Aristotle suggests giving it a try anyway; after all, attitudes change when people change their practices.

The Pictures on the Wall

In Chapter 14, I mentioned a colleague who gathered pictures of some of the people who influenced who she became and to whom she believed she owed debts of gratitude. Some of the people in her collection were family, friends, and colleagues. Others were writers and thinkers she had never met. Though she does not teach in a Montessori classroom, she said she sometimes looks up at her picture of Maria Montessori and asks, "What would Maria do?" Determining which characters in the screenplay of your life would warrant inclusion on your wall will likely lead to gratitude and to a deeper sense that you are growing not only in years but in depth.

Conclusion

This chapter and the book end together. Repeatedly, I have noted that, as teachers we do hard work. And I have repeatedly claimed that doing so need not wear us out or make us cynical. In the introduction, I noted that teachers—like most people in humanistic professions—tend to work with a grand vision in mind; that we go to work day after day because we want the world to be a better place. And we hope that our efforts help move the world in that direction. I also argued that grand visions are realized in the nitty-gritty of life. In the case of educators, that nitty-gritty involves spending most of our days in classrooms with students.

This book is not the first word on that tension between vision and task, and it will not be the last. But my hope for my readers is that in this book you will have found life-giving ways to rethink and reframe your work. Barring highly unusual circumstances, I will not be in attendance at your retirement tea. But if I were to turn up there, I hope that the broad smiles I would see on your face would have their origins in your having flourished for decades in that noble work to which you were called. Indeed, teachers' work is part of a grand thing, and you will have been part of that.

Notes

1 Parker Palmer, *The Courage to Teach: Exploring the Inner Landscape of a Teacher's Life* (San Francisco, CA: Jossey-Bass, 1998).
2 Ivan Illich, "To Hell with Good Intentions," http://www.ciasp.ca/CIASPhistory/IllichCIASPspeech.htm. Also see "Who Wants to be a Volunteer?" (Oslo: Norwegian Students and Academics' International Assistance Fund, 2014), https://www.youtube.com/watch?v=ymcflrj_rRc.
3 This idea originated with Sam Keen, *Fire in the Belly: On Being a Man* (Toronto: Bantam, 1991).

Bibliography

Aguilar, Elena. *Onward: Cultivating Emotional Resilience in Educators.* San Francisco, CA: Jossey-Bass, 2018.

Alexander, Christopher. *The Timeless Way of Building.* New York: Oxford University Press, 1979.

Alexander, Christopher; Ishikawa, Sara; Silverstein, Murray; Jacobson, Max; Fiksdahl-King, Ingrid; and Shlomo, Angel. *A Pattern Language: Towns, Buildings, Construction.* New York: Oxford University Press, 1977.

Aristotle. *The Nicomachean Ethics.* Edited by Robert C. Bartlett and Susan D. Collins. Chicago, IL: The University of Chicago Press, 2011.

Ayers, William. "A Teacher Ain't Nothin' but a Hero: Teachers and Teaching in Film." In *Images of Schoolteachers in America*, 2nd ed., edited by Pamela Boliton Joseph and Gail E. Burnaford, 201–9. Mahwah, NJ: Lawrence Erlbaum, 2001.

Badley, Ken. *Curriculum Planning with Design Language: Building Elegant Courses and Units.* New York: Routledge, 2018.

Badley, Ken. *Engaging College and University Students: Effective Instructional Strategies.* New York: Routledge, 2022.

Badley, Ken, ed. *So, You Have a Teaching Practicum.* Amazon Direct, 2019. Independently published.

Badley, Ken, and Patrick, Margaretta, eds. *The Complexities of Authority in the Classroom: Fostering Democracy for Student Learning.* New York: Routledge, 2022.

Bandura, Albert. *Self-Efficacy: The Exercise of Control.* New York: Freeman, 1997.

Bandura, Albert. "Self-Efficacy: Toward a Unifying Theory of Behavioral Change." *The Psychological Review* 84 (1977): 191–215.

Berger, Peter. *Invitation to Sociology.* New York: Doubleday, 1967.

Borgmann, Albert. *Crossing the Postmodern Divide.* Chicago, IL: The University of Chicago Press, 1990.

Buber, Martin. *Between Man and Man.* New York: Macmillan, 1965.

Bulman, Robert C. *Hollywood Goes to High School: Cinema, Schools and American Culture*. New York, NY: Worth, 2005.

Bunyan, John. *Pilgrim's Progress*. London: Nathaniel Ponder, 1677, 1684.

Clavell, James, director. *To Sir with Love*. Los Angeles, CA: Columbia Pictures, 1967.

Cockburn, Bruce. *Wondering Where the Lions Are*. Toronto: True North Records, 1979.

Code, Lorraine. *What Can She Know?: Feminist Theory and the Construction of Knowledge*. Ithaca, NY: Cornell University Press, 1991.

Coe, David Allen. "*Take This Job and Shove It*" (song sung by Johnny Paycheck). Los Angeles, CA: Columbia Recording Studios, 1977.

Corbley, Andy. "How a High-School Class Solved Six Murders and Identified the Bible Belt Strangler." *Good News Network*, May 29, 2024. https://www.goodnewsnetwork.org/how-a-us-high-school-class-solved-six-murders-and-identified-the-bible-belt-strangler/.

Costa, Arthur L.; and Kallick, Bena. *Dispositions: Reframing Teaching and Learning*. Thousand Oaks, CA: Corwin/Sage, 2014.

Cousins, Norman. *Head First: The Biology of Hope*. New York: Dutton, 1989.

Csikszentmihalyi, Mihalyi. *Flow: The Psychology of Optimal Experience*. New York: Harper and Row, 1990.

Danckert, James; and Eastwood, John. *Out of My Skull: The Psychology of Boredom*. Cambridge, MA: Harvard University Press, 2020.

Danielson, Charlotte. *The Framework for Teaching: Evaluation Instrument*. Princeton, NJ: The Danielson Group, 2014.

Danielson, Charlotte, with Thomas L. McGreal. *Teacher Evaluation to Enhance Professional Practice*. Alexandria, VA: ACSD, 2000.

Dee, Amy; and Badley, Ken. "Creating an Educational Ethos where Innovation and Accountability Flourish: A New Model for Transparency in Educational Organizations." *The International Journal of Educational Leadership Preparation* 5, no. 4 (October–December 2010). https://digitalcommons.georgefox.edu/soe_faculty/52/.

Dewey, John. *Experience and Education*. New York: Macmillan, 1938.

Dewey, John. *The Child and the Curriculum*. Chicago, IL: The University of Chicago Press, 1902.

Dilthey, Wilhelm. *Wilhelm Dilthey: Selected Works, Volume VI, Ethical and Worldview Philosophy*. Edited by Rudolf A. Makkreel and Frithjof Rodi. Princeton, NJ: Princeton University Press, 2019.

Duckworth, Angela. *Grit: The Power of Passion and Perseverance*. New York: Simon and Schuster, 2016.

Duckworth, Eleanor. *The Having of Wonderful Ideas and Other Essays on Teaching and Learning.* New York: Teachers College Press, 2006.

Einhorn, Randall; Celotta, Jennifer; Karas, Jaime Eliezer; Sohn, Matt; Davani, Shahrzad; Tan, Justin; Kosar, Melissa; Scanlon, Claire; Whittingham, Ken; Cherry, Matthew A.; Davis, Dime; Malik, Geeta; Edelson, Richie; Ghalayini, Razan; and Soni, Karan, directors. *Abbott Elementary. 2021-2024.* Los Angeles, CA: Warner Brothers, 2021.

Eisner, Elliot. "From Episteme to Phronesis to Artistry in the Study and Improvement of Teaching." *Teaching and Teacher Education* 18, no. 4 (May 2002): 375–85.

Erikson, Erik. *Identity and the Life Cycle.* New York: W. W. Norton, 1994.

Erikson, Erik. *Adulthood.* New York: W. W. Norton, 1978.

Erikson, Erik; and Erikson, Joan Mowat. *The Life Cycle Completed.* New York: W. W. Norton, 1998.

Estevez, Emilio, director. *The Way.* Los Angeles, CA: Elixir Films; Filmax; Icon Entertainment, 2010.

Etzioni, Amitai. *A Comparative Analysis of Complex Organizations: On Power, Involvement and Their Correlates.* New York: Free Press, 1975.

Farhi, Adam. "Hollywood Goes to School: Recognizing the Superteacher Myth in Films." *The Clearing House* 72, no. 3 (1999): 157–9.

Flett, George L. *The Psychology of Mattering: Understanding the Human Need to be Significant.* Boston, MA: Academic Press/Elsevier, 2018.

Freytag, Cathy E.; and Shotsberger, Paul, eds. *Self Care for Educators: Soul-Nourishing Practices to Promote Well Being.* Central, SC: Freedom's Hill Press, 2022.

Giddens, Anthony. *The Consequences of Modernity.* San Francisco, CA: Stanford University Press, 1969.

Gollan, Doug. "Inside the Challenges of the Post-Covid Travel Industry's Soaring Demand." *Forbes*, August 18, 2023. https://www.forbes.com/sites/douggollan/2023/08/18/inside-the-challenges-of-the-post-covid-travel-industrys-soaring-demand/.

Groopman, Jerome. *The Anatomy of Hope: How People Prevail in the Face of Illness.* New York: Random House, 1998.

Grossman, Pam; Hammerness, Karen; and McDonald, Morva. "Redefining Teaching, Re-Imagining Teacher Education." *Teachers and Teaching: Theory and Practice* 15, no. 2 (2009): 273–89.

Guarino, Cassandra M.; Santibañez, Lucrecia; and Daley, Glenn A. "Teacher Recruitment and Retention: A Review of the Recent Empirical Literature." *Review of Educational Research* 76, no. 2 (2006): 173–208.

Hauke, Elizabeth. "Make Classroom Connections by Drawing from the Slow Movement." *Times Higher Education,* August 25, 2022. https://www.timeshighereducation.com/campus/make-classroom-connections-drawing-slow-movement.

Herek, Stephen, director. *Mr. Holland's Opus.* Los Angeles, CA: Hollywood Pictures, Buena Vista Pictures, 1995.

Hickman. Richard. *The Art and Craft of Pedagogy: Portraits of Effective Teachers.* New York: Routledge, 2011.

Hill-Jackson, Valerie; Hartlep, Nicholas D.; and Stafford, Delia. *What Makes a Star Teacher: 7 Dispositions That Support Student Learning.* Alexandria, VA: ASCD, 2019.

Hollabaugh, Jaliene. *Exploring the Perceptions and Experiences of Inductive Teachers in Secondary Education: How do Inductive Teachers Find Their Place in the Teaching Profession, and What Motivates Them to Remain in the Field?* Doctoral dissertation, George Fox University, 2011. https://digitalcommons.georgefox.edu/edd/1.

Hollis, James. *Finding Meaning in the Second Half of Life.* New York: Gotham/Penguin, 2005.

Hollis, James. *The Middle Passage: From Misery to Meaning in Mid-Life.* Toronto: Inner-City Books, 1993.

Howells, K. *Gratitude in Education: A Radical View.* Rotterdam: Sense Publishers, 2011.

Hughes, John, director. *Ferris Bueller's Day Off.* Los Angeles, CA: Paramount Pictures, 1986.

Hughes, Michelle C. *Dispositions are a Teacher's Greatest Strength: Mindful Pedagogical Practices to Develop Self-Awareness to Flourish in the Classroom.* New York: Routledge, 2024.

Hughes, Michelle C., and Badley, Ken, eds. *Joyful Resilience as Educational Practice: Transforming Teaching Challenges into Opportunities.* New York: Routledge, 2021.

Illich, Ivan. "To Hell with Good Intentions." http://www.ciasp.ca/CIASPhistory/IllichCIASPspeech.htm.

Inman, Duane, and Marlow, Leslie. "Teacher Retention: Why Do Beginning Teachers Remain in the Profession? *Education* 124, no. 4 (2004): 605–14.

Jackson, Shirley. "The Lottery." *The New Yorker,* June 26, 1948.

Jewison, Norman, director. *Fiddler on the Roof.* Los Angeles, CA: Mirisch, Cartier, 1971.

Johnson, Kelly. *Kelly: More than My Share of it All.* Washington, DC: Smithsonian, 1985.

Kasdan, Jake, director. *Bad Teacher.* Los Angeles, CA: Sony/Columbia Pictures, 2011.

Keen, Sam. *Apology for Wonder.* New York: Harper and Row, 1969.

Keen, Sam. *Fire in the Belly: On Being a Man.* Toronto: Bantam, 1991.

LaGravenese, Richard, director. *Freedom Writers*. Los Angeles, CA: Paramount Pictures, Double Feature Films, MTV Films, Jersey Films, Kernos Film, 2007.

Lakoff, George; and Johnson, Mark. *Metaphors We Live By*. Chicago, IL: The University of Chicago Press, 1980.

Latifoglu, Ahmet. "Staying or Leaving? An Analysis of Career Trajectories of Beginning Teachers." *International Studies in Educational Administration* 44, no. 1 (2016): 55–70.

Leder, Mimi, director. *Pay it Forward*. Los Angeles, CA: Bel-Air Entertainment, Tapestry, Warner Brothers, 2000.

Leonhardt, David. "The Case for $320,000 Kindergarten Teachers." *New York Times*, July 27, 2010. https://www.nytimes.com/2010/07/28/business/economy/28leonhardt.html.

Locke, John. *An Essay Concerning Human Understanding*, edited by Kenneth Winkler. Indianapolis, IN: Hackett, 1996.

Lortie, Dan. *Schoolteacher: A Sociological Study*. Chicago, IL: The University of Chicago Press, 1975.

Lowe, Robert. "Teachers as Saviors, Teachers Who Care." In *Images of Schoolteachers in America*, 2nd ed., edited by Pamela Booth Joseph and Gail E. Burnaford, 211–25. Hillsdale, NJ: Lawrence Erlbaum, 2001.

Mali, Taylor. "What do Teachers Make?" https://www.youtube.com/watch?v=RxsOVK4syxU.

Maxwell, Scott. "Florida Teacher Shortage: Veterans Take Pass on Filling the Gap." *Orlando Sentinel*, May 3, 2024. https://www.orlandosentinel.com/2024/05/02/teacher-shortage-veterans-say-no-maxwell/.

McAulay, John D. "A Teacher's Week." *Peabody Journal of Education* 33, no. 5 (1956): 308–10.

McCartney Matthews, Melissa Lee. *A Funny Thing Happened on the Way to the Hippocampus: The Effects of Humor on Student Achievement and Memory Retention*. Doctoral dissertation, Arizona State University, 2011.

McCullick, Bryan; Belcher, Don; Hardin, Brent; and Hardin, Marie. "Butches, Bullies and Buffoons: Images of Physical Education Teachers in the Movies." *Sport, Education and Society* 8, no. 1 (2003): 3–17.

McGreal, Chris. "It Got Vile Very Quickly: How Alex Jones Turned a Tragedy into a Battleground." *The Guardian*, March 26, 2024. https://www.theguardian.com/tv-and-radio/2024/mar/26/alex-jones-sandy-hook-shooting-documentary.

McTigue, Jay; and Wiggins, Grant. *Understanding by Design*. Alexandria, VA: ASCD, 1998.

Meyerson, Debra E.; and Scully, Marueen A. "Tempered Radicalism and the Politics of Ambivalence and Change." *Organizational Science* 6, no. 5 (1995): 585–99.

Mockler, Nicole. *Constructing Teacher Identities: How the Print Media Define and Represent Teachers and their Work*. London: Bloomsbury, 2022.

Mockler, Nicole. "No Wonder No One Wants to Be a Teacher: World-first Study Looks at 65,000 News Articles about Australian Teachers." *The Conversation*, July 10, 2022. https://theconversation.com/no-wonder-no-one-wants-to-be-a-teacher-world-first-study-looks-at-65-000-news-articles-about-australian-teachers-186210.

Mockler, Nicole; and Groundwater-Smith, Susan. *Questioning the Language of Improvement and Reform in Education*. New York: Routledge, 2020.

Natanson, Hannah; and Balingit, Moriah. "Caught in the Culture Wars, Teachers Are Being Forced from Their Jobs." *Washington Post*, June 22, 2022. https://www.washingtonpost.com/education/2022/06/16/teacher-resignations-firings-culture-wars/.

Negussie, Tesfaye; and Ahmed, Rahma. "Florida Schools Directed to Cover or Remove Classroom Books that are not Vetted." https://abcnews.go.com/Politics/florida-schools-directed-cover-remove-classroom-books-vetted/story?id=96884323.

Nichols, Tom. *The Death of Expertise: The Campaign against Established Knowledge and Why It Matters*. Old Saybrook, CT: Tantor, 2017.

Noddings, Nel. *Caring: A Feminine Approach to Ethics and Moral Education*. Oakland, CA: University of California Press, 1984.

Noddings, Nel. *The Challenge to Care in Schools*. New York: Teachers College Press, 1992.

Norwegian Students and Academics' International Assistance Fund. "Who Wants to be a Volunteer?" Oslo: iKind Media; NEFDT Films, 2014. https://www.youtube.com/watch?v=ymcflrj_rRc.

Ortony. Andrew. "Why Metaphors Are Necessary and Not Just Nice." *Educational Theory* 25, no. 1 (April 2007): 45–53. https://doi.org/10.1111/j.1741-5446.1975.tb00666.x.

Orwell, George. *1984*. London: Secker & Warburg, 1949.

Pallasma, Juhani. *The Thinking Hand: Existential and Embodied Wisdom in Architecture*. Chichester: Wiley, 2009.

Palmer, Parke. *The Courage to Teach: Exploring the Inner Landscape of a Teacher's Life*. San Franciso, CA: Jossey-Bass, 1998.

Palmer, Parker. *To Know as We are Known: A Spirituality of Education*. New York: Harper, 1983.

Pietarinena, Janne; Pyhältö, Kirsi; Soinic, Tiina; and Salmela-Arod, Katariina. "Reducing Teacher Burnout: A Socio-contextual Approach." *Teaching and Teacher Education* 35 (October 2013): 62–72.

Poehler, Amy. *Yes, Please*. New York: Harper, 2014.

Ricoeur, Paul. *The Rule of Metaphor: Multi-Disciplinary Studies of the Creation of Meaning in Language*. Translated by Robert Czerny, with Kathleen McLaughlin and John Costello. Milton Park: Routledge and Kegan Paul, 1978.

Rogers, Carl. *Freedom To Learn: A View of What Education might Become*. Indianapolis, IN: Charles Merrill, 1969.

Santoro, Doris A. "Good Teaching in Difficult Times: Demoralization in the Pursuit of Good Work." *American Journal of Education* 118, no. 1 (2011): 1–23.

Scull, W. Reed; and Peltier, Gary. "Star Power and the Schools: Studying Popular Films' Portrayal of Educators." *Clearing House* 8, no. 1 (2007): 13–17.

Seligman, Martin. *Learned Optimism: How to Change Your Mind and Your Life*. New York: Knopf, 1991.

Shine, Kathryn. "Are Australian Teachers Making the Grade? A Study of News Coverage of Naplan Testing." *Media International Australia* 154, no. 1 (2015): 25–33. https://doi.org/10.1177/1329878X1515400105.

Sima, Richard. "Want to Feel Happier? Try Snacking on Joy." *Washington Post*, November 22, 2022. https://www.washingtonpost.com/wellness/2022/11/17/feel-happier-joy-flourishing/.

Sinclair, Murray; with Mazina Giizhik. *Who We Are: Four Questions for a Life and a Nation*. Toronto: McLelland and Stewart, 2024.

Smith, Gordon T., *Consider Your Calling: Six Questions for Discerning Your Vocation*. Downers Grove, IL: InterVarsity Press, 2015.

Smith, Gordon T., and Badley, Ken. "Called to Teach." *Teaching Theology and Religion* 1, no. 3 (October 1998): 171–6.

Snowdon, David. *Aging with Grace: The Nun Study*. New York: Bantam, 2001.

Steeg Thornhill, Susanna; and Badley, Ken. *Generating Tact and Flow for Effective Teaching and Learning*. New York: Routledge, 2020.

Stegner, Wallace. *The Angle of Repose*. New York: Vintage Books, 1971.

Stotland, Ezra. *The Psychology of Hope*. San Francisco, CA: Jossey-Bass, 1969.

Syborn, Freddy; Hegarty, Elliot; Gosling-Fuller, Ben; and Campbell, Al, series directors. *Bad Education*. London: Tiger Aspect Productions, 2012–2024.

Taylor, Charles. *The Malaise of Modernity*. Toronto: Anansi, 1991.

Thompson, Greg. *The Global Report on the Status of Teachers, 2021*. Brussels: Education Research International, 2021. https://www.ei-ie.org/en/item/25403:the-global-report-on-the-status-of-teachers-2021.

Thompson, Greg; Creagh, Sue; Stacey, Meghan; Hogan, Anna; and Mockler, Nicole. "Researching Teachers' Time Use: Complexity, Challenges and a Possible Way Forward." *The Australian Educational Researcher* 51 (2024): 1647–70.

Toohey, Peter. *Boredom: A Lively History*. New Haven, CT: Yale University Press, 2011.

Trikonis, Gus, director. *Take This Job and Shove It*. Los Angeles, CA: Metro-Goldwyn-Mayer, Embassy Pictures, 1981.

Tucker, Tiana. *Bridging the Research-to-Practice Gap: Factors Affecting Teachers' Efficacy About Instruction*. Doctoral dissertation, George Fox University, 2015. https://digitalcommons.georgefox.edu/edd/55/.

Tykwer, Tom, director. *Run, Lola Run*. Berlin: X-Filme Creative Pool; WDR, Arte, 1998.

Van Brummelen, Harro; and Badley, Ken. *Metaphors We Teach By: How Metaphors Shape What We Do in Classrooms*. Eugene, OR: Wipf and Stock, 2012.

Van Manen, Max. *The Tact of Teaching: The Meaning of Pedagogical Thoughtfulness*. Albany, NY: SUNY Press, 1991.

Varkey Foundation. *Global Teacher Status Index, 2018*. London: Varkey Foundation, 2018. https://www.varkeyfoundation.org/global-teacher-status.

Volf, Miroslav. *The End of Memory: Remembering Rightly in a Violent World*. Grand Rapids, MI: Eerdmans, 2006.

Voyage, Matthew. "How is Instagram Changing the Way We Travel?" *Medium*, 2023. https://medium.com/@matthieuvoyage/how-is-instagram-changing-the-way-we-travel-a406a1841cd3.

Walker, Jennifer D.; Johnson, Kimberly M.; and Randolph, Kathleen M. "Teacher Self-Advocacy for the Shared Responsibility of Classroom and Behavior Management." *Teaching Exceptional Children* 53, no. 3 (2021): 216–25.

Walker, Tim. "Where Do Teachers Get the Most Respect?" *NEA Today*, November 28, 2018. https://www.nea.org/nea-today/all-news-articles/where-do-teachers-get-most-respect.

Wang, Hongyu. *The Call from the Stranger on a Journey Home: Curriculum in a Third Space*. Lausanne: Peter Lang, 2004.

Weir, Peter, director. *Dead Poet's Society*. Los Angeles, CA: Touchstone Pictures, Buena Vista Pictures, 1989.

Weir, Peter, director. *The Truman Show*. Los Angeles, CA: Scott Rudin Productions, Paramount Pictures, 2000.

Whiteman, Honor. "Laughter Releases 'Feel Good Hormones' to Promote Social Bonding." *Medical News Today*, June 3, 2017. https://www.medicalnewstoday.com/articles/317756.

Yee Brandy; and Yee, Diane. *International Perspectives on Ethical Educational Leadership: Lessons from Workplace Cultures That Have Lost (and Found) Their Way*. London: Palgrave Macmillan, 2024.

Yost, Deborah S. "Reflection and Self-Efficacy: Enhancing the Retention of Qualified Teachers from a Teacher Education Perspective." *Teacher Education Quarterly* 33, no. 4 (Fall 2006): 59–76.

Index

accompaniment, teaching as 76
administrators 13, 20, 53, 162, 173, 184–7
adventure, teaching as 76–8, 143–4
aerospace 62, 77, 103, 111
AI, see artificial intelligence
aircraft, see aerospace
Alberta 1, 63, 111–12, 118, 121, 139
Alexander, Christopher 74–5, 192
allies 154–6, 160, 162, 193
anthropologists 48, 53, 184–5
apprentices and apprenticeships 12, 113
 apprenticeship by observation 7–8
Aristotle 12, 167–8, 176, 181
art 116
artificial intelligence 11, 42
artistry, teaching as 25
assessment 29–32, 42, 65, 71–9, 158–9, 186–7
 shared with students 63
authority 33, 63, 85–6, 156–7, 169, 186–7
 authorizing oneself 85
awe, see wonder

backward design 71
Bandura, Albert 84
boredom 95–6
boundaries, professional 5, 76, 113–15, 125, 134, 154
brain 171–2, 194–5, 198
Building 20 (MIT) 102
burnout 112, 131, 174

calling, teaching as 17, 24–6
career, teaching as 17, 20, 97–9, 121, 143, 198
 landmarks in 178–9
China 23
CIA rope, see core cycle
classroom community 62
climate, classroom, see ethos, classroom
climbing, see mountains and mountaineering
colleagues and collegiality 88, 149–56, 162–3, 177, 187
complexity (of teaching) 22–3, 31, 39–41, 168
consent (form of authority) 63, 156–7
contentment 25, 167, 172
contract, teaching 37, 85, 156
core cycle (curriculum, instruction, assessment) 31, 40, 59, 65, 154–6
courage 19, 85, 167
COVID-19 44, 116, 118, 130, 143
craft, teaching as 43, 78–9
creativity 10, 43, 62, 101–3, 188
Csikszentmihalyi, Mihaly 33, 67, 158, 160, 188, 192
culture
 classroom (see ethos, classroom)
 school 184–9
curriculum 29–32, 35–6, 42, 71, 73–5, 154–5
 district committees 101
 models of 29
 pilot teaching 101
cynicism 71–2, 130, 151, 186–7, 191

Danielson, Charlotte 90
depression, moral 131

design   25, 71, 73–5, 192
developmental stages   132
Dewey, John   35, 154–5
dispositions   5–6, 167–81
doctoral degree   197–8

elementary schools   110–11, 123, 175, 186
empathy   87, 167, 174
endorphins, *see* brain
engineers and engineering   20–3, 103
environmental care (as an ideal)   62
Erikson. Erik   132, 136, 155, 157, 160, 169
ethos, classroom   3–4, 29–33, 159–60, 162, 164
    safety   63
    shaping   32–3, 40, 191
Everest, Mount   127–9
expertise   8, 12, 135, 155, 160, 169

faith   24, 101, 117
fatigue   41, 111, 118, 131
films about teachers   7, 9–10, 12–13
fit in teaching, *see* place
Florida   8, 22
flow, *see* Csikszentmihalyi, Mihalyi
forgetting, *see* memory

generativity   132, 136, 148
geology, concepts in   183–4
goodwill, *see* consent (form of authority)
government   21–2, 39, 44, 55, 121, 156
    role in education   110
grading   19, 42, 44, 132, 180, 193, 196
gratitude   3, 100, 167–9, 173–6, 202
Gretzky, Wayne   12
grit, *see* persistence
guides   128, 130, 135, 146–8, 150–1, 153

Hollabaugh, Jaliene   87–8
Hollis, James   96
hope   173
Howells, Kerry   173
humility   155–6, 167, 169
humor, *see* jokes

ideals of teachers
    articulating   200
    baseline ideals   108
    definition of   59–60
    lists of ideals   60–1, 107–8
    maintenance of   117, 132–3
    overall ideals   1, 36, 56, 59–65, 88, 107–9, 118–21, 132–3
identity of teachers   88, 96
images of teachers   7
    anyone can teach phrase   44
    effects of social media on   11
    teacher as hero image   9
    teacher as martyr image   9
improvisation, teaching as   75–6
inclusion   108, 154
induction years of teaching, *see* pre-service teachers
initiative fatigue   41
instruction   19, 30–3, 40–3, 75–8, 101–2, 154–8, 187–8
    differentiation   34–5, 64
    strategies   62, 89, 101, 143, 191–2
intellectual stimulation   100, 195
intensity (of teaching)   41–3, 64, 103, 108, 140, 160–71
interns, *see* pre-service teachers

job, teaching as   17–20, 24–6, 33
jokes   24, 36, 75–6, 139, 140, 177, *see also* laughter
Johnson, Mark   72
journalism, journalists   10–11
journals, scholarly   103, 198
journal-keeping   53, 90–1, 100, 172, 182, 202
journeys   139–40, 145–6, 149, 180, 184–90, *see also* travel
Jungian psychology   96

kentopia, definition of   168
Kenya   36, 64, 121–2, 142, 147–8, 199
kindergarten   45, 71, 72, 76, 112, 175

Lakoff, George   72
language   34, 50–3, 71–7, 90, 160–1
    pattern language in curriculum design   73–5
    renaming life events   177
    school within a school, phrase   189
    teaching of   112–13
    used to describe teaching   17–27

Index   215

laughter   63, 113, 167, 171–2, *see also*
    jokes
leadership   132, 134
learning, students'   62
    from mistakes   84–5
    joy in   63
listening   169
literature   184, 195
Lockheed Martin, *see* Skunk Works
Lortie, Dan   7–8, 12

Macbeth   26, 92, 193
maps and mapping   72, 90–2, 128,
    178–9, 182, 200
marking, *see* grading
media, social   11, 44, 115
memory   176–80
mentors and mentoring   84–7, 125,
    132–4, 147–8, 177–8, 195–6
    counter-mentors   136
metacognition   102–3, 188–9, 193
metaphors   4, 55, 68, 71–82, 91, 150, 199
    functions of   71–2
    puzzle of teaching metaphor   39–45
    summit push metaphor   127–37
    views of metaphor   72–3, 77–8
mindset   1, 72, 84, 112, 144
Minecraft   35, 38
mission statements   66, 96
mistakes   63, 85, 112, 142, 147–8
Mockler, Nicole   10–11
mountains and mountaineering   127–9,
    133–4, 144

networks, personal   118–19, 162
Nichols, Tom   8
novice teachers, *see* pre-service teachers

objectives, curriculum   31, 76, 77, 122,
    155–6

Palmer, Parker   24–5, 33, 62, 155–6, 169,
    191
pandemic, *see* COVID-19
Paris   74, 140
passion (for teaching)   115, 174
perseverance, *see* persistence
persistence   20, 83–4, 167, 169, 171
philosophy   36, 48, 60, 65–8, 91, 118–19

philosophy of education   65
    applications of   67–8
    effects of articulating   192
    statements   66
pilgrims, teachers as   144–6, 151
place, finding one's place   85–6, 111
Poehler, Amy   75
practices   50–1, 56, 60, 108, 173–4,
    184–6, 202
pre-service teachers   8, 60–1, 83, 89, 135,
    180, 194, 201
    hosting   89
principals, *see* administrators
privilege, recognition of   174
profession, teaching as   3, 6, 8, 11–12,
    17, 20–6
    attractiveness to young people   11
    autonomy (professional)   78
    public respect for   21, 24
    qualifications normally
        required   22–3
    retention in   83–8, 118
    self-governance of profession   21–2
professional learning communities
    (PLCs)   89, 102
psychologists   95–6, 156, 173

refugees, teachers as   149–51
reinvention, personal   201
relationships   20, 33, 84, 87–8, 186
    with students   156–62
    with colleagues   87, 111, 153, 187,
        195
    with friends and family   96, 133, 195
repose, angle of   6, 79, 183–9
research, conducting   89, 102
resilience   41, 167
retirement   44, 96, 128, 133, 136, 180
retreats (reflective)   88–9, 199–200
rewards (of teaching)   7, 9, 25, 33, 40–5,
    95, 127, 145, 170–2
    good will of students (*see* consent)
    financial (*see* salaries, teachers)
Ricoeur, Paul   72
Rogers, Carl   62, 156

salaries, teachers'   8, 20–6, 43, 45, 55, 197
Santoro, Doris   131
schools, building dynamics   130, 184–9

secondary education   42–3, 101, 155, 159, 161
self-efficacy   84
service   26, 63, 97, 125, 146, 199
   service trips   199
   educational ideal   63
Skunk Works   62, 77–8, 102–3, 188, 192
slow movement   103
Smith, Gordon   96–7
social interaction   195
social media, *see* media, social
sociologists   48, 53–4, 156, 174, 184–5
Stegner, Wallace   183–9, 190 n.1
students
   cohort characteristics   35–6
   discoveries made by   161–2, 169–70
   flourishing of   174–5
   individual differences (*see* instruction, differentiation)
   interactions with   41
   questions   75
   respect   63–4, 157
   support of teachers   154, 156–62
subway maps, *see* maps and mapping
supervision (of the teaching profession)   20–2
supporters   100, 133, 154–65
surprise, openness to   170
syllabi   107–8

teachers
   challenges   96–7, 133
   change in responsibilities   99
   complexity of (*see* complexity of teaching)
   components of work   30
   core cycle of activities (*see* core cycle)
   criticisms of   130, 140, 142
   final decades of teaching   127–37
   identity of   33–4, 120
   images of   44
   induction years of career   83–92
   intensity of (*see* intensity of teaching)
   joy in   98
   leadership, involvement in   134
   legal aspects   36–7, 77
   middle years of career   95–104
   models of   29
   outstanding   89
   psychological demands of   130
   rewards of (*see* rewards of teaching)
   self-care   167
teams   122, 162–4, 195
textbooks   101, 134–5, 196
theatre   75–6, 119
thinking   11, 29, 59, 62, 167, 192–4
   critical and creative   62, 116
to-do lists   192
Tolkien, J. R. R.   143
tourists   139–1, 147, 151
travel, travelers   122, 140–6, 151, 178, 180, 196, 199
trauma-informed practice   34

unions   109–10, 119, 121, 125, 134
university   29, 83, 107, 178, 191, 198, 201
   advanced degrees   89, 196–8

Van Manen, Max   12, 192
Varkey Foundation   21, 23–4
vocation   13, 17–26, 33, 43, 88, 96
   confirmation that teaching is right vocation   25–6
   etymology of word   24
   questioning choice of   8

wisdom   117, 132, 136
wonder   62, 167, 169–71, 189
worldviews   4, 47–55
   changing worldviews   54–5
   definition and characteristics of   47–50
   formation and maintenance of   50–3, 87, 91
   influences of   49, 91
   teachers' worldviews   48–9, 55–6
writing for publication   198

Yukon   142, 178, 180, 197

zone, *see* Csikszentmihalyi, Mihalyi

About the Author

Ken Badley serves as Research Professor in Education at Tyndale University in Toronto, Canada. Besides writing secondary textbooks, he has published extensively on the foundations of education, curriculum, instruction, teacher self-care, and school cultures. He has taught in four Canadian provinces and two American states, at the secondary, undergraduate, graduate, and doctoral levels. Ken lives in Edmonton, Canada.